THE POWER OF THE WORD

JOHN BRECK

THE POWER OF THE WORD
In the Worshiping Church

ST VLADIMIR'S SEMINARY PRESS
CRESTWOOD, NEW YORK 10707
1986

Library of Congress Cataloging-in-Publication Data

Breck, John, 1939-
    The power of the word.

    Bibliography: p.
    Includes index.
1. Orthodox Eastern Church—Doctrines. 2. Word of God
(Theology). 3. Bible—Hermeneutics. 4. Orthodox Eastern
Church—Liturgy. 5. Orthodox Eastern Church—Creeds.
6. Icons—Cult. I. Title.
BX323.B74   1986   230'19.   86-24773
ISBN 0-89281-153-6 (pbk.)

THE POWER OF THE WORD

© Copyright 1986

by

ST VLADIMIR'S SEMINARY PRESS

ISBN 0-89281-153-6

PRINTED IN THE UNITED STATES OF AMERICA
BY
ATHENS PRINTING COMPANY
New York, NY 10018

*To the faculty of the St Sergius Institute,
Paris, and its Rector, Protopresbyter Alexis
Kniazeff: in gratitude.*

Table of Contents

Abbreviations

The names of many periodicals and series are given in full. The following are the most important abbreviations.

ANF: Ante-Nicene Fathers
CBQ: Catholic Biblical Quarterly
IDB: Interpreter's Dictionary of the Bible
Jerome Bib Comm: Jerome Biblical Commentary
JBL: Journal of Biblical Literature
NF:Neue Folge (New Series)
NovTest: Novum Testamentum
NPNF: Nicene and Post-Nicene Fathers
NRTh: Nouvelle Revue Théologique
NTD: Das Neue Testament Deutsch
NTS: New Testament Studies
OCA: Orientalia Christiana Analecta
PG: Migne, Patrologia Graeca
PL: Migne, Patrologia Latina
RB: Revue Biblique
RechScRel: Recherches de science religieuse
RevBib: Revue biblique
RevOrChr: Revue de l'Orient chrétien
RGG: Religion in Geschichte und Gegenwart (3rd ed.)
SourcesChr (= SC): Sources Chrétiennes
SuppDictBib: Supplément au Dictionnaire de la Bible
SVTQ: St Vladimir's Theological Quarterly
ThLZ: Theologische Literaturzeitung
TWNT: Kittel, Theologisches Wörterbuch zum NT
ZNW: Zeitschrift für die ntl. Wissenschaft
ZThK: Zeitschrift für Theologie und Kirche

Abbreviations for books of the Bible follow the usage of the Revised Standard Version [Thomas Nelson, 1952], with the following exceptions; Ac = Acts; Isa = Isaiah; Phlm = Philemon; 1-2 Thess = 1-2 Thessalonians.
For patristic references, see G.W.H. Lampe, *A Patristic Greek Lexicon*, Oxford, 1961.

NB: *The essays in this collection were written between 1975 and 1983. While they have been revised to develop the title-theme, with few exceptions no attempt has been made to update the secondary literature.*

Foreword

The Word of God expressed in the form of Holy Scripture and traditional creedal formulas possesses an inherent power by which it communicates divine grace and truth.

The essays in this collection were written to explain and to emphasize the importance of this "power of the Word" as the means by which saving events of the past become "actualized" in each present moment within the life and experience of the Church. For this "actualizing power" to become operative, however, it must be perceived and comprehended on the level of both mind and heart. Like sacramental grace, the operation of the divine Word depends upon a "synergism" or "co-operation" between divine initiative and human receptivity. This act of receptivity is essentially one of perception, known in patristic tradition as *theōria*: a spiritual vision or contemplation of the divine presence and the divine economy, revealed within the framework of salvation-history.

From an Orthodox perspective, both interpretation and confession of the Word of God are grounded in this "theoretic perception" of the saving power of the Word. In contemporary Orthodoxy, however, the dynamic quality of the Word, the "power of the Gospel for salvation," has become largely obscured by a general neglect of Scripture study and a failure to perceive doctrine, liturgy and iconography as vehicles of *biblical* revelation. One of the most pressing needs within the Church today is to recover the patristic vision of the dynamic quality of the Word as the instrument of God's self-disclosure and self-communication. It is my hope, therefore, that this volume might contribute to a much needed reawakening of our Orthodox consciousness of the power and the beauty of the divine Word, not to serve esthetic interests, but to enable us to rediscover the central place of Holy Scripture within Orthodoxy as the primary source of Christian truth and life.

The Sacramental Power of the Word

"There is one God who manifested Himself through Jesus Christ His Son, who is His Word, proceeding from silence..."
— St Ignatius (Mag VIII. 2)

"Silence is the sacrament of the world to come; words are the instrument of this present age."
— St Isaac the Syrian
(Letter no. 3)

Within Orthodoxy, the relationship between Word and Sacrament is one of essential unity, grounded in silence.

"In the beginning," God speaks out of silence to create heaven and earth by the power of His Word. Divine speech has a dynamic, creative quality that may be termed "sacramental," in that it accomplishes what it signifies (Isa 55:11). Through His *dabar* or "word-reality," Yahweh determines the growth and destiny of His chosen people while uniting Himself to them in a covenant of love. As the Old Covenant draws to a close in order to make possible a new and deeper relationship of love between God and man, the Spirit of prophecy withdraws from Israel, prompting the rabbis to explain the ensuing silence as a sign of divine wrath and consequent judgment. St Ignatius, with the whole of Christendom, interprets this crucial moment in Israel's history as

11

a prelude to "the fullness of time," when God will once again "speak out of silence" to utter the promise of a new creation through the person and teaching of His incarnate Word. This new and final creative act the apostle calls a "mysterion," a "sacrament" hidden in God from before all time, but now revealed and accomplished in the person of the divine Logos, the crucified and risen Son of God (I Cor 2:2,7; Eph 1:9f; 3:1-12; Col 1:25-27; 2:2f, etc.). The purpose of this sacramental act, like the original work of creation, is to call mankind "from nothingness into being," from a non-being of man's own making into a radically new existence bestowed by grace, from fragmentation and hostility into reconciliation and unity, an eternal participation in the very life of God. To accomplish this "sacrament," which is nothing less than the divine economy of universal salvation, the divine Word summons and introduces fallen humanity into a new order of reality, the eternal life of the Kingdom. There He brings His saving work to fulfillment by submitting Himself, with all of creation, to God the Father (I Cor 15:20-28).

According to St Isaac and Eastern mystical tradition, once this mission of the Word is completed, human words of proclamation, of supplication and of praise will be forever transformed into the silence of contemplation.

This rooting of Word and Sacrament in the divine *sigē*, the "silence" from which God articulates the economy of salvation, will perhaps seem strange and unwarranted to non-Orthodox Christians, as will the insistence upon their fundamental unity (which is not to say "identity"). For centuries Catholics and Protestants have been enmeshed in controversy over the relative importance of the two, indicating by the very nature of their arguments that both confessions consider Word and Sacrament to be separate, if complementary, realities that together constitute the *esse* of the Church. Calvin well expressed the Western conception when he defined the Church as God's instrument of salvation through the "preaching of the Gospel" and the "institution of the sacraments" (Institutes IV.1,1). Such a definition presupposes a distinction, even a dichotomy, between Word and Sacrament, preaching and liturgy, proclamation and celebration, that is quite foreign to Orthodox theology. In the thought of the Eastern Fathers, grounded as it is in the wholistic nature of the apostolic vision, Word and Sacrament are inseparable. Together they form a unique and unified medium of *communion* between God and man, a reciprocal participation between divine and human life.

From the perspective of Orthodox Christianity, the relationship between Word and Sacrament, proclamation and celebration, must be explained in such a way as to stress the fundamental unity between the two. This is necessary not only to clarify matters for the sake of ecumenical dialogue. It is also vitally important for the continuous and arduous task of bringing *orthopraxis* into line with *orthodoxia*. For the Orthodox, like Roman Catholics, have known long periods during which Scripture was neglected and the Church's celebration often became reduced to formalized and sterile ritual. And like many Protestants, the Orthodox have often deformed authentic, traditional eucharistic practice by justifying infrequent communion on the grounds of piety and ethics (the question of individual "worthiness"). Such attitudes, however, spring not from doctrinal motives, as in the Western Churches, but from a failure to understand fully the traditional Orthodox position concerning the inherent unity between proclamation of the Word and its celebration. The continuing challenge to Orthodoxy, therefore, and one of its most important contributions to ecumenical discussion, is to preserve and affirm what we may call the "kerygmatic" character of the Sacrament and the "sacramental" character of the Word.

The first step in this ongoing renewal involves overcoming a purely "verbal" understanding of the Word. Protestant theology has rightly insisted on the indispensable role of preaching in the Church's inner life as well as in its mission to the world (Rom 1:16; 10:14-17; I Cor 1:17,

etc.). All too frequently, however, the concept of the "Word
of God" in Reformed tradition has been reduced to the
canonical Scriptures or even to the sermon, as though one or
the other possessed in and of itself the capacity to transmit
knowledge of God and to establish communion with Him.
As Luke 18:34 and similar passages make clear, though, the
scriptural Word is not necessarily self-revealing. Human
words can become the very Word of God only through the
inspirational and interpretive *dynamis* or power of the Holy
Spirit (cf. Lk 24:45-49; Ac 1:4-8). Only the risen Christ,
the eternal divine Logos operating through the Spirit, can
open men's minds to understand the Scriptures, bringing to
their remembrance the fullness of His teaching and declaring
the hidden truths of the eschatological age, to His own glory
and to the glory of the Father (Jn 14:26; 16:13-15).

The fact that even Christ's own words are not automatically self-revealing explains why He invariably links
proclamation of the "good news" of the Kingdom with concrete, material *signs* that reveal the deeper meaning and
confirm the truth of His words. At the beginning of His
ministry, He concludes and "validates" His teaching in the
Temple by healing a man with an unclean spirit (Mk
1:21-27; cf Mt 4:23). Similarly, the apostolic commission
consists of the double imperative to preach and to heal:
"Whenever you enter a town... heal the sick in it and say
to them, 'The Kingdom of God has drawn near to you'"
(Lk 10:8f). The prophet's oracle was dramatically sealed
by a "sign-act" that associated some material object with the
pronouncement of divine judgment (e.g., Jer 19, 28; Ez
4, 5). In this case, the object participated in the prophecy
by enabling those to whom the oracle was addressed to
visualize the consequences of their refusal to repent. The
sign-acts of Jesus and the apostles (Lk 10; Ac 3, etc.),
however, actually accomplish the work of salvation, albeit
proleptically (that is, "symbolically," and not merely "by
anticipation"), by actualizing the promise of the *kerygma*
in the life of the diseased or possessed individual. This
healing—accomplished through the power of the spoken
word—is a true "symbol" of salvation in that it enables the

restored person to participate immediately in the new creation, the eschatological and cosmic reality of which Christ
is Author and Head. That reality is nothing other than the
Church: the "new life in the Spirit." "The Church of Christ
is not an institution," affirms Fr Sergius Bulgakov, "it is a
new life with Christ and in Christ, guided by the Holy
Spirit."[1] Within the life and experience of the Church, the
Word is confirmed and actualized by the ritualized sign-act
of the Sacrament. For just as with the healings performed
by Jesus during His earthly ministry, the sacraments, particularly Baptism and Eucharist, communicate to the believer
forgiveness of sins and participation in the new life of
the Kingdom (cf. Mk 2:10f; Jn 5:14).

To perceive the essentially sacramental character of the
Word, then, we first have to pass beyond a strictly verbal
notion of the Word and rediscover its *dynamic* quality, its
revelatory and saving *power* as an instrument of the
divine will.

As the self-effecting action of the prophetic oracle and
the irreversible character of blessings and curses illustrate,
the "power of the Word" was recognized, with joy or with
dread, throughout the Old Testament period. Under Stoic
influence, the Alexandrian Logos-theology of Philo, with
other currents of late-Judaism, offered the earliest Christians, and particularly the Evangelist John, a fresh, incisive
terminology to express the ineffable mystery of the Word-
made-flesh. The New Testament itself bears witness to the
process of reflection, grounded in Christ's self-revelation and
deepened by the inspirational-interpretive activity of the
Spirit, that unites the teaching of Jesus and the christology
of the Church into a single "Gospel of God" (Rom 1:1;
15:16; I Thess 2:2,8-9; I Pet 4:17). Beginning with the
words *of* Jesus, the *ipsissima verba/vox Jesu* transmitted by
oral tradition, the apostles soon developed a lapidary message
about Jesus, formulating in various but similar ways the redemptive meaning not only of His words, but of His actions:
the ultimate sign-acts of His crucifixion, resurrection and
glorification. This proclamation of the *kerygma,* or salvation-

[1]S. Bulgakov, *The Orthodox Church,* New York, 1935, p. 9.

message based upon Christ's saving activity, led finally to the Johannine identification of Jesus *as* the Word, the Logos of God.

The Word *of* Jesus. The power of His Word, as we have seen, becomes literally visible with the healing miracles. Evil spirits are exorcized by His word (Mt 8:16; Lk 4:36), a word that can heal even at a distance if it is received with faith (Mt 8:8). By His word, "even the winds and sea obey Him" (Mk 4:41, par.): the nature-miracles attest to His authority over creation itself. Yes His words are directed particularly towards men, establishing the criteria for salvation or judgment (Mk 8:38; Jn 12:48; cf. Heb 4:12f) and affirming His ultimate authority to forgive sins, a power that only God can exercise (Mk 2:7).

The Word *about* Jesus. Throughout the New Testament we encounter the expression "Word of truth" as a synonym for the Gospel or kerygmatic proclamation (Eph 1:13; Col 1:5; II Tim 2:15; Jas 1:18; cf. I Pet 2:25). "Truth" (*alētheia*) signifies both the message of revelation and the divine reality that is revealed. Christ Himself *is* the truth (Jn 14:6; cf. 8:31f) in that He both announces and embodies that truth. The "Word of truth" is a creative word that engenders "children of God" (cf. Jn 1:12f; I Jn 5:1) by introducing them into the new life of the Kingdom, implicitly or explicitly through the sacrament of baptism (Jn 3:3-5; I Jn 5:6-8; Tit 3:5; I Pet 1:3; 3:21f. etc.). Thus St Paul can declare that "the Gospel is the power of God for the salvation of all who believe" (Rom 1:16), precisely because "the Word of God operates (*energeitai*) in you who believe" (I Thess 2:13). The amended passage of I Pet 1:22-25,[2] also makes clear the fact that in apostolic times the saving power of the word—like that of the sacraments—was known to be contingent upon faith and repentance: "Having purified (their) souls by obeying the truth through the Spirit, to exercise unfeigned fraternal love . . . having been regenerated not by corruptible seed, but by incorruptible, through the living and abiding Word of God," the faithful

---

[2]The words "through the Spirit" are probably secondary, interpolated by a scribe who quite accurately grasped the meaning of the text.

are joined to Christ through a constant renewal of their baptismal commitment. Because of the indispensable role of faith and repentance in the work of salvation, the sacrament can only be conceived *ex opere operantis,* expressed in Orthodox terminology as a "synergy" or co-operation between man and God.

Jesus *as* the Word. The Logos-doctrine of the fourth Gospel represents the summit of New Testament christology. Here the power of the divine Word is revealed in all its fullness: He is Creator and Redeemer, the eschatological Judge and the sacrificial Lamb, the High Priest and the Servant of servants. Paradoxically—or rather, in the language of the Fathers, "antinomically"—His power is revealed through self-abasement, suffering and death, just as those who assume His ministry of reconciliation will be called to manifest their strength through weakness (II Cor 12:10). It is this antinomy that reveals the true nature of the Word: the Word of God is a Person, a divine hypostasis of the Holy Trinity, who becomes incarnate in the person of Jesus of Nazareth. The Word *becomes* flesh; therein alone lies His power to assume human life and to raise it to an eternal, glorified order of existence.

In a valuable essay on the "Mystery of the Word,"[3] Paul Evdokimov notes that "A sacrament is essentially 'mystical' or spiritual; and yet it is the most concrete act of all, for the liturgical word is filled more than any other with transcendant presence." This insight, founded upon ecclesial experience, permits us to affirm that the "power of the Sacrament" is derived from the "power of the Word" that it enshrines and celebrates.

In authentic Orthodox experience, the Word comes to its fullest expression within a sacramental context. Whether proclaimed through Scripture reading and preaching, or sung in the form of antiphons (psalms) and dogmatic hymns (festal troparia, the Monogenês and Credo), the Word of God is primarily communicated—expressed and received—by

---

[3]"Le Mystère de la Parole," in *Le Buisson Ardent,* Paris, 1981, p. 63.

the ecclesial act of *celebration,* and in particular, celebration of the eucharistic mystery.

As the resurrection appearance at Emmaus indicates, the first generation of Christians situated proclamation of the Word in an ecclesial-liturgical setting. The risen Lord draws near to two of His disciples and inquires as to the subject of their conversation. As in other resurrection appearances, "their eyes were kept from recognizing Him" (Lk 24:16; cf. Jn 20:14; 21:4). In response to His question, Cleopas offers a summary of the events concerning Jesus' condemnation, passion and death, as well as an account of the empty tomb. In all, his account represents a portion of the earliest *kerygma,* modified by the Evangelist Luke to provide a dramatic setting for Jesus' reply: "Was it not necessary that the Messiah should suffer these things and enter into His glory?" Then, retracing the typological events of the Old Testament that He Himself fulfilled in His life and sacrificial mission, Jesus "interpreted to them in all the Scriptures the things concerning Himself" (Lk 24:26f).

Although their "hearts burned within them" at Christ's proclamation (24:32), their eyes remained veiled. Only at the table of which He is both guest and host, do they finally recognize this stranger to be their crucified and risen master. "When He was at table with them, taking bread He blessed;[4] and having broken it, He gave it to them. And their eyes were opened, and they recognized Him" (24:31). As the parallel passages recounting the institution of the Lord's Supper make unmistakably clear (Lk 22:19; cf. Mk 14:22f; Mt 26:26ff; I Cor 11:23ff), the meal at Emmaus, shared by the risen Christ and His disciples, is an image of the eucharistic celebration of the early Church.

What will subsequently be called the "Liturgy of the Word," proclamation on the basis of scriptural revelation,

---

[4]Following Jewish custom, Jesus blesses *God* in an act of thanksgiving. While later Church practice will pronounce a blessing upon the bread (giving rise in various traditions to a conception of "metamorphosis," "transubstantiation," "consubstantiation" or, more recently, "transignification"), such a ritual act has meaning only after Christ's ascension, when through the blessing, pronounced as an epiklesis, the Spirit transforms the material substances of bread and wine into the Body and Blood of the glorified Lord.

occurs on the Jerusalem road leading to the village. In ancient Byzantine rites, preserved and celebrated today by the Orthodox Churches, this act of revelation and proclamation is preceded by the Lesser Entrance. Originally the bishop entered the church at this moment. Today the bishop vests in the nave, the center of the church, and at the Lesser Entrance he makes his "entry" into the altar, preceded by the elevated Word. Until this moment, the Gospel book has rested upon the altar table: the Word of God remains invisible, yet is ever present, as in the period of the Old Covenant. With the singing of the Beatitudes, the celebrant venerates the Gospel and hands it to the deacon to begin the procession that will lead from the altar to the bishop, and back into the altar, where it will be "enthroned" once again. It will be brought forth a second and last time to be read, interpreted, and thus "reactualized" in the midst of the people, to close the Liturgy of the Catechumens or Liturgy of the Word.

Nevertheless, however enriching the Gospel reading may be, however eloquent the sermon, revelation of the divine Word remains incomplete before celebration of the eucharistic mystery. As in the experience of the disciples at Emmaus, the gathered community only "perceives" the full revelation, it only opens its eyes to a true understanding and acceptance of the divine economy, through a personal and intimate *communion* in the divine gifts of Christ's Body and Blood. The Liturgy of the Word thus comes to fulfillment in and through the Liturgy of the Eucharist, the Sacrament of sacraments that alone transforms the Word from a message about Jesus into a true participation in His divine life.

Despite the necessity of such a "eucharistic fulfillment" of the Word, in actual practice vast numbers of Orthodox Christians still refuse frequent communion in favor of a more passive attendance at the liturgical service. For some, this is the result of simple negligence or indifference. For many others, this refusal to communicate other than at feasts such as Pascha and their names day is due to a genuine feeling of unworthiness. We have learned to approach the Mystery with such awe and reverence that we can never feel truly "worthy" of our Lord and of the gifts He offers. But that is precisely why the Orthodox Church insists upon the necessity of regular confession and reception of the sanctifying grace of absolution.[5] Frequent communion without adequate preparation can indeed lead to the "despising of the Church of God" and the failure to "discern the Body" of our Lord that St Paul roundly condemns in I Corinthians 11. The Body of the Church, however, is constituted and continually nourished by the Body of Christ. Without that nourishment, the Word itself loses meaning because it is no longer *actualized* in the experience of the ecclesial community. The Bible then has no more interest and significance in the life of the believer than any other ancient historical document. Although the Word finds expression in the dogmatic and scriptural portions of the Liturgy, it can only become a "Word of life" insofar as it leads from repentance to participation, from conversion to communion.

And conversely, partaking of the Holy Mysteries can only fulfill and sustain Christian existence to the degree that the Sacrament truly actualizes the divine Word within the gathered community and in the daily life of God's people. Within the Church's celebration the Word assumes sacramental value: the sacramental rite itself is the framework in which the Word comes most eloquently and most powerfully to expression. This is true, however, only because within the Sacrament, the Word Himself is rendered present

[5]"Regular confession," however, should not lead to another misconception of the sacraments that consists in making confession an obligation to be automatically fulfilled before each communion. Although an intimate link exists between the two, and should definitely be respected, confession should not, as often happens, be reduced to a simple "passport" that grants access to the Eucharist. Confession is the sacramental act of repentance by which we open ourselves to God's reconciling grace. As such, it should be preserved in the Church as a sacrament in its own right, a "synergism" of our conversion and God's forgiveness. It should be neither systematically associated with (and thereby subordinated to) the Eucharist, nor should it be totally replaced by "general confession," practiced as an expedient to facilitate frequent communion. As for the question of our "worthiness": it is precisely at the chalice that we confess ourselves to be "the first among sinners" and pray that our communion will be "for the healing of soul and body."

as "the Offerer and the Offered," the Celebrant and Sacrifice of the eucharistic mystery.

Ultimately, proclamation and celebration of the Word must resolve into silence. This characteristically Orthodox intuition is rooted in the apostolic witness and elaborated most fully in "hesychasm," the interior pilgrimage charted by the spiritual tradition of the Philocalia. Yet this pilgrimage is largely misunderstood and little appreciated even by Orthodox Christians. At the heart of this "way that leads to silence" is the voluntary self-abasement known as "kenotic obedience." In Christian existence it reflects the attitude of the Baptist before the mystery of the incarnate Logos: "He must increase, but I must decrease" (Jn 3:30). This attitude of humble self-effacement, however, is itself the reflection of Christ's own "kenosis," the obedient self-renunciation that He willingly assumes as the sacrificial Lamb of God.

The Word of God Himself, the Paschal Lamb slain before the foundation of the world (Rev 13:8), is the true and ultimate Sacrament of our salvation. As such, He offers the most compelling and eloquent expression of His power, authority and love, by concluding His earthly ministry in silence: silence before His accusers, before Pilate, and before the Cross.

God reveals Himself by speaking out of silence. But for silence itself to become the matrix of revelation, it must assume its own objective reality. Far from being a mere absence of noise, a momentary suppression of ambiant sounds, silence is an attitude or state of both mind and heart. Like solitude, its purpose is essentially spiritual: it creates a sacred space within the life of the person, enabling one to sense an invisible presence and to hear inaudible speech. At the same time, silence permits the person to articulate thoughts, feelings and longings to which ordinary human speech can give no shape or expression.

If the world is suspended in the twin dimensions of time and space, transcendent existence—what has been traditionally called the "mystical life"—unfolds in other dimensions of silence and solitude. As time and space are complementary expressions of a single, unified material reality, silence and solitude determine another immaterial reality: the "sacred space of the heart" that the apostle identifies as the Temple of the Holy Spirit. It is there, in the hidden depths of personal existence, that the Word reveals itself to be a Person, the source and sustainer of all that renders truly "personal" those created in His divine image. There, in the silence of the inner sanctuary, the Word discloses the mystery of the divine will by creating a deep and genuine "communication," a *koinonia* or communion, between divine and human life.

God speaks from silence to silence. As the ultimate expression and realization of the divine mystery of His saving grace, silence, in the words of St Isaac the Syrian, is "the sacrament of the world to come." Through this process, by which proclamation in this age resolves into the divine silence of the age to come, the Word of Scripture and of liturgical celebration derives its power as a source of authentic knowledge and eternal life.

PART I

INTERPRETING THE WORD

CHAPTER I

The Hermeneutic Problem

Despite a renewed emphasis upon biblical studies in our seminaries today, critical exegesis of the Bible remains an enterprise little understood and still less appreciated by most Orthodox Christians. The Holy Gospel, they feel, should be heard and venerated in the Church as the divine Word, "full of grace and truth." By what pretension, they ask, do we presume the right to "criticize" God's self-revelation?

This way of posing the question does not mean that the Orthodox share with fundamentalists a notion of biblical literalism and inerrancy. Even those who are theologically least sophisticated appreciate the divine-human character of Scripture; they are fully aware that God discloses His Person and will through human experience interpreted by human language. The question does indicate, however, that most Orthodox consider historical-critical research into the origin, authorship, purpose, and meaning of biblical writings to be somehow suspect, even a blasphemous tampering with the canon that can only lead to distortion of its inspired message. While the blood of the martyrs may be the seed of the Church, as Tertullian affirmed, the sweat of the exegete can only be the seed of heresy...

This widespread attitude is due largely to an inadequate knowledge or plain misunderstanding of the methods and results of exegesis as it is practiced by scholars of other Christian confessions. Even in the "diaspora," Orthodox Christians have long tended to reject the technical language of exegesis ("historical-critical method," "form" and "redaction" analysis, etc.) as though the terms themselves betrayed some sinister motive on the part of the exegete to demolish traditional views of apostolic authorship, compositional unity and doctrinal teaching. It is true that many exegetes have called into question such views. Only in the rarest of cases, however, has personal polemic totally invalidated their research for biblical studies in general and for Orthodox scriptural teaching in particular.

Recent studies by Orthodox exegetes[1] have in fact confirmed what our Protestant and Catholic brethren have long been saying, that exegetical method as such is neutral. It is an instrument, a working tool, that like any sharp implement can be used for good or ill. With the growth and deepening of ecumenical relations, Orthodox lay people, as well as theologians, are gradually discovering that scientific study of the biblical texts is both useful and necessary for hearing the true message of the written Word of God and for proclaiming that message in a language that speaks clearly and convincingly to their contemporaries who live in a world of instinctive scepticism and spiritual confusion.

As the title of this chapter indicates, the following remarks are offered as general reflections upon the scientific discipline that guides the exegete as he moves from an initial "listening to the text" to interpreting that text for today: the discipline of biblical hermeneutics. Our purpose is to suggest an Orthodox answer to what biblical scholars call the "hermeneutic problem," an answer that gives full weight to the need for a rigorously scientific approach to biblical studies, while remaining faithful to Orthodox convictions concerning inspiration and the relationship between Holy Scripture and Holy Tradition.

I.

The aim of exegesis is to understand and to interpret the

[1]See especially V. Kesich, *The Gospel Image of Christ: The Church and Modern Criticism*, Crestwood, N.Y.: SVS Press, 1972.

meaning of written documents, particularly the Bible, by applying to the text pertinent insights of the historical, philological, archaeological and philosophical sciences. Exegesis itself is a scientific discipline insofar as it uses historical-critical methodology to answer questions concerning the origin of the text (who wrote it, when and where), its purpose (why it was written), its aim (to whom and to what situation it was written), and its function within the life of the community (its *Sitz im Leben* or "life-setting," as well as its "form" or literary genre). At the level of "lower criticism," exegetical research attempts to establish the original text of a biblical document as the author or "school" of authors composed it, and to lay the ground-work for "higher criticism" that seeks to determine the meaning or message of a given pericope within its original context. Developed chiefly by German Protestant scholars since the beginning of the 19th century, historical-critical methodology is accepted today by virtually all exegetes, regardless of their confessional background, as an indispensable tool of textual criticism and the scientific discipline of "introduction."

Biblical scholars do not agree, however, on the value and use of such methodology for determining the *meaning* of a given passage. The problem involved is two-fold: to determine the meaning of the apostolic writing in its original historical context, and to discern its significance for today in the internal life of the Church and for Christian mission to the world. Strictly speaking, the first aspect concerning the original message communicated by the biblical author is a scientific problem. In seeking its solution, exegetes are divided only by their selection of different critical methods used to study the text: for example, literary and form criticism, redaction criticism or structuralism. Most exegetes today employ a combination of these tools, and their differences concern the particular accent they place upon one or another of these diverse methods.

More serious disagreement occurs when the exegete attempts to interpret the doctrinal content of a biblical passage and to elaborate its significance for Christian life and faith.

Holy Scripture is unique in that it contains a universal message of divine origin. Understood by faith to be God's Word addressed to man, and not simply man's words about God, Scripture speaks to every age, irrespective of the latter's historical and cultural peculiarities. Of course, individual biblical writings were addressed to specific communities at given moments in the past. As the "Word of God," however, those same writings are timeless. They speak to man in the 20th century as directly and with as much authority as they did to the early Church. Yet because their message is couched in language and thought-forms that are historically and culturally conditioned, the message of the biblical writings is seldom transparent. Consequently, it must be interpreted anew by every generation: it must be translated into a modern idiom and explained in terms that are accessible to the modern mind. Only through such a procedure can God's Word of the past become God's Word for the present. On one level, this reinterpretation is the task of the preacher and the teacher. It is first of all, however, the problem of the exegete, who alone is qualified to undertake the arduous work of "interpreting" the text to lay bare its original meaning and to determine its importance for Christian doctrine.

But therein lies the difficulty. What criteria is the exegete to use in order to move from a scriptural Word of the past to a living Word for the present? How can he proceed from an historical-critical evaluation of the biblical text to an interpretation of its universal doctrinal signification? If God has revealed Himself in biblical language, a language conditioned by its time and its milieu, how can we interpret that language so that it speaks to us today in our own historical-cultural context? This is the question that lies at the heart of what biblical scholars call "the hermeneutic problem."

The word "hermeneutic" comes from the Greek *hermeneia,* which means "translation" or "interpretation/ explanation." As an independent scientific discipline hermeneutics has existed in Protestant theology since the beginning of this century. Its basic principles, which originated with Aristotle, were taken up and developed in various ways by specialists such as G. Heinrici, W. Dilthey and M. Heidegger. Influenced especially by the latter two, Rudolph Bultmann and his disciples transformed hermeneutics into a program of biblical interpretation that sought answers to questions concerning the origin and meaning of human existence. The fact should not be overlooked, however, that exegetical procedures employed by New Testament authors already presupposed certain fundamental hermeneutic principles. The program of "promise and fulfillment" woven throughout the Gospel of St Matthew is a well known case in point.

Generally speaking, we may say that hermeneutics establishes the rules that govern the interpretation of Scripture. Its primary aim is to apply the fruits of exegetical research to concrete situations within the Church and world of today. This essentially theological task, according to a popular formula, seeks to "make the Bible relevant for modern man," a formula that identifies "modern man" with the average literate and cultivated citizen of Western technological societies.

To accomplish this basic task, however, hermeneutics must begin by identifying "modern man" such as he actually is, in order to address him in ways consistent with his cultural and spiritual heritage. It is commonplace to affirm that the 20th century has experienced a prodigious progress in the descriptive and applied sciences, to the point that philosophy has given way to technology as the chief inspiration and preoccupation of our contemporaries. The result has been the transformation, perhaps more accurately the deformation, of 20th century man into a truncated being whose world-view is grounded primarily in sensory perception and whose major concerns are limited to practical application of the means of production. His personal and collective vision no longer embraces transcendent phenomena and ultimate values. Because miracles, for example, can be neither rationally explained nor produced at will, they do not and can not exist. As for death, it is no longer perceived as a "paschal" event, a "pass-over" into a fullness of life beyond earthly existence. To the contrary, death is dreaded as an arbitrary limitation, imposed upon the unwary and the unwilling by capricious forces beyond human control. "Technological man" is a stunted being, a caricature of the true Adam, devoid of ultimate meaning and transcendent destiny. To his eyes, God, neighbor and the world about him are prized above all for their utilitarian value. The bumper-sticker slogan "Prayer works!" is often his most noble expression of religious belief. His ardent quest for comfort and pleasure drives him to flee even the most elementary forms of asceticism, rendering him insensitive to the presence and demands of the God of love and judgment. Having suppressed a natural sense of awe before the *mysterium tremendum,* he has deprived himself of the sacred and precious gift of wonder. Although his science is often reduced to "scientism," it represents his sole source of value and consolation, and he clings to it with sectarian passion. In short, he is the willing victim of a severe spiritual crisis.

Profoundly sensitive to this crisis and its consequences for their contemporaries, Protestant theologians such as Bultmann and his followers tried to develop a biblical hermeneutic that would allow Scripture to speak in a language both accessible and acceptable to men and women of today. The famous program of "demythologization" attempted to interpret elements of biblical tradition that Bultmann considered to be symbolic or mythological, such as the nature miracles, healings and the bodily resurrection of Jesus. The problem raised by this program is essentially a hermeneutic one: what criteria should be used to distinguish an historical fact (a particular event) from a mythical image (an interpretation of the event in figurative, non-scientific language)? As Bultmann himself admitted, the exegete's presuppositions inevitably determine the results of his research.[2] To the extent that it attempts to "render the Bible relevant for today," therefore, exegesis necessarily departs

---

[2]R. Bultmann, "Ist voraussetzungslose Exegese möglich?", in *Theologische Zeitschrift* XIII (1957) 409-417; (ET: *Existence and Faith,* "Is Exegesis Without Presuppositions Possible?", N.Y., 1960, pp. 289-96); and "The Problem of Hermeneutics," in *Essays Philosophical and Theological* (= *Glauben und Verstehen,* Gesammelte Aufsätze II), S.C.M., London, 1955, pp. 234-261.

from the limits of a rigorously scientific discipline; it leaves the domain of objective historical investigation and enters into the realm of theological speculation. The question is whether or not such a step is legitimate.

What in fact is the proper relationship between exegesis and theology? Should the two be radically separated, as was the case until recently in Roman Catholic tradition, and to an extent remains the case in Protestantism with its heavy emphasis upon often non-biblical systematic and philosophical theology? This raises an even more basic question: Does the Bible actually speak to the life and faith of 20th century man? And if so, what are the hermeneutic presuppositions that will allow the interpreter to enlighten the present by the past? How can we break the so-called "hermeneutic circle" that results from the fact that while we seek to understand a given phenomenon in relation to its historical context, the context itself can only be properly understood on the basis of a prior understanding of the phenomena that determine it? The only way to resolve such a conundrum, and answer the multitude of questions that arise from it, is to identify the "hermeneutic bridge" or link that directly relates the life situation of Christians today with the Word of God as that Word comes to expression in Holy Scripture.

The three major Christian confessions, Protestant, Catholic and Orthodox, have suggested very different answers to the question, "What unites (and thus makes 'relevant') the apostolic witness to the present life of the Church?" Each of these answers appears to have been chiefly influenced by a particular conception of the work of the Holy Spirit within the Christian community. At the risk of over-simplifying, we can say that Protestant pneumatology is essentially "charismatic" insofar as it insists upon the spiritual illumination of the individual in his personal reading of the Bible.[3] This individualistic, charismatic accent, based upon biblical accounts of prophetic activity in Israel and in the early Church, became the cornerstone of Protestant theology in the 16th and 17th centuries. Reacting against the policy of the Roman

---

[3]See in this regard the monograph by Théo Preiss, *Le témoignage intérieur du Saint-Esprit*, Delachaux et Niestlé, Neuchâtel, 1946.

Church that denied lay people the right to read the Scriptures
for themselves, the Reformers not only rejected the authority
of the magisterium. They also eliminated the sacramental,
ecclesial context that had been proper to biblical proclamation and interpretation throughout the apostolic and patristic
periods. Rightly insisting that the Spirit is bound by no human
institution, the Reformers promulgated their principle of
sola scriptura: Scripture alone, the divinely inspired Word
of God, contains the fullness of revelation and thus suffices
for the faith and salvation of the believer who receives interior illumination by the operation of the Holy Spirit.

This conception of the Spirit, working through Scripture
to elicit faith and bring about the believer's personal justification (or "righteousness," *dikaiosynē*), had definite merit.
On the one hand it situated the Bible, and particularly the
New Testament, at the very center of Christian life and
faith, and thereby it managed to restore to Scripture its
"canonical" (that is, normative) value for determining
Church doctrine. On the other hand, it succeeded at least
partially in surmounting the division between exegesis and
dogmatic theology that subsists in the Catholic Church to
our day. From an Orthodox point of view, however, the
Protestants did not go far enough towards elaborating a
truly "spiritual" hermeneutic. By isolating pneumatology
from ecclesiology, they lost sight of the proper context in
which the message of the Holy Scriptures should be interpreted and proclaimed. The liturgy and sacraments were no
longer seen to be essential means for actualizing and ap-
propriating the Word of God. This vital work was to be
accomplished by preaching alone. The very expression "Word
of God" was restricted to the Bible and its exposition. "The
Word" thus became a purely verbal phenomenon. As a result,
the *hypostatic character of the Word*—the personal reality
of the divine Logos—became obscured by an exaggerated
accent placed on *words*: the written and spoken words of
Scripture and preaching.

This state of affairs provoked within Protestantism a
certain crisis, still unresolved, concerning the place of exegesis
in the elaboration of Christian doctrine. (The lack of a

clear solution to this problem, by the way, has tended to transform Protestant "systematic theology" into philosophical speculation that is by and large independent of the biblical witness. A notable example is the monumental but theologically unsatisfying *magnum opus* of Paul Tillich.) Protestant theologians affirm unreservedly that the Word of God is contained in the written documents of the Bible. Nevertheless, as they themeslves have so skillfully demonstrated, these writings are marked by the history and culture of their times to such an extent that they must be constantly reinterpreted in a new language, using new thought-forms, in order to speak in a pertinent fashion to each new generation.[4] But since modern Protestant hermeneutics accepts the presuppositions of a secularized, "demythologized" world-view, the question remains: What meaning can biblical writings have today, given the fact that they were addressed to a world that perceived the sacred at the very heart of daily experience and accepted as historical fact what we today would dismiss as "myth"?[5]

Bultmann tried to resolve this dilemma by attributing to authors of the New Testament, and especially to the Fourth Evangelist, a fundamental concern to eliminate mythological elements from the apostolic witness. His attempt was far from convincing. More to the point for the interpretation of Scripture was his program, taken up and variously adapted by his disciples, called "existential hermeneutics." Accentuat-

[4]This basically correct observation is carried by Protestant exegetes to an extreme that denies the possibility of a *theologia perennis*: "theology" must be recreated *sui generis* in and for each new age (see, e.g., the beginning of O. Kaiser's introduction to OT exegesis, in Kaiser and Kümmel, *Exegetical Method*, Seabury Press, N.Y., 1981). Such a view implies that there is no living Tradition within the Church, no doctrinal formulations of truth (divine revelation), and that truth itself is mutable and relative. This implication, a logical and indeed necessary deduction from the (immutable?) reformed doctrine *sola scriptura*, poses a formidable obstacle in the pathway towards theological unity between the Protestants and the Orthodox. For a perceptive critique of this position, with a call for creating within Western Christendom a "post-modern orthodoxy," see Thomas C. Oden, *Agenda for Theology*, Harper and Row, N.Y., 1979.

[5]Using "myth" in the incorrect, popular sense. "Myth" as defined by specialists in the history of religions, as well as by exegetes of the Bultmann-school, signifies a linguistic image that gives expression to an ineffable transcendent reality.

ing the dynamic aspect of the Word of God, certain major currents of Protestant theology characterize the biblical witness as a "language-event" (*Wortereignis,* G. Ebeling) that creates a personal encounter between man and God. Through (the preaching of) the Word, man is called to make a decision for or against the object of faith, for or against obedience to the divine will. From this perspective, the aim of hermeneutics is well summarized by the title Bultmann gave to his collected essays, *Glauben und Verstehen,* "Faith and Understanding," or rather "faith through understanding," the reverse of Anselm's maxim, *credo ut intelligam,* "I believe in order to understand." This means that Scripture serves first of all to answer fundamental questions concerning the meaning of human existence. By "hearing the Word," the individual attains self-knowledge: he knows himself to be a child of God, the object of divine grace and love.

This kind of existential hermeneutics is problematic for two reasons. In the first place, it makes subjective "understanding" an essential condition of faith. The consequent risk is to replace the apostolic imperative by the comparatively pedestrian exhortation of the Delphic oracle: "Know thyself!". Then again, it relegates to a secondary position the historical event in which faith is grounded. For over a decade, Protestant theologians such as W. Pannenberg and E. Fuchs have struggled to correct a tendency, especially prevalent among Bultmann's disciples, to devaluate history. Christian faith, they rightly insist, must be rooted in the concrete facts of its historical origins, that is, in the life and mission of Jesus as Christ and Lord, the incarnate Son of God.

If their efforts have not been entirely successful, it is due to a fundamental principle of Protestant hermeneutics that *a priori* limits the possibility for the exegete to span the temporal gulf that separates the age of Jesus from later generations of the Church. This principle holds that the primary aim of exegesis is to discern what is called the "literal" meaning of Scripture, that is, the meaning that the biblical author himself understood and intended to transmit. Although the literal sense must be the point of departure and the basis for any valid interpretation of a given text, its nearly exclusive role in Protestant exegesis tends to reduce the concept of "the Word of God" to this meaning alone. All the exegete can and should do is determine and explicate the author's intended meaning within his own historical-cultural framework. This means, however, that *revelation itself* is limited by the understanding of the biblical author and his ability to communicate that understanding through the written word. For from this perspective, revelation *by* the Word in the person of Jesus Christ is nothing more than revelation *of* the Word in the form of written *paradosis* or "tradition."

This tendency, resulting from dogmatic adherence to the principle of *sola scriptura,* inevitably leads the exegete into a sort of "hermeneutic impasse." This is because the strictly literal meaning of a biblical text is incapable of speaking in a direct, personal and relevant way to men and women of our day. Reduced to its purely literal sense, Scripture is no different from other ancient religious writings that purport to speak to man of God and divine reality. It remains an interesting collection of historical documents, on the level of philosophy and ethics perhaps even an inspiring one. It is not, however, understood and appreciated as the vehicle of revelation itself, the personal, self-disclosing communication of God to man. To span the centuries that separate the world of today from the world of the prophets and apostles, therefore, we must discover the "hermeneutic bridge," the key to interpretation that can unlock the mystery of the divine Word and render it both intelligible and accessible at every new moment and in every new historical situation.

II.

To the question, What is the "hermeneutic bridge" between the witness of Scripture and the present life of the Church, Protestant theology replies: the Word and its exposition.[6] This principle was articulated especially in Lutheran

[6]See especially G. Ebeling, "Zeit und Wort" in *Zeit und Geschichte* (Bultmann Festschrift), Tübingen, 1964, pp. 341-356, where the author

circles as a rebuttal to the Catholic claim that the hermeneutic
bridge was assured by the Church through the institution of
the magisterium. Neither "the Word" nor "the Church" as
institution, however, represents an adequate response to the
hermeneutic problem. For neither one nor the other, in and
of itself, has the capacity to *actualize in the present the
saving events of the past.* The Word bears witness to those
events, and the Church is the locus of their actualization.
The object of the biblical witness is actualized, however, only
by God Himself, acting within the eucharistic community
through the presence and power of the Holy Spirit. The
hermeneutic bridge between the biblical event and its actualization in the Church, then, is neither the preached Word
nor the ecclesial institution. It is the *person of the divine
Spirit.* This holds true even if we mean by "the Word" not
only Scripture and its proclamation, but also and primarily
Jesus Christ, the Logos of God. For although the risen and
glorified Christ continues His revelatory and saving work
within the Church, He does so through the person of the
Spirit (Jn 14:26; 16:13-15).

Since the Second Vatican Council, Catholic theologians
have gone far towards rediscovering the "hermeneutic function" of the Holy Spirit. In an interesting evaluation of "the
new hermeneutic,"[7] Fr Henri Cazelles proposes in the place
of an existential hermeneutic one that centers upon the
interpretive work of the Spirit within the liturgical-sacra-
mental community of the Church. From the point of view of
such a hermeneutic, he maintains, "Scripture presents itself
less as a Word of God than as the witness to a new, life-
giving gift of God, a creative power . . . Catholic hermeneutics
will perceive (in the Bible) an historical witness to human
life 'in the Spirit,' what we call 'grace.' " We want to

speaks of a "Zeitmacht des Wortes." See also his "Wort Gottes und
Hermeneutik" in *Wort und Glaube,* Tübingen, 1960, pp. 329-48. The latter
article was originally published in *Zeitschrift für Theologie und Kirche* 56
(1959), pp. 224-51, and has appeared in English translation in *Word and
Faith* (Philadelphia, Fortress Press, 1968), pp. 305-32. See also Ebeling's
"Die Bedeutung der kritisch-historischen Methode für die protestantische
Theologie und Kirche," *Wort und Glaube,* pp. 1-49 (=ZThK 47 [1950],
pp. 1-46; ET: *Word and Faith,* pp. 17-61).

[7]"La nouvelle herméneutique biblique" (Bruxelles 1969), p. 10f.

develop this insight from an Orthodox perspective by re-formulating our original question: In what way does the Spirit serve as the hermeneutic bridge that actualizes the past in the present life of the Church? What solution, in other words, can Orthodox pneumatology propose towards resolving the "hermeneutic problem"?

Before attempting to answer this question, we need first to modify the traditionally accepted distinction between the various "senses" of Scripture. Catholic scholars such as H. de Lubac and J. Coppens have sought to correct a one-sided Protestant hermeneutic that limits itself to a quest for the literal sense of a biblical passage. Acknowledging the value and necessity of historical-critical methodology for discerning the literal meaning of a text, Fr Coppens in particular adopted and refined the patristic theory of a fuller "spiritual sense," a *sensus plenior,* which means the sense that God Himself seeks to communicate through the biblical account. The question of whether or not the biblical author understood this fuller meaning is secondary. The essential point is that each passage of Scripture contains a "double sense," at once literal and spiritual.

This conclusion, however, first spelled out by Origen, betrays a certain misunderstanding of the limits of the Spirit's operation within history. Can we hold that the Spirit inspires biblical authors to communicate certain truths (II Tim 3:16; II Pet 1:10-12) and yet ignore His influence upon the historical events to which those authors bear witness? Or ignore His influence upon those who interpret the biblical witness in each successive generation? Scripture itself attests to the fact that the operation of the Spirit is not limited to the inspiration of the biblical author. The sphere of His influence extends also to the development of historical events, as well as to the interpretation and actualization of those events within the preaching of the Church and its liturgical celebration.

This means in the first place that every true sense of Scripture is, properly speaking, a "spiritual" sense, in that it ultimately stems from the operation of the Spirit Himself. It is, of course, both necessary and useful to distinguish between a literal sense (that is, what the biblical author understood and intended to communicate) and a *sensus plenior* (i.e., what God seeks to convey through the biblical witness, regardless of whether the author perceived that message). The "literal sense," however, is also a "spiritual sense" insofar as both the author's witness and the saving events to which he bears witness are inspired and molded by the Holy Spirit. From a Christian perspective, based upon personal and communal experience, "fallen" human history is preserved from anarchy and chaos by God who performs His mighty acts of salvation within it. This is not to affirm a naïve liberal view of inevitable progress within history, nor even an evolutionary theory that would situate eschatological fulfillment within the "space-time continuum." It means simply that events are not random, that the Creator and Redeemer works out His economy of salvation within that continuum and thereby establishes a veritable "salvation-history" within the created order. We have little difficulty conceiving of the inspirational activity of the Spirit upon persons, be they prophets, apostles or even later interpreters. Less evident is the activity of the Spirit in shaping historical events. The conviction that the Spirit does so operate, however, underlies the principal hermeneutic method employed by both the apostolic witnesses and the Church Fathers: the method of *typology*.

In his important study entitled *The Face of Christ in the Old Testament*, Prof. Georges Barrois remarks that "the first condition of validity for typological interpretation is that there be an ontological relationship between the type and the typified mystery, by reason of the gradual realization, within time, of God's eternal design."[8] Thus the Exodus from Egypt foreshadows the return of Israel from captivity in Babylon, and both events are prophetic images of our salvation accomplished through Christ's death and resurrection. Similarly, the crossing of the Jordan by Joshua prefigures the baptism of Jesus in the Jordan, which is itself "a prototype of our regeneration and of our deliverance

---

[8]*The Face of Christ in the Old Testament*, Crestwood, N.Y.: SVS Press, 1974, pp. 43-44.

from sin and death." Thus, Prof. Barrois continues, "the Old Testament types prepare the revelation of the New, and the Gospel illumines the mysterious events of the past. Typology, therefore, appears to be an integral part of the divine economy, essentially linked with the progression of Sacred History toward its *telos,* its ultimate goal, the kingdom that is to come."[9]

Typology is based upon the premise that historical events in Israel's history are related in terms either of "promise and fulfillment" or of "prototype to antitype." The above statement by Prof. Barrois stresses the role of typology in the unilateral movement of salvation-history toward its *telos* or fulfillment in the Kingdom of God. From this viewpoint, a type may be defined as a prophetic image that points forward to and is fulfilled by some future antitype or eternal archetype.

Typological relationships, however, are characterized by a double movement: from the past towards the future, but also from the future towards the past. What is often forgotten in discussions of typology is the crucial point that a type is not merely a sign that points toward a future or transcendent reality. It is also an historical locus in which that reality is proleptically realized. For the *telos* is an *eschatological reality* that breaks into the historical order, to render itself accessible to those who approach it with faith. A *crux interpretum* of New Testament exegesis well illustrates this point.

In 1 Corinthians 10, St Paul presents his two-fold interpretation of the "Body of Christ" as the eucharistic bread and as the *ekklēsia,* the assembly of baptized believers. He introduces this passage by an enigmatic reference to the experience of Israel during its desert wanderings, when the people were "baptized" in the cloud and sea, ate a common "spiritual food" and drank a common "spiritual drink." The apostle continues, "They drank from a spiritual rock that followed them, and this rock was Christ" (*hē petra de ēn ho Christos*). This image of a spiritual rock that followed the Israelites through the desert is found neither in the

[9]*Ibid.,* p. 43.

Exodus 17 and Numbers 20 accounts that relate the desert
crossing, nor elsewhere in the Old Testament. Whether its
origins are to be traced to rabbinic exegesis or, as Prof.
Barrois suggests, to reflection upon the Divine Wisdom in
Hellenistic Judaism,[10] need not concern us here. The crucial
point is that to the apostle's mind, *Christ was present among
the people of Israel in pre-incarnate form.* A virtual identification is established between the rock and Christ, between
the prototype and its antitype, such that the eschatological
antitype is conceived as being present to or existing in the
historical prototype. Conversely, we may say that the historical prototype, the rock, *participates* in the eschatological
antitype (Christ), insofar as the rock serves as the locus
at which the antitype reveals itself. "The rock is Christ"
because and insofar as "Christ is the rock." That is, Christ,
the eternal Son of God, enters into Israel's history as the
source of living water that sustains the people during their
sojourn in the desert. The rock is thus a *typos* in the double
sense of the word. On the one hand, it points forward to
the incarnate life and historical ministry of Jesus Christ,
from whose side flowed life-giving water and blood, themselves typological images of the sacraments of baptism and
eucharist. On the other hand, the rock as a prototype serves
as the locus at which the future saving work of Christ is
proleptically realized in Israel's history: the people's thirst
is actually assuaged by the living water that flows from the
rock. This is not because of some magical quality inherent in
the rock itself, but because the rock—unbeknownst to the
people—has been selected by the divine will as the historical
locus where the Son of God, the eternal, creative and life-
giving Word, manifests Himself to them.

The fact that this theophany appears as a revelation of
the Son of God only to the later Christian interpreter does
not alter the objective reality of the typological relationship
that exists between the historical prototype and the future
antitype. The desert rock points forward to the future incarnation and activity of Jesus Christ; but in Prof. Barrois'
terms, an *ontological relationship* exists between the type

10*Ibid.,* p. 85 and p. 165 n. 12; cf. the reference to Dt 32, p. 156.

and the typified mystery, such that St Paul can affirm, "the rock *was* Christ."

A similar typological interpretation must be made of the manna in the desert and the paschal lamb. Each of these Old Testament images is a prototype of the coming Son of God, He who proclaims Himself to be the true Bread from heaven and who gives His life as a vicarious offering for the sins of the world. Yet the prototype itself "contains," so to speak, the future reality. Church Tradition sees in the manna and in the paschal lamb the operation of the eternal, divine Son, who nourishes Israel in the desert and expiates the people's sins through the temple sacrifices. Accordingly, Melito of Sardis could affirm in his well-known pashal homily that "Christ suffered in Able, was exposed in Moses, etc.", and he could speak of Old Testament types as *mysteria* or "sacraments" of Christ's presence among the people of Israel.

This digression concerning typological relationships has been necessary to illustrate a key point in our discussion of hermeneutic method. the fact that God acts continually *within history* to shape events towards realization of the divine economy. History and eternity must not be conceived as two distinct dimensions of reality, utterly separate from one another. Historical events must not be interpreted as though they belonged to a "secular realm" in which God is absent, dead, or at best relegated to the status of a strictly future *telos*. Eschatological reality manifests itself actively in the present historical order. Therefore the late Fr George Florovsky could speak of an "inaugurated eschatology," a divine consummation already in the process of realization. This means that no hermeneutic can do justice to the correlation and significance of historical events unless it takes seriously the patristic conception of Sacred History, consisting of events that are related to each other according to the laws of typology. For "typology" is not simply a human mode of interpretation. It is first of all a *divine mode of activity within history*. God acts in terms of promise and

fulfillment, coordinating historical events in such a way that
the future fulfillment is continually being realized throughout the history of Israel and in the subsequent history of
the Church.

Divine activity within history, however, is the activity
of the three divine Hypostases or Persons of the Father,
the Son and the Holy Spirit. Insofar as typological interpretation discerns "the face of Christ in the Old Testament,"
it must take full account of the complementary operation of
the Spirit in guiding Israel's salvation-history towards ultimate
fulfillment in the Kingdom of God.

The Nicene Creed affirms that the Spirit "spoke by the
prophets," and Christian faith accepts without question His
inspirational activity in shaping both the prophetic word
and the written text of Scripture. (This does not imply,
however, a doctrine of literal or verbal inspiration. The
Spirit acts by "synergy," i.e., by cooperating with the human
agent in such a way that the inspired word remains a human
word, subject to the historical, cultural and linguistic conditions of its time.) As we have seen, the economy of the
Spirit is by no means limited to prophetic inspiration, despite
the fact that the Credo alludes only to this particular activity.
From the creation recounted in Genesis 1, through the
charismatic ministry of the Judges and on to the spiritual
renewal of Israel following the captivity in Babylon, the
ruach-Yahweh or Spirit of the Lord is active in creating and
shaping historical events as well as prophetic words. Known
throughout the Ancient Near East as a transcendent power
active within history, the divine ruach reveals itself at
Pentecost to be God Himself, the Holy Spirit who distributes
the various charismata, the "spiritual gifts," necessary for
the growth and organization of the Church as well as for
its mission within the world.

The relationship between the activity of the Spirit and
the activity of the Son in Israel's history is evident to the
apostolic witnesses, although none of them attempts to describe it in a systematic way. The Old Testament speaks of
the Spirit and His operation; it does not, of course, speak
explicitly of the Son. Yet the prophetic words and events

inspired by the Spirit point to the Son, thereby preparing the people for the inauguration of the messianic age in the historical person of Jesus Christ. We may affirm, then, that it is the Spirit Himself who correlates words and events in such a way that they find their fulfillment in Christ. It is the Spirit, in other words, who creates typological relationships within history. The Spirit and the Son thus work together for the salvation of Israel, the one creating and the other fulfilling the conditions of the divine economy.

A similar complementarity characterizes the activity of the Spirit and the Son within the New Israel of the Church. Just as the eternal Word manifested Himself to Israel in the form of prophetic utterance inspired by the *ruach* of God, that same Word, risen and glorified, continues His revelatory activity within the Christian community through the Person of the Spirit of Truth. The essential point is that the influence of the Spirit extends beyond the work of stimulating and guiding the thought processes of the biblical authors. For inspiration is a *global* phenomenon that encompasses not only the author, but also the *interpreter* of Scripture.

We should recall that to the authors of the New Testament documents, Holy Scripture consisted of what we call the "Old Testament." Their own writings, therefore, are in large measure interpretations of the Law, the Prophets and the other Writings of Israel. Once these apostolic works were themselves accepted as inspired "scripture" and acquired canonical status alongside the books of the Old Testament, successors to the apostles continued the activity of scriptural interpretation, not as a personal exercise undertaken on their own authority, but *under the continuing guidance of the Spirit within the ecclesial community.* Those who most faithfully reflect that guidance are recognized, venerated and studied as Fathers of the Church. The Spirit of Pentecost, however, never ceases to dwell within the community of believers, to lead them progressively into "all the truth" (Jn 16:13). His chief inspirational activity under the new covenant in Christ takes the form of "interpretation of the Scriptures." It is essentially a *hermeneutic* function, begun among the people of Israel and pursued throughout the present age and into the age of the Kingdom.

This hermeneutic activity of the Spirit of Truth involves three interrelated elements: 1) the historical event; 2) proclamation of the soteriological significance of that event by the biblical author; and 3) interpretation and actualization of that proclamation by the Church in each new generation. The work of the Spirit consists in *supplying* the event with typological significance and in leading the prophetic, apostolic or later witness to *discern* that significance and then to *proclaim* and *transmit* it as an element of Church Tradition. St Paul's affirmation to Timothy, "all Scripture is inspired by God" (II Tim 3:16), should be understood as referring to this global inspirational activity of the Holy Spirit. For it is the Spirit who inspires first the prophets to *hear* and to *announce* the divine Word of judgment and grace; then Jesus, the eternal Word of God, to *proclaim* His message with full divine authority (Jn 3:34); then the apostles to *interpret* and *transmit* the Word; and finally the later prophets, teachers, and particularly bishops, to *preserve* the Word of Truth: all of this, so that the faithful might receive and translate that Word into works of love "for the life of the world and its salvation."

III.

It is incumbent upon Orthodoxy to preserve exegesis as a function of the worshiping Church. This is because exegesis is properly a *theological* discipline. Although based upon scientific procedure, it transcends the limits of pure science to delve into the realm of divine mystery, a realm that by its very nature exists beyond the field of empirical research. This awareness, that the object of theological inquiry remains forever beyond the limits of scientific procedure, obliges Orthodoxy to reject the popular Western image of theology as *die Königin der Wissenschaften,* the Queen of the Sciences. As a contemplation of divine life and its relation to human existence, theology is infinitely more than a science, however exalted scientific method and aims may be. Otherwise, theology is mere illusion.

In order to proclaim a living and life-giving Word for the Church, exegesis must go beyond the critical tasks of establishing the text and deciphering the message intended by the biblical author. To recover the proper doctrinal and doxological dimensions of Scripture, *the exegete himself must participate in the process of divine revelation.* He must submit himself and his skill to the guiding influence of the Holy Spirit, if his efforts are to bear fruit for faith and salvation. For exegesis, as an integral part of the Church's theological activity, is a *theandric* process, a divine-human enterprise based upon *synergy* or cooperation between the divine Spirit and the human interpreter.

Viewed in this light, the role of the modern interpreter (exegete or preacher) is recognized to be every bit as important as the role of the biblical author in receiving and transmitting the divine Word. Protestant theology has developed this intuition into a doctrine that lays primary emphasis upon proclamation of the Word. "How are men to hear without a preacher?," asks St Paul in Romans 10; and the Reformers responded to this rhetorical question by defending the truth of another Pauline affirmation, "the Gospel is the power of God for salvation to everyone who has faith" (Rom 1:16). Our Protestant brethren have a great deal to teach us about the central place of the Word of God in Christian life and missions. As Orthodox, however, our responsibility is to insist upon the fact that the true place of the Word—its exegesis as well as its proclamation—is within the liturgical, sacramental community of the Church. This is a point of utmost importance, one that has been neglected or denied by many of the main currents of Protestant theology and exegesis.

For its part, Roman Catholic theology has yet to rediscover the essential unity that exists between Scripture and Tradition. The danger among contemporary Catholic exegetes, liberated by Pope Pius XII and his successors from undue submission to the demands of dogmatic theology, is to assume with their Protestant counterparts that Scripture can be interpreted *in vacuo,* apart from the illumination provided by the whole of ecclesial Tradition. Scripture and Tradition must not be conceived as two opposed or even complementary realities. Scripture is an integral part of Tradition that serves as the norm or canon of Truth, the measure by which all authentic Tradition is recognized and verified. This fact explains the Orthodox insistence that Holy Scripture belongs *in the Church,* the Church being the locus or sphere of that living Tradition, the point of encounter between mankind and the divine Word.[11] For it is only in the Church that the Spirit actualizes the Word in the *liturgy,* in the *sacraments* and in the *preaching* of the Gospel. This He does by virtue of His "hermeneutic function," the continual inspirational activity that permits the Word of God to be interpreted anew in every present moment and for every new generation.

The doing of exegesis thus requires a "leap of faith" that takes it beyond the realm of the empirical sciences. That leap of faith presupposes—without objective proof, yet on the basis of ecclesial experience—that the Holy Spirit is the principal agent in the work of interpretation. It is He who creates of apparently random events a veritable history-of-salvation and reveals the meaning of those events through the hermeneutic activity of the Church. Without this presupposition, affirming the interpretive function of the Spirit, the so-called "hermeneutic circle" remains closed: no key exists to unlock the mystery of a past phenomenon so as to render it constantly "actual" and "relevant" for the present. Without such a presupposition, the Word of Scripture remains a lifeless word of the past, a mere dead letter. For if the preached Word possesses "the power of God for salvation," it is only because of the divine origin and inspiration of that Word.

The Holy Spirit, as Spirit of Truth, can alone break the "hermeneutic circle" by serving as the "bridge" or hermeneutic link that reactualizes and renders accessible the

[11]See the article by Fr Thomas Hopko, "The Bible in the Orthodox Church," *St Vladimir's Theological Quarterly* vol. 14, no. 1-2/1970, pp. 66-99; reprinted in *All the Fullness of God,* SVS Press, N.Y., 1982, pp. 49-90.

Word of God at every moment within the ongoing life of the Church through its preaching and its liturgical celebration. As the ultimate *source, interpreter* and *fulfillment* of Scripture, and therefore of theology itself, the Spirit thus guides the Church "into all the Truth," towards its *telos*, its final consummation in the Kingdom of God.

CHAPTER II

The Patristic Setting for "Theoretic" Hermeneutics

The Orthodox Church is faced today with the challenge of rediscovering and developing a biblical hermeneutic which remains faithful to the contemplative, spiritual vision (*theōria*) of the Greek Fathers, while addressing itself with relevance and conviction to the modern world.[1] The aim here is to make some small contribution to this truly awesome task.

We begin with a survey and evaluation of the exegetical methods used by the theologians of Alexandria and Antioch from the third to the fifth centuries. They, above all, established guidelines for exegetical method, and no Orthodox hermeneutic can fail to take seriously their immense contribution to the Church's understanding of Holy Scripture. In the following chapter, we propose a reinterpretation of *theōria* as the basis of a hermeneutic which can respond faithfully and adequately to the present needs of the Church.

I. *Philosophical and exegetical background*

Two related but opposing schools of Greek philosophical thought played major roles in shaping the methods of biblical exegesis in use at Alexandria and Antioch during the third

[1]An important group of articles on exegetical method and biblical interpretation can be found in The Greek Orthodox Review, vol. 17, no. 1, 1972 (S. Agourides, V. Kesich, Th. Stylianopoulos).

and fourth centuries A.D. The older school, which originated
with Plato (ca. 429-347 B.C.), inspired the allegorical interpretation favored by the Alexandrians. The younger, reflecting the historical rationalism of Aristotle (384-322 B.C.),
influenced Antiochian as well as medieval Western hermeneutics. It also left its mark upon the historical-critical method
developed by German Lutheran and other Protestant scholars
in the latter half of the 19th century.

According to Plato's theory of knowledge, ultimate reality
(*alētheia*) is apprehended by the intellect rather than by
sense perception. The sphere of *alētheia* is the transcendent
world of "forms" or "ideas" in which the immortal human
soul has its origin. Salvation consists in an escape: through
"recollection" (*anamnēsis*) of its celestial origins, the soul
breaks free from the fetters of material existence and passes
into the transcendent realm of eternal truth.

Similar soteriological ideas were spawned in a great
variety of esoteric cults influenced by Persian religion, especially Mythraism and other "mysteries" such as those of
Osiris, Isis, and Orpheus. Today it is widely recognized that
second-century Christian gnosticism received its chief inspiration from sources such as these. Reitzenstein, Bultmann, Jonas,
and others have proven beyond reasonable doubt the existence
of a pre-Christian gnosticism which, although highly diverse
in its many expressions, taught an essentially Platonic doctrine of salvation. Of equal importance is the early gnostic
anthropology which was taken over and reworked by Christian
heretics such as Valentinus and Basilides. This doctrine of
man teaches a rigorous exclusivism. As we know from the
polemical writings of Irenaeus and Tertullian,[2] the Christian
gnostics asserted that humanity is divided into three classes
or types of persons who differ according to their nature: the
hulikoi or *sōmatikoi* (who are "earthly" or carnal), the
psychikoi ("psychics," animated by the *psychē* or life-principle
of heavenly origin), and the *pneumatikoi* ("spirituals," who
know their celestial origins by virtue of *gnōsis* or saving
knowledge). The *sōmatikoi* are the "simple," condemned to

[2]Irenaeus, adv. Haer. 1:7:5 (PG 7:35); Tertullian, adv. Val. 29 (PL
2:583f).

a purely mundane existence without hope of salvation. The *psychikoi* can be saved by acquiring a limited *gnōsis* and by practicing a moral *imitatio Christi*. Only the *pneumatikoi*, however, can attain perfect union with God through divine *gnōsis* or knowledge of Jesus Christ as the "saved Savior."

Anthropological and soteriological ideas of this kind were destined to influence, for better or worse, the hermeneutic method developed at Alexandria in the early centuries of our era. By opposing the eternal realm of truth to the historical world of matter, the heirs of Platonic philosophy tended to devaluate the concept of history and, consequently, the historical framework of revelation. From their point of view, a temporal event as such has no ultimate or final meaning. It is nothing more than the vehicle of expression for an invisible, eternal reality which has no true ontological insertion in the ephemeral domain of history. Interpretation of historical events consists in discerning their "spiritual sense"; that is, the deeper significance of the eternal, celestial reality which expresses itself within human life. Stated as a hermeneutic principle, the aim is to discern the "hidden meaning" of an event by laying bare the eternal truth enshrined within it. The purely historical or "literal sense" (i.e., the sense understood and intended by the author of the report in question), while valuable for situating the revelation in its temporal context, is of merely secondary importance. It should be noted that this kind of mystical idealism is incapable of grasping the true meaning of either incarnation (the assumption of flesh or physical existence) or resurrection (the transformation of a physical body into a spiritual body).

It was in just such a conceptual milieu that the hermeneutic method of "allegory" developed. Long before the Christian era, Greek philosophers had employed allegory to interpret the poems of Homer and Hesiod. Stoics used the same method to discern in ancient myths the roots of their monistic philosophy. In the same spirit, the Alexandrian Jew Philo (ca. 30 B.C. to 45 A.D.) made use of allegory in his quest to reconcile the teachings of the Old Testament with Greek philosophy. As did his predecessor Aristobulus, Philo used allegory to eliminate embarrassing anthropomorphisms in the Hebrew Scriptures. Attempting to uncover the spiritual meaning of the law of Moses and of prophecy, Philo abandoned the literal meaning of Scripture when passages spoke in terms he deemed unworthy of God, or when repetitions or contradictions appeared in the text. Thereby he managed to reveal the "true" spiritual sense of the biblical witness which was concealed behind the shadow of the literal sense. Allowing his hermeneutic method to color his theology, Philo depicted God not as a Lord of love, anger and judgment, but as pure transcendent Being who reveals Himself in the mediating Logos.[3]

In the period of late-Judaism, Alexandria became the chief center of encounter between Old Testament faith and the mystical, metaphysical speculation of the philosophers. Here the Septuagint was produced, incorporating Greek modes of thought into a translation of the Hebrew Scriptures. Alexandrian influence also bore heavily upon the midrashic method of exegesis developed by the Rabbis.[4] This method distinguished four different but complementary meanings within Scripture: 1) *peshat* (the literal or historical sense), 2) *remez* (the hidden sense of the Mosaic law and of Halakah, the corpus of legal decisions based on the law), 3) *darush* (the allegorical sense, expressed in the form of Haggadoth or legends), and 4) *sod* (the mystic or kabbalistic sense). Emphasis was often given to the allegorical interpretation in such a way as to downgrade history as the sphere of the divine economy. In reaction against the excesses of allegory, certain Rabbis such as Hillel promulgated various hermeneutic rules, of which one of the most important was the principle of interpreting one passage of Scripture by another which was less obscure. Hermeneutics of this kind, of course, are only possible where Scripture is viewed as integrally and uniformly inspired by the Spirit of God.

If the philosophy of Plato can be characterized as a

[3]De migr. Ab. 174; de opif. mun. 20, 24.
[4]E. L. Dietrich, art. "Schriftauslegung im Judentum," RGG[3] 1515ff; R. Greer, *Theodore of Mopsuestia, Exegete and Theologian*, London 1961, p. 86ff.

mystical, speculative idealism, that of his disciple Aristotle represents rather an empirical realism. According to Aristotle, the material world is ontologically real; "forms" or "universals" exist only within particular "substances" (*ousiai*). The soul, for example, constitutes the universal of the material body, the two being united in the individual human being. Aristotelian thought was also marked by a rationalism which unequivocally rooted the meaning of events within history.

This radical modification of Platonic dualism had important repercussions upon the hermeneutics as well as upon the theology of the school of Antioch. On the one hand, its realistic conception of the material world and of history remained faithful to the Old Testament view of God who reveals Himself in and through concrete events. On the other hand, it gave rise to an unfortunate tendency towards historical positivism which often refused to accept a typological interpretation of biblical passages, even where such interpretations were sanctioned by apostolic authority. As we shall point out, this tendency is particularly evident in the works of Theodore of Mopsuestia. This same positivism inevitably led to the exaggerations of Antiochian christology represented by Theodore and Nestorius, as well as to a soteriology which substituted the theme of communion with God by adoption (*koinonia*—Theodore) for that of the deification of man by grace (*theōsis*—Athanasius).

It would be a mistake, however, to stereotype Alexandrian exegesis as purely allegorical and Antiochian as purely historical, as though the former were uniquely concerned with the spiritual sense of the text, while the latter sought only the historical or literal sense. The exegetes of both schools were primarily concerned with the quest of revealed truth, pursued by means of *theōria*, an interpretive vision which sought to discern the spiritual meaning of the Word of God. It is significant in this regard that Cyril, an Alexandrian *par excellence*, often stressed historical precision (*tēs historias to akribes*) over the spiritual vision of a biblical passage (*tēs pneuma-*

tikēs theōrias tēn apodosin),[5] whereas Theodore of Mopsuestia, the arch-enemy of allegory, held that the most exalted sense of Scripture was the sense revealed by typology.[6]

Although the schools of Alexandria and Antioch favored two very different methods of exegesis, their concern was the same: to define and explain the relationship between the Scriptures of the Old Testament and the apostolic writings of the early Church. From the time of the resurrection (Lk 24:44ff), Christians lived by the conviction that the Old Testament bore witness to the divine economy which was fulfilled in the person and ministry of Jesus Christ. The Hebrew Scriptures were cherished as a preparation for the New Covenant. The Old Testament was thus regarded as an essentially Christian book. But this raised a difficult hermeneutic question: in what sense and under what form is the Christian proclamation to be found there? What method of interpretation (*hermēneia*) would enable the Church to discover and elucidate the images of Christ and His saving work which were hidden behind the persons and events of Jewish sacred history?

Before we turn to the different answers to these questions proposed by Alexandrian and Antiochian exegetes, it would be useful to note two hermeneutic principles defended by both camps.

In the first place, they were persuaded by the influence of their common Jewish heritage that Holy Scripture is uniformly inspired and, indeed, "written" by the Spirit, who expresses Himself in the language of the human author.[7] Two key passages from the apostolic writings affirmed this principle: "All scripture is inspired by God" (2 Tim 3:16) and "no prophecy was ever inspired [lit. borne] by the will of man, but men inspired by the Holy Spirit spoke from God" (2 Pet 1:21). The authors of these two passages were speak-

[5]Prologue to Isaiah comm., (PG 70:9).

[6]In Ioel (PG 66:232); in Ionam Praef. (PG 66:317ff).

[7]Origen, c. Cels. 5:60 (PG 11:1:1276); Basil, hom. in pss. 1:1 (PG 29:1:210) *Pasa graphē theopneustos . . . dia touto sungrapheisa para tou pneumatos;* Theodoret, praef. in pss. (PG 80:865) *tou theiou pneumatos tēn aiglēn* (lumen) *edexato;* Kelly, J.N.D. *Early Christian Doctrines,* London 1960, p. 60f.

ing of the Old Testament, which was sacred Scripture to early Christians prior to the establishment of a New Testament canon. But it is not impossible that the quotation from 2 Timothy includes in the term "scripture" the words of Jesus together with certain elements of the apostolic kerygma.[8] In any case, the epistles of St Paul and the Synoptic Gospels, which themselves interpreted the Old Testament in the light of the incarnation and resurrection, were acknowledged to have the authority of sacred Scripture by the beginning of the second century.[9] According to the perspective of the post-apostolic Church, then, the Holy Spirit inspired not only the books of the Old Testament, but also (selected) writings of the apostles which commented upon those books. Further on we shall consider the importance of this understanding of inspiration as it concerns the problem of Scripture and Tradition.

The second major hermeneutic principle recognized by both schools held that since Jesus as Christ had fulfilled the prophecies of the Old Covenant, the true meaning of prophecy could only be discerned by means of typology. As discussed in the previous chapter, a "type" (*typos*) may be defined as a prophetic image (a person, place, object, or event) that points forward to and is fulfilled by a corresponding future reality (the antitype). As applied to the Old Testament, typology seeks to uncover the deeper spiritual significance of various types of prophetic images which foreshadow New Testament antitypes. Its justification lies in the conviction that God Himself, as author of history as well as of Scripture, ordains events in terms of "promise and fulfillment." This presupposes that history is sacred rather than secular. It is truly a *Heilsgeschichte* or salvation-history, the sphere of divine economy in which man and the cosmos progress under the guidance of God towards eternal salvation.

Jesus Himself used, explicitly or implicitly, various typological images from the Old Testament and intertestamental writings to communicate to His disciples the meaning of His

[8]Compare, e.g., I Tim 5:18 with Lk 10:7.
[9]II Pet 3:15f; Ignatius, Smyrn. 5, 7, 8; Phil 5; Clem Rom, ad Cor 63:2; II Clem 2:4.

person and work (Son of Man, Servant of Yahweh, Davidic King or Son of God, etc.) He is proclaimed by the Church to be the new Moses who fulfills the Torah of Israel: His sacrifice on the cross manifests the perfect law of love incarnate in His person (Mt 5:17; Jn 13:34; Gal 5:14, etc.). By combining Jesus' quotation of Psalm 22 with other verses drawn from the psalter and prophecies,[10] the Evangelists affirm that the promises of the Old Covenant have been fulfilled in the crucified Christ. From beginning to end, St Luke's Gospel displays a hermeneutic program of promise and fulfillment: the economy of God in Jesus Christ is brought to completion "according to the Scriptures" (cf. 1 Cor 15:3f). The most typical expression of this program is given by St Matthew: "All this took place to fulfill what the Lord had spoken by the prophet . . ." (1:22 et passim, RSV). The same theme dominates the Acts of the Apostles, the Epistle to the Hebrews, and such post-apostolic writings as the letter of Ignatius to the Magnesians (chs. 8f).

Typological interpretation of the Old Testament was thus normative from the very beginnings of Church tradition. What distinguished and separated the schools of Alexandria and Antioch were their respective methods of developing typology into two very different hermeneutic systems: the Alexandrians sought to uncover allegorical symbolism, whereas the Antiochians insisted on preserving the historical meaning revealed in and through the prophetic image or type.

II. The exegetical school of Alexandria

We have noted that Alexandrian hermeneutics bore the imprint of a Hellenistic philosophy which was firmly embedded in the speculative idealism of Plato. Among Jewish interpreters, Philo and the Rabbis drew deeply from this dualistic, mystical wellspring. Accordingly, they often used allegorical methods to discern the spiritual sense of sacred Scripture, convinced that this method would more fully and

[10]Pss. 22, 31, 69; Hos 10; cf. Ps. 2:7 and the narratives of Jesus' baptism and transfiguration.

adequately reveal eternal truth than would a strictly historical interpretation of the text.

When St Paul distinguishes the "spirit" from the "letter" (Rom 2:29; 7:6; 2 Cor 3), he is not speaking of two distinct meanings which stand side by side in Scripture. He is distinguishing instead between two covenants. This is especially evident in Gal 4:21-31, where Hagar and Sarah are "allegorically" (actually by a form of typology) interpreted to represent Israel and the Church. On the one hand, there is the Old Covenant of the law of Moses, which demands an obedience beyond man's capacity, and which, as a result, holds him in a captive state of slavery and death. On the other hand there stands the New Covenant based upon the law of life, the law of freedom in the Spirit, by which the Christian becomes progressively transfigured into the image of the glorified Christ. Under Hellenistic influence, however, certain schools of Christian exegesis misinterpreted this Pauline dualism and attempted to distinguish the spiritual sense of a scriptural passage from its historical-literal sense. To be sure, Paul himself employed such a method to proclaim the meaning of Christ as Second Adam, the perfect, divine man who recapitulates in His person the whole of humanity, thereby restoring within man the image of God obscured by sin (Rom 5; 1 Cor 15). And in 1 Cor 10, he evokes Israel's desert experiences as types (*typoi*) or prophetic figures which announce what is to come in the eschatological age.[11] Nevertheless, his typology remains firmly anchored in history. The two poles, type and antitype, possess revelatory and soteriological value insofar as they link two moments in salvation-*history*. Indeed, New Testament tradition is unanimous in affirming that the divine economy is worked out precisely within the concrete sphere of human life and activity.[12]

[11]A. Robert and A. Feuillet, *Introduction à la Bible* I, Tournai (Belg.) 1959, p. 181.

[12]The fact that historical-critical exegesis denies the historicity of Adam, Abraham and even Moses (cf. M. Noth, *The History of Israel*, N.Y. 1958-60, ch. 3) has no bearing upon the typology employed by those who took such historicity for granted. The crucial requirement is that the proto-type (the prophetic figure) must have "existed" in Israel's spiritual consciousness (and consequently in its religious history) before the antitype became manifest. Typology, and the *theōria* based upon it, depends upon the historical reality

Those who adopted the allegorical rather than a genuinely typological method of interpretation did so, in fact, on the basis of a world-view which implicitly denied that ultimate truth can incarnate itself within space and time. By seeking truth in the antitype or second pole of the analogy, allegory tended to divest the divine plan of its historical context. The result was to make of Christian faith a kind of mystery religion for those "initiates" who had been perfected in *gnōsis*. Quite against their intent, the allegorists undermined both the incarnation (die *Mensch*werdung) of the Redeemer and His appeal addressed to the simple, the poor and the sinful.

Allegory had been employed by Christian writers well before the foundation of the catechetical school in Alexandria. The Epistle of Barnabus (chs. 4-6), for example, criticized the Jews for their naive insistence upon a purely literal exegesis. It further asserted that the wisdom of Christ is only accessible through allegorical interpretation of the Old Testament. Among the apologists, Justin made reluctant use of allegory in his dialogue with the Jew Trypho, preferring however the historical to the purely figurative sense. In Christian gnostic thought of the second century, allegory played an important role in Heraclean's commentary on the Gospel of John. Similarly, Ptolemaeus bore witness to the possible uses of allegory when, in his Epistle to Flora, he spelled out certain gnostic exegetic principles to be applied to the Pentateuch.

In the anti-heretical writings of Irenaeus and Tertullian, we find the first systematic refutations of gnostic allegorization. Attempting to define a "canon of truth" (Irenaeus) or *regula fidei* (Tertullian), these ardent defenders of the apostolic faith established their own hermeneutic principles by which Christian truth could be unveiled in the biblical texts. Each took as his norm the apostolic tradition of the catholic (*katholikē*) Church, defined in the fifth century by Vincent of Lerins as "*quod ubique, quod semper, quod ab omnibus*

of the *antitype*: a person or event which is ulterior to and in some way fulfills the type. This is not the case with allegory, where in the final analysis neither pole need be historically grounded, since truth is ultimately an eternal, celestial reality.

creditum est," "that which has been believed everywhere, always and by all." If the formula is somewhat naive in view of the immense diversity of creedal expressions in the pre-Nicene period, it nonetheless states quite admirably the conviction that the Orthodox Faith had been preserved by the Holy Spirit from the time of the Church's foundation. This *depositum fidei,* it was held, is contained chiefly in the sacred Scriptures of the Old Testament and in the inspired writings of the apostles.

The school of Alexandria was thus endowed with a double heritage: allegory as a hermeneutic method, and apostolic faith in the inspired Word of God as the unique source of Christian truth. Founded in the second century by the former Stoic philosopher Pantaenus, this school was the first major Christian center of biblical science. Its chief representatives were Clement, Origen, Athanasius, Didymus the Blind and Cyril. Since we are concerned simply to illustrate the chief principles of allegory, we shall restrict this section to a rapid summary and evaluation of the interpretive methods of Clement and Origen.

A philosopher rather than an exegete, Clement († ca. 215) devoted his efforts to reconciling apostolic faith with the prevailing Hellenistic spirit. Greek philosophy and Jewish law, he maintained, represent twin pathways which converge in Christ.[13] This theme is elaborated throughout his most important works, which include an apology against paganism (*Protreptikos pros Hellēnas*), pedagogical writings addressed to new converts (*Paidagōgos*), and a miscellaneous group of reflections dealing with the relationship of Greek philosophy to the Christian faith (*Strōmateis*). In addition, he composed commentaries on the Old and New Testaments called "sketches" (*Hypotypōseis* or *Adumbrationes*), of which only fragments have been preserved.[14]

Although Clement never develops a system of exegesis, he offers a theory of allegorical interpretation based upon the axiom that the most sublime truths are uniquely expressed

---

[13]Strom. 1:5:331 (PG 8:1:717; for Clement's works, see PG 8-9); cf. Strom. 6:17:823.

[14]Ed. Dindorf, 1868 (PG 8:9).

in the form of symbols.[15] The exegete must seek the "deep sense" of Scripture which goes beyond the purely literal sense. Reviving certain elements of gnostic anthropology, Clement distinguishes the "simple" from the "perfect": those for whom the literal sense suffices, from those who attain union with Christ by means of divine *gnōsis*. To the "perfect," the letter of the text is simply a vehicle for the spirit; it is a cipher through which truth expresses itself. In relation to the symbolic or spiritual sense, the historical meaning of a passage is clearly secondary. This doctrine, wholly foreign to biblical tradition, is rooted, in the words of J.N.D. Kelly, in "the Platonic conception, shared by Origen too, that there is a hierarchy of beings, . . . the lower [of which] reflect, and can be treated as symbols of, the higher."[16]

Photius, who knew the *Hypotypōseis,* roundly condemned their author for holding still other beliefs which were influenced by gnostic mythology.[17] Although Clement was a devoted disciple of Jesus Christ and a willing defender of apostolic faith, he allowed the excesses of his exegetic method to influence his theology to the point of deforming it into heresy. By using allegory, he tried to distinguish between faith and *gnōsis.* Although faith is essential to salvation, it represents merely a preliminary step towards pure knowledge. In other words, faith is the foundation—but only the foundation—of knowledge.[18] The true gnostic attains salvation by an "initiated contemplation" (*epoptikē theōria*)[19] which consists in a mystical apprehension of saving truth. Such a notion

[15]Strom. 5 passim. See Th. Camelot, "Clément d'Alexandrie et l'écriture," Rev Bib 53 (1946), p. 244: [according to Clement] "God, or rather the Logos, is the sole author of the two Testaments. He hides Himself in the Old to reveal Himself in the New. Thus the Old Testament is in its entirety a symbol of the New, just as the New Testament is a symbol and prefiguration of the coming Kingdom. Man's religious history is the history of the progress of this revelation of the Logos in the world, in Scripture and in the soul." See also the important art. by Cl. Mondésert, "Symbolisme chez Clément d'Alexandrie," Rech Sc Rel 26 (1936), p. 158-180; and his book *Clément d'Alexandrie. Introduction à l'étude de sa pensée . . .,* Paris, 1944, p. 142-159.

[16]J.N.D. Kelly, *Doctrines,* p. 74.

[17]Photius, Bibl. Cod. 109 (PG 103:3:384); quoted by Quasten, J., *Patrology,* vol. II, Maryland, 1964, p. 17.

[18]Strom. 7:10:864f.

[19]Strom. 1:2:327; cf. 6:10.

is not without merit insofar as it conforms to biblical and patristic tradition.[20] It is dangerously at variance with that tradition, however, to the degree that the vision of the divine mysteries (*theōria*) is reserved for the "initiated" alone. By developing their conception of *theōria* on the basis of typology rather than allegory, the Antiochians offered an important corrective to the gnosticizing tendencies of Clement and other Alexandrians. Their major criticism, however, was reserved for Clement's eminent disciple, Origen.

Origen (ca. 185-254) succeeded Clement as head of the catechetical school in Alexandria from 203 until 231. Excommunicated by his bishop Demetrius, Origen was subsequently obliged to leave Alexandria and settle in Cesarea. There he founded another school of biblical studies which he directed for nearly twenty years. An exegete and theologian of remarkable talent, energy and faith, Origen was condemned by the Council of Constantinople in 543 on a variety of grounds, particularly for his teachings on universal restitution (*apokatastasis,* defended as well by Gregory of Nyssa), the pre-existence of the human soul, and his allegorical method of interpretation.

Origen worked out his exegetic principles in the fourth book of his dogmatic treatise, *De principiis* (*Peri archōn*). On the dubious basis of a textual error in Proverbs 22:20f, he sought to distinguish three different levels of meaning within Scripture: bodily or somatic, psychic, and spiritual or pneumatic.[21] These three levels correspond to the three aspects

[20]See P. Evdokimov, *La Connaissance de Dieu selon la tradition orientale,* Lyon 1967, ch. 5; and for classical works on the theme of mystical knowledge, J. Daniélou, *Platonisme et Théologie mystique,* Paris 1944, esp. parts II-III (on the mystical theology of Gregory of Nyssa), and V. Lossky, *The Mystical Theology of the Eastern Church,* London 1957, esp. chs. 10-11.

[21]"The way, then, as it appears to us, in which we ought to deal with the Scriptures and exact from them their meaning is the following, which has been ascertained from the Scriptures themselves. By Solomon in the Proverbs we find some such rule as this enjoined respecting the divine doctrines of Scripture: 'And do thou portray them in a threefold manner, in counsel and knowledge, to answer words of the truth to them who propose them to thee' " [Prov 22:20f]; in Quasten II, p. 60 (from ANF). (For parallel Greek and Latin texts, in translation, see G. W. Butterworth, ed.,

of human nature distinguished by Platonic anthropology:
the flesh (corresponding to the historical or literal sense),
the soul or *psychē* (the moral sense discerned by typology),
and the spirit (the allegorical sense). "The individual," says
Origen, "ought then to portray the ideas of Holy Scripture
in a threefold manner upon his own soul in order that the
simple man may be edified by the *flesh* as it were of the
Scripture, for so we name the obvious sense, while he who has
ascended a certain way [may be edified] by the *soul*, as it
were. The perfect man again [may receive edification] from
the spiritual law, which has a shadow of good things to
come. For as a man consists of body, soul and spirit, so in
the same way does Scripture, which has been arranged to be
given by God for the salvation of men."[22]

Following his teacher Clement, Origen denies that all
men possess the potential to pass from "flesh" through "soul"
to "spirit" by acquiring divine knowledge. Only the "perfect"
can enjoy the vision of future blessedness, the "good things
to come," whereas the "simple" must be satisfied with a
meager "fleshly" edification. Such a notion seriously jeopar-
dizes the biblical doctrine of salvation and was rightly rejected by later Christian tradition.

In practice, Origen's hermeneutic rules distinguish three
methods for interpreting the meaning of Scripture: historical,
typological and allegorical. The first reveals the obvious
meaning of the text without resorting to figures or metaphors.
The typological method establishes a relationship between two
persons or events, in which the former prophetically prefigures the latter. Finally, the allegorical method deciphers
the most exalted spiritual sense of the passage, which means
its relevance or application in the daily life of the believer.
Prof. Kelly offers a typical example of this threefold interpretation as applied to a single passage. "When the Psalmist
cries (3:4), 'Thou, O Lord, art my support, my glory, and

Origen On First Principles, N.Y. 1966, p. 275, quoting De princip. 4:2:4.)
Instead of "threefold," the original Prov. text surely read "thirty," corresponding to the thirty chapters of the Egyptian "Instruction of Amen-em-ope,"
on which this section of the OT text is based; see commentaries, ad. loc.
   [22]Quasten II, ibid.

the lifter up of my head,' [Origen] explains that it is in the first place David who speaks; but secondly, it is Christ, Who knows in His passion that God will vindicate Him; and, thirdly, it is every just soul who, by union with Christ, finds his glory in God."[23]

Embarrassed by the literal meaning of certain passages in the Old Testament, Origen, like Philo before him, employed allegory to interpret statements which seemed unworthy of God, in order to discover their more lofty spiritual significance.[24] It is in fact the quest for this higher sense which defines the chief thrust of all of Origen's exegetical work. For to his mind, every passage, indeed, every word of Scripture bears spiritual meaning.[25]

[23]Sel. in ps. 3:4; Kelly, *Doctrines,* p. 73. In his study, *L'oeuvre exégétique de Théodore de Mopsuèste* (Rome 1913, p. 38-41), L. Pirot summarizes Origen's hermeneutic principles: "a) Understand in the literal sense, and do not interpret allegorically, everything in the Sacred Books concerning orders, commandments, laws or moral precepts; but take in the allegorical sense all ceremonial laws. b) Take as referring to the heavenly dwelling of the Blessed information concerning Jerusalem, Babylon, Tyr and other places, for the prophets often spoke of the earthly Jerusalem while meaning the Heavenly Jerusalem. c) Explain in the allegorico-mystical sense everything which, taken in the literal sense, seems impossible, false, contradictory, absurd, useless, or unworthy of God." See also, H. Kihn, "Ueber *theôria* und *allêguria* nach den verlorenen hermeneutischen Schriften der Antiochener," *Tübinger Quartalschrift,* 1880, p. 531ff.

[24]In Numer. hom. 26:3 (PG 12:744); In Jerem. hom. 12:1 (PG 13: 377); De princip. 4:9 (PG 11:361).

[25]De princip. 4:3:5, "For our contention with regard to the whole of divine scripture is, that it all has a spiritual meaning, but not all a bodily meaning"; Butterworth, *Origen,* p. 297. Other Alexandrians sought a "hidden meaning" in the Scriptures: Dionysius, On the Promises (Eusebius, Eccl. Hist. 7:25:4f), Didymus the Blind, De Spiritu sancto 57 (PG 39:1081), who distinguishes the literal from the "pneumatic sense." Didymus is more circumspect than others in his use of allegory to interpret the NT, preferring instead the literal sense. Cyril made the most liberal use of allegory to discover the spiritual sense of Scripture. See his De ador. in sp. 1:1 (PG 68:137); Glaphyres praef. (PG 69:9): "We elevate ourselves above the historical sense, we progress from the image and the shadow to the reality (itself)." See G. Bardy, *Supp. Dict. Bib.* 4:579, who notes that Cyril at times prefers the typological method. Among the Cappadocians, Gregory of Nyssa used both methods. In De hom. opif. and Explic. apol. in Hex., he seeks a purely literal sense, whereas at the beginning of his commentary on the Song of Songs he stresses the limits of the literal sense for instruction in morality (Bardy, col. 578). In a well known passage in De Vita Mosis (see J. Daniélou, Sources chr. I bis, Paris 1955, p. 81f), Gregory speaks of Moses' ascent into the cloud of divine darkness. He attempts to ground his apophatic

As the late Cardinal Daniélou rightly noted, Origen did
not in general deny history, but he often neglected or down-
graded it.[26] This dangerous weakness was virtually inherent
in the allegorical method. The Alexandrians, says Vaccari,
"call 'allegory' any transposition of a saying or discourse
from one object (real or not) to another by virtue of a real
or ideal similarity between them."[27] All too often the unreal
or ideal relationship between two objects outweighed and
obscured every other. As a consequence, legitimate typology
was neglected, and the meaning of a biblical passage was
presented in the form of a figure or metaphor which was often
devoid of any historical grounding. Bolotov has said that the
danger for the Alexandrians was to invent their own Holy
Scripture.[28] More precisely, the real danger with the allegorical
method, insofar as it transgressed the historical limits of
typology, was to transform the divine economy from *Heilsgeschichte* into mythology.

III. *The exegetical school of Antioch*

During the third century A.D., christological thought was
marked by two major tendencies which the Church later defined as heretical: docetism and adoptionism. The former
characterized Alexandrian teaching, while the latter, in the
form of modalistic monarchianism, was prevalent at Antioch.
In the following paragraphs we want to point out and suggest an explanation for the close relationship between christology and exegetical method which was characteristic of both
schools. It will become clear that the doctrine of the person
of Christ, originally shaped to combat diverse forms of here-

doctrine in a biblical passage which allows such interpretation only through
allegorization. What is essential is not Moses' own experience and its meaning for the people of Israel, but rather the mystical experience of the Christian who seeks to penetrate the "luminous darkness" of spiritual reality.

[26]J. Daniélou, *Origène,* Paris 1948, p. 180f.

[27]Quoted by P. Ternant, "La *théoria* d'Antioch dans le cadre des sens de
l'Ecriture," Biblica 34 (1953), p. 139 (three arts. in the same vol.).

[28]Quoted by G. Florovsky, *The Eastern Fathers of the Fourth Century,*
Paris 1931, vol. I; ch. on "St John Chrysostom as exegete," p. 217-223 (in
Russian).

tical teaching, played a decisive role in the development of both Alexandrian and Antiochian hermeneutics.

Influenced by the mystical dualism of the Platonists, Christian gnosticism exercised a major, although predominantly negative influence upon the early Church. Its so-called "docetist" christology was preached throughout Asia Minor and at Antioch, where it was combatted with impressive vigor by St Ignatius. The term "docetism" means "appearance" (etym: *dokein*, to appear). According to traditional docetic teaching, the human body of Christ was mere appearance. That is, it denied that "Jesus Christ had come in the flesh" (1 Jn 4:2).[29] Affirming the divinity of the Word, it in effect did away with His humanity. In his defense of the apostolic faith, St Ignatius attacked docetism by insisting that Christ was in reality both man and God. As man, His suffering was real.[30] After His resurrection, the Son was spiritually united with the Father (*pneumatikōs hēnōmenos*); and yet He remained *en sarki*, in the flesh.[31] By this subtle antinomy, St Ignatius laid the foundation for the faith of Nicea: Jesus Christ is truly God[32] and truly man, resurrected in the two natures of divinity and glorified humanity.

With few exceptions, Christian theologians of Alexandria and Antioch failed to maintain this fine christological balance. As a result, docetist and adoptionist influences continued to be felt well into the post-Nicene period. At Alexandria, a major center of gnostic mystical speculation, the Church opted to assimilate rather than to reject these and other elements of Hellenistic thought. Clement, for example, represents a form of gnostic docetism when he denies that Christ suffered His passion in the depths of His soul (*apathēs tēn psychēn*).[33] The Savior was indeed the God-man,[34] but as such He was completely "impassible"; if He ate and drank,

---

[29]It is far from certain that the Antichrists of I John are docetists; other passages suggest that those who "deny Christ" (= Jesus) as Son of God are in fact Sectarian Jews. Nevertheless, the formula of 4:2, taken alone, well expresses the docetist tendency.

[30]Tral. 10; Smyr. 2, 12; Polycarp 3; Eph. 7.

[31]Smyrn. 3.

[32]Polyc. 8:3; Rom. 3:3; 6:3; Eph. 18:2.

[33]Strom. 6:9; cf. Paed. 1:2 (PG 8:1:252).

[34]Paed. 3:1.

it was simply to hide His divinity from human eyes. Origen avoided the docetic pitfall with greater success than did his teacher. Yet with the majority of Alexandrians, he emphasized above all the divinity of Christ and His equality with the Father (*homoousios*) as a second divine hypostasis.[35] This remained true despite the fact that he tended unquestionably towards subordinationism,[36] calling the Son *theanthrōpos,* but also *deuteros theos.*[36a]

The study of the history of religions has clearly demonstrated the diversity of gnosticism within the early Church.[37] Among the multiple forms of docetic christology, the teaching of Cerinthus very likely contributed to the typically Antiochian tendency to accentuate the humanity of Christ while distinguishing sharply between Jesus and the divine Word, the *homo assumptus* and the *verbum assumens* (Theodore). According to St Irenaeus,[38] Cerinthus professed that the Christ (Christos, possibly an emanation from the Godhead) descended upon the man Jesus at His baptism in the Jordan and ascended from Him prior to the crucifixion. This radical separation of the "Jesus of history" from the "Christ of faith" preserved the heavenly being from the fetters of mundane existence as well as from suffering and death. But its implicit denial of biblical soteriology helped to spark a patristic reaction summed up in the formula, "What is not assumed cannot be saved." The historical records place Cerinthus at Ephesus; but his influence was widely felt throughout Asia Minor by the beginning of the second century.

The diverse and incompatible christological teachings of Alexandria and Antioch had as their common aim an explanation of the person of Jesus Christ and the soteriological meaning of His life and work. To the degree that they pre-

[35]c. Cels. 8:12 (but cf. 8:15); De princip. 1:2:12.
[36]De princip. 1:2:13; 4:35; c. Cels. 5:39; In Joh. 6:23; 13:25; etc.
[36a]In Ezek. hom. 3:3; c. Cels. 5:39; In Joh. 6:202.
[37]See esp. W. Bauer, *Rechtgläubigkeit und Ketzerei im ältesten Christentum,*[2] Tübingen 1934 (1963); and R. Bultmann, *Das Urchristentum im Rahmen der antiken Religionen,* Zürich, 1949. For a critical evaluation of certin tendencies of this school, see C. Colpe, *Die Religionsgeschichtliche Schule,* Göttingen 1961.
[38]adv. Haer. 1:26:1; 3:11:1.

served both the humanity and the divinity of Christ in a single, undivided person, the theologians of the two schools were recognized as orthodox doctors of the Church. Their reflections, however, were inevitably influenced by the cultural and philosophical milieux in which they lived and taught. Consequently, the Alexandrians stressed the divinity of the incarnate Word and the union between the two natures (shading towards monophysitism), whereas the Antiochians clearly and sharply distinguished the divine from the human nature, tending towards a conception of Jesus as the man in whom the Word of God dwelt.[39]

It is especially difficult to weigh the relationship between hermeneutics and theology in terms of cause and effect. We have noted in the case of Clement and Origen how deeply the former can influence the latter. Yet it is undeniable that philosophical and theological presuppositions condition the hermeneutic method of the interpreter who seeks to expound the very Scriptures which provide the norm (*kanōn, regula*) for his theology. Such is the dilemma posed by the "hermeneutic circle." If Alexandrian christology was to a certain degree tainted with docetism, this was due to its positive attitude towards the mystical, idealistic philosophy of its cultural milieu. The same was true, *mutatis mutandis*, at Antioch. There where Aristotelian thought held sway, Christian theology was characterized by an empirical rationalism which refused to sacrifice historicity on the altar of spiritual significance. Accordingly, the Antiochians stressed the historical quality of biblical events and the human nature of Christ. These two distinct christological tendencies, both of

[39]S. Cave, *The Doctrine of the Person of Christ,* London 1925, p. 105: "Each type of view had its advantage and its peril. The Alexandrian preserved the unity of Christ's person, and presented to Christian faith the God made man in Him, but it tended to ignore Christ's real humanity. The Antiochene view preserved Christ's true humanity, and could speak of His actual sorrows and real development, but it tended to destroy the concrete unity of the person, or to preserve it only by relapsing into a lower view of Christ, to see in Him not the God-man but a man whom God inspired." R. V. Sellers, *The Council of Chalcedon,* London 1961, p. 158ff, explains the different point of departure for the two schools: whereas the Alexandrians presupposed a trinitarian concept of God, the Antiochians began with His unity which manifests itself in three hypostases.

which were *a priori* faithful to apostolic tradition, bore a marked influence upon the two methods of exegesis, allegory and typology.

The exegetical school of Antioch originated primarily in reaction to the excesses of allegorization as practiced by Origen.[40] Founded around 260 by Lucian († 312), this "school" was far less homogeneous than its Alexandrian counterpart. If it can be said that theological minds as different as those of Theodore of Mopsuestia and John Chrysostom belonged to the same school, it is because of their similar method of exegesis rather than because of a common theology. Close friends for many years, these two great theologians represent the antipodes of Antiochian thought, Theodore being the more radical and rationalistic, and St John, the more conservative and mystical.

Lucian, the teacher of Arius, had been exposed to the heretical influence of Paul of Samosata. A confirmed enemy of the Alexandrian Logos-theology, Paul was named bishop of Antioch around 260. In 268 he was condemned and deposed for his doctrine of monarchian modalism which implicitly defended the heresy of adoptionism. Paul denied the personality (*hypostasis*) of the Son and the Spirit. Consequently, he refused to accept the divinity of Jesus, holding that He was merely a chosen human being to whom God communicated Himself in a purely accidental union. This adoptionist christology, which divided Jesus Christ into two realities without a common nature, paved the way for the christological dualism of Theodore and Nestorius.[41] Thus, from its inception, the school of Antioch was marked by adoptionist tendencies rooted in an empirical rationalism of Aristotelian origin. Although problematic in many respects, this philosophical bent nevertheless prevented the Antiochians

[40]The remark of Pirot is worth noting: "Rien de plus dangereux pour la rectitude d'un mouvement intellectuel qu'une tell origine"; *L'oeuvre exégétique*, p. 38ff.

[41]See F. Cayré, *Précis de patrologie et d'histoire de la théologie* I, Paris 1931, p. 166-169; Quasten II, p. 142ff. Quasten speaks of Lucian as "the father of Arianism."

from jeopardizing Christ's humanity. In the remainder of this section we shall examine the impact of these philosophical and theological presuppositions upon Antiochian hermeneutics.

The chief theoretician of the school of Antioch was unquestionably Diodore, bishop of Tarsus from 378 until his death in 392. He received his theological education at Antioch and went on to Athens to pursue classical studies. A student of Eusebius of Emessa, who was himself a disciple of Lucian, Diodore was exposed to the subordinationist and adoptionist teachings which crystalized respectively in the doctrines of Arius and Nestorius.

With regard to the controversy surrounding the adoptionist leanings of Paul of Samosata, Eusebius speaks of a certain presbyter Malchion, who was revered at Antioch for the purity of his faith in Christ.[42] Malchion, Eusebius notes, had forced Paul to clarify his doctrinal opinions at the Antiochian synod of 268. The action brought to light the nature and extent of Paul's heretical views and set the stage for his condemnation. Subsequently, Malchion was himself attacked by Diodore in a polemical treatise which is no longer extant. We may assume, however, that Diodore defended a "separatist" christology similar to Paul's own. In any event, Photius alludes to a work by Diodore entitled "On the Holy Spirit," which, he maintains, proves that the author "is already infected by the taint of the Nestorian heresy."[43]

In the sixth decade of the fourth century, Apollinarius, then bishop of Laodicea, attempted to combat Arianism with a christology that exalted Christ's divinity at the expense of His humanity. Diodore attacked this teaching in two dogmatic works, "Against the Synousiasts" and "On the Incarnation." The former[44] was directed against certain disciples of Apollinarius who had defended a doctrine of consubstantiality (*synousiōsis*) between the flesh and the divinity of Christ,

---

[42]Eusebius, Eccl. Hist. 7:29.
[43]Photius, Bib. Cod. 102; Quasten III, p. 400.
[44]PG 33:1550-1560.

thereby prefiguring monophysitism.[45] For this ardent defense of Christ's humanity, Diodore was himself attacked in 438 by Cyril of Alexandria. In his work *Contra Diodorum et Theodorum,* Cyril charged Diodore with direct responsibility for the Nestorian heresy. This unjust judgment was ratified in 499 by a synod of Constantinople, which condemned the bishop of Tarsus, thereby causing a number of his writings on doctrine and exegesis to be destroyed.

The judgment was indeed unjust, for Diodore had defended with equal vigor and conviction, against Julian the Apostate, the traditional teaching regarding Christ's divinity.[46] The misunderstanding concerning Diodore's actual position was chiefly due to the imprecision of theological language in the pre-Nicene period. From the time of Ignatius, if not before, the messianic titles "Son of Man" and "Son of God" had lost the historical and eschatological significance attributed to them by certain psalmists, prophets, and late-Judaism in general. To Ignatius, these titles expressed the double origin of Christ: born of Mary of the tribe of David, yet born of the Holy Spirit by the power of God.[47] While attempting to refute Apollinarianism, Diodore had the misfortune of overstressing the distinction between these two titles, declaring that the Son of God had assumed the Son of David (Son of Man), and that the man born of Mary was not God by nature.[48] Little wonder, then, that Diodore was charged, especially by Alexandrians, with laying the foundation for the dualistic christology of Nestorius.

We should keep in mind, however, that Diodore's christological concepts were formulated in an atmosphere of polemic. Depending upon his adversary, he found himself obliged to stress at one moment Christ's humanity and at another His divinity. When isolated from the total corpus

[45]Cayré, *Patrologie,* p. 440; J. Meyendorff, *Byzantine Theology,* N.Y. 1974, p. 32-41.

[46]Theodoret, Hist. eccl. 4:22.

[47]Smyr. 1:1; Eph. 7:2; 18:2.

[48]See L. Mariès, "Le commentaire de Diodore de Tarse sur les Psaumes," Rec Or Chr 4 (24) (1924), p. 148f; R. Seeberg, *History of Doctrines* I, Eng. tr. Michigan 1961, p. 247-249; and A. Grillmeier, *Christ in Christian Tradition,* N.Y. 1965, p. 260-270.

of his works, many of his christological formulas indeed seem one-sided. And there can be no doubt that both Theodore and Nestorius drew upon his teachings as inspiration for their own more radical distinction between the two natures of Christ. Nevertheless, it is important to recall that Diodore was recognized by the Emperor Theodosius I as a thoroughly dependable witness to orthodox belief.[49]

The origins of the exegetical methods practiced by the school of Antioch, like the origins of its christology, go back to the third century. Lucian himself was a specialist in textual criticism. His knowledge of Hebrew enabled him to complete a revision of the Septuagint which, according to St Jerome, was used by a majority of the Eastern Churches.[50] From its beginning, his school gave priority to historical, grammatical and philological research, with the aim of expounding the literal meaning of Scripture. Eustathius, bishop of Antioch from 324 to 330, employed these exegetic tools in his polemical writings against Arianism and Origen's use of allegory.[51] Although he represented something of a bridge between Lucian and Diodore, Eustathius nevertheless seems to have avoided their tendency toward christological dualism.

Well before Diodore, Antiochian exegesis was thus characterized by concern for a rigorously scientific interpretation of the text. As we have noted, its philosophical basis was principally Aristotelian. As a student in Athens, Diodore was exposed to Aristotle's thought as interpreted by followers of Porphyry (234-305), himself a disciple of Plotinus. With questionable success, Porphyry had tried to fashion a synthesis of Aristotelian and Neo-platonic philosophy based upon allegory. Perhaps it was by reaction to this particular allegorical tradition that Diodore began to construct his hermeneutic principles, taking as his inspiration the rationalistic, historical empiricism of Aristotle.

Around 360, Diodore founded in Antioch a monastic

---

[49]In the Imperial Edict of the Council of Constantinople of 381 (Cod. Theod. 16:1:3).

[50]Jerome, Praef, in paral; adv. Ruf. 2:27; cf. Quasten II, p. 142. A contemporary of and co-martyr with Lucian, the priest Dorotheus was also a specialist in biblical science and in Hebrew (Euseb., Eccl. Hist. 7:32).

[51]Cayré, *Patrologie,* p. 318f; Quasten III, p. 302ff.

center (askētērion) dedicated to teaching asceticism and theology. His two most important disciples, Theodore and John Chrysostom, bore eloquent testimony to the high quality of his ascetic and moral life. Diodore's exegetical work comprises commentaries on the entire Old Testament, the Gospels, Acts, and several Epistles. Most of these writings have come down to us in the form of fragments or heavily interpolated passages (In psalm., for example).

In an important study of Diodore's exegetical method, E. Schweizer notes the following traits.[52] Although he spelled out in considerable depth the etymological meaning of certain of its key words, Diodore did not know the Hebrew language. Due in part to his classical education and in part to the influence of Lucian, he unfailingly oriented his exegesis in such a way as to illuminate the historical and literary context of the passage in question.[53] He investigated etymology, sentence structure, grammar, and attempted to reconstruct the primitive text. His concern for "lower criticism" was matched by his interest in the historical situation of the author and his readers. To his mind, the chief goal of exegesis is to clarify the intention of the biblical writer by adapting a genuinely scientific method of interpretation which had already been long employed in the study of secular literature.

The value of Professor Schweizer's study is diminished by his relative silence regarding the most important contribution that Diodore made to hermeneutics: his principle of theōria. Orthodox tradition was unanimous in its conviction that the Old Testament represented essentially a preparation for the coming of Jesus Christ. Accordingly, one must read the spiritual history of the Jewish people in the light of the Gospel. Diodore accepted this supposition unconditionally, even to the point of proclaiming Abraham to be the "father

[52]E. Schweizer, "Diodor von Tarsus als Exeget," ZNW 40 (1941), p. 33-75. Here the author erroneously identifies theōria with typology; similarly, R. Greer, Theodore.

[53]Schweizer notes, for ex., "In R [Comm. on Rom.] achtet Diodor sehr auf den Zusammenhang. Der Gedankenfortschritt des Paulus festigt eine These, wiederholt das Gesagte, führt es weiter aus, erklärt es genauer oder fasst es zusammen, begründet das Gesagte, wehrt Misverständnisse ab, läuft auf ein bestimmtes Ziel hin oder ergibt ein Problem," p. 54.

of the Church."[54] The challenge to the Christian exegete, therefore, is to develop hermeneutics which take fully into account the relationship of promise and fulfillment which unites the two Testaments.

Diodore worked out his solution to this problem in a treatise, now lost, on the "difference between *theōria* and allegory" (*tis diaphora theōrias kai allēgorias,* where *diaphora* perhaps means "disagreement"). Other extant works such as his prologue to Psalm 118, however, offer enough information for us to sketch the main lines of his conception of *theōria* as a method of interpretation.

To Clement and other Alexandrians, the word *theōria* denoted the spiritual sense of a scriptural passage as revealed by allegory. As Fr de Lubac has shown, *theōria* in Alexandrian terminology is virtually synonymous with *allēgoria.*[55] Origen held that every passage and every word of Scripture possessed its own spiritual meaning, even where the literal sense had to be discarded as unworthy of God and of His revelation.[56] The goal of exegesis, he maintained, is to decipher the symbolic language of the Bible in order to discern its "interior" significance. In practice, this meant that the exegete sought the meaning of a text in the words themselves, that is, in biblical symbols rather than in historical events. Despite his preference for allegory, Origen generally paid due respect to history as the realm of revelation and the working out of the divine economy. To more radical allegorists, however, the historical event bore meaning only to the degree that it represented symbolically a mystical or moral experience in the life of the believer. Such a conception destroys typology, since the historical continuity between the two poles of the analogy is broken. Thus the cross of Christ, according to Origen's own allegorical interpretation, becomes the antitype

---

[54]Comm. on the Octateuch 26:16; in J. Deconinck, *Essai sur la chaîne de l'Octateuch,* Paris 1912.

[55]H. de Lubac, "Typologie et allégorisme," Resch Sc Rel 34 (1947), p. 202; *Histoire et Esprit: l'intelligence de l'Ecriture d'après Origène,* Paris 1950, p. 123.

[56]E.g., De princip. 4:12:20; cf. In Joh. 10:18:189. Similarly, Clement, who affirms that Scripture is inspired in its very syllables and letters, Protr. 9:87.

of the ritual holocaust prescribed by Mosaic law, while its true (spiritual) significance lies in "the sacrifice which each Christian, in imitation of Christ, should reproduce and accomplish in his heart."[57] The essential point is not the objective fact of the crucifixion with its cosmic and eschatological consequences. It is rather the personal, interior apprehension by the Christian of the meaning of that event. The exegesis, as it were, becomes more important than the text itself. Historical objectivity gives way to a subjectivism which denies the temporal dimension of eschatology and projects the economy of salvation into a celestial sphere conceived in terms of Platonic idealism.

A healthy reaction against this relative disregard of the historical meaning of Scripture motivated Antiochian theologians from the time of Lucian. Often their critique exaggerated the degree to which the Alexandrians abused allegory (this was especially true in the case of Origen). However, they recognized the danger inherent in the method itself, and consequently they took pains to distinguish precisely between allegory and typology. Like typology, allegory is based upon two poles, type and antitype. But the fact that allegory situates the true, spiritual meaning within the interior life of the believer rather than in the historical event itself obliges us to regard it not merely as an extension or logical development of typology, but as an altogether different method of interpretation.[58]

Diodore and his disciple Theodore began with a hermeneutic presupposition which was the opposite of Origen's: not every passage of Scripture has a spiritual meaning, but every

[57]Hom. in Lev. 1:4f (PG 12:2:409ff); Kelly, *Doctrines*, p. 73.

[58]Thus we cannot accept the opinion of J. Daniélou, who holds that allegory is essentially typological. Speaking of *allēgoria* and *theōria*, he states that "l'une et l'autre sont également typologiques. Elles ne s'opposent pas, ainsi qu'on le dit, comme littéral et allégorique. Mais dans cette exégèse typologique, également christologique, les Antiochiens mettent davantage l'accent sur l'aspect sacramentaire de la tradition catéchetique, les Alexandrins sur l'aspect mystique de la tradition, l'un et l'autre étant également traditionnels"; (quoted by P. Ternant, "La *theōria*," p. 141.) The acual opposition is not between "literal" and "allegorical," but between typology and allegory as two different methods, each of which seeks the spiritual sense (see below).

passage does have its own historical and literal meaning.[59] According to Diodore, the task of the exegete is to discern within the historical event both its literal and its spiritual sense. The literal sense refers to the meaning of the event as understood and expressed by the biblical writer. It includes a "spiritual" dimension to the extent that *the writer himself* recognized the event to be a type of some eschatological reality. An example is the psalmist or prophet who speaks of contemporary persons or events while consciously anticipating, by the grace of divine inspiration, the fulfilment of these historical types in the messianic age (e.g., Isa 9:2-7; 11:1-9). Thus the king of Israel and the collective Servant-figure were conceived as images of the Messiah.

It must be said, however, that in recent studies dealing with patristic hermeneutics, undue stress has been laid upon this element of conscious anticipation on the part of the biblical author.[60] Whether or not the author himself was conscious of a typological relationship between two images, historical and eschatological, is ultimately of little importance. What matters is the perception of "spiritual divination" by the *interpreter,* who beholds in a past event the actual presence of an eschatological and soteriological reality. It is this spiritual perception or divination which Diodore and his followers term *theōria.*

The exegete applies *theōria* to the biblical text by means of typology. Like allegory, typology establishes a relationship of promise and fulfillment between two poles, type and antitype. These poles or types are related to each other in one of two ways. They may both be historical, one being situated in the Old Covenant and the other in the New (e.g., Adam or Moses as types of Christ). Or the antitype may be "transhistorical" or eschatological, in which case the type is situated in the present age and the antitype in the age to come (e.g., the Eucharist as a figure of the Heavenly Banquet). In either case, a typological relationship can only exist between the

---

[59]See H. Kihn, *Theodor von Mopsuestia und Junilius Afrikanus als Exegeten,* Freiburg im B. 1880, p. 26ff. Socrates, Hist. eccl. 6:3 (PG 67:668) speaks of the double accent of the Antiochians: *Psilō tō grammati tōn theiōn prosechōn graphōn, tas theōrias autōn ekterpomenos.*

[60]A case in point is the study by P. Ternant, "La *theōria*," art. cit.

two images or poles when the type finds its realization or fulfillment in the antitype, and the eschatological antitype is firmly rooted in salvation-*history*.[61] Whereas allegory views the event as a mere "sign" which points toward the eschatological reality, typology stresses the *symbolic* character of history: the type actually participates in the transcendent reality of the antitype and derives its ultimate meaning from it. Thus understood, typology can legitimately discover "the face of Christ in the Old Testament,"[62] and affirm that the eucharistic celebration enables the Church to participate proleptically in the festival of the heavenly Kingdom.

Allegory discovers two quite distinct meanings within the words of the written account: an historical or literal sense and a spritual sense. Only the second of these is ultimately important for the life of faith. To a *theōria* based on typology, however, it is not the words of Scripture which contain the essential meaning, but the *events* to which those words bear witness. And within the historical event itself, *theōria* discerns not two different senses, but rather what we may call a "double sense," of which the spiritual dimension is firmly grounded in the literal, historical dimension. Put another way, *theōria* discerns a typological relationship at the very heart of the event itself.[63] This relationship expresses a double meaning: the one intended by the author (the literal sense) and th one which points forward to and finds its fulfillment in the messianic age.[64] Unlike allegory, *theōria* affirms that the spiritual sense is in no way separable from the literal sense, for the eschatological antitype is itself inseparable from the

[61]See on this subject the art by R. Bultmann, "Ursprung und Sinn der Typologie als Hermeneutischer Methode," ThLZ 75 (1950), p. 202-212; and G. Florovsky, "Revelation and Interpretation," in *Bible, Church, Tradition: An Eastern Orthodox View,* Belmont, Mass. 1972, p. 30-36; as well as chapter 1 above.

[62]The title of Prof. Georges Barrois' study, of which ch. 3 is particularly devoted to typology; St Vladimir's Seminary Press, N.Y. 1974.

[63]In the words of P. Ternant, "la *theōria* sert à déceler une véritable typologie au creux du sens littéral," "La *theōria,*" p. 143.

[64]J. Guillet, "Les Exégèses d'Alexandrie et d'Antioche. Conflit ou malentendu?", Rech Sc Rel 34 (1947), p. 286, n. 36: "Le sense littéral adéquat est un seul; un seul substantiellement, mais, si l'on peut ainsi parler, virtuellement double. Il y a une seule prédiction, qui se verifie deux fois: une première fois partiellement, une seconde fois totalement."

historical event which it employs as a vehicle of expression. Christ, for example, is in a mysterious way *present* in the person of Moses. Or, to use St Paul's metaphor, "the Rock was Christ" (*hē petra de ēn ho Christos*).[65] As developed by Antiochian theologians, this notion is admittedly problematic insofar as it fails to make clear exactly how the antitype is present within the type (without separation but without confusion, one might say). But the great merit of *theōria* is its single-minded concern to preserve the historical foundation of eschatology. The type is a prophetic symbol which participates in the antitype as a "premise" or "foretaste" (*arrabōn*). And conversely, *the eschatological antitype is truly (ontologically) present in the historical type*. Allegory, on the other hand, treats the type as a simple metaphor or parabolic sign whose spiritual meaning lies not within history, but within the abstract realm of Platonic ideas.

Diodore insisted that Scripture faithfully preserves this double "theoretic" sense: literal and spiritual. It is useless, even pernicious, to look for a "foreign meaning" apart from the literal sense of the text, since the results of such a quest would lead the exegete away from typology and into allegory.[66] To remain faithful to the historical meaning of the text, then, just how does *theōria* discern the eschatological reality in the typical event? It does so, Diodore affirms, by virtue of the *hyperbolic* character of the biblical narrative.

Explaining the double sense of Scripture discerned *kata theōrian,* Diodore holds that the prophets, in predicting future events, adapted their oracles both to their contemporaries

---

[65]This Pauline image, which could conceivably be translated, "Christ was the rock," originated in Jewish Wisdom tradition and underscores the apostle's conviction of the pre-existence of the Son of God. Cf. H. Conzelmann, *Der erste Brief an die Korinther,* Göttingen 1969, p. 196f, and chapter one above.

[66]Praef. in pss., L. Mariès, art. cit., p. 88. Cf. Severian of Gabala, who attempts to preserve history while discerning within it a superior *theōria*: "Haec non per allegoriam inducimus, sed in historia conspicimus. Aliud est allegoriam in historiam vi inducere; aliud historia servata allegoriam excogitare," de mundi creat. 4:2 (PG 56:459). St Jerome is especially severe in his critique of the Antiochians: "si turpitudinem litterae sequatur et non ascendat ad decorem intelligentiae spiritualis." In Amos 2:1 (PL 25:1003). We might recall that Jerome accepted Origen's distinction of three senses in Scripture, although he was not a true allegorist.

and to future epochs. To the former, their words were "hyperbolic" (*hyperbolikoi*) or exaggerated in that they contained
a meaning which was not yet fully disclosed. But for the age
in which the prophecies were realized, the oracles were seen
to be in complete harmony with the events which marked their
fulfillment.[67] Interpreted from a historical point of view
(*histōrikōs*), persons and events of the Old Covenant possess
their own significance within the context of Israelite history.
Interpreted from the point of view of *theōria* (*theōrēma-
tikōs*), however these same persons and events reveal a
superior, eschatological meaning. Thus the Psalms, according
to Diodore, are both history and prophecy. As history they
are spoken with hyperbole (*kath' hyperbolēn*), but as prophecy they are realized in actuality (*kat' alētheian*)[68] in the
person of Christ and in the life of the Church.

This holds true for all Old Testament types. According
to the typological *theōria* of Diodore, historical realities such
as Israel, David, Solomon, and the paschal lamb find their
fulfillment in Christ.[69] Far from being neglected as a mere
sign, the historical event is accentuated by *theōria* in such a
way as to preserve its revelatory value. This, in fact, is the
chief characteristic of typology which distinguishes it from
allegory. *Theōria* can discern the true spiritual meaning of
scriptural passages, precisely because the texts bear witness to
concrete events which constitute the historical context in
which the divine economy is accomplished.

Theōria thus provided Diodore with a middle road between the excesses of allegory and of what he called "Judaism," meaning a concern for the literal sense of Scripture
alone.[70] The two extremes are equally dangerous, since the
first leads to sheer fantasy while the second ends in a kind
of verbal rationalism that deprives Scripture of its eschatological and mystical significance. Through proper application,

---

[67]Mariès, art. cit., p. 97. Cf. P. Ternant, "La *theōria*," p. 146.

[68]Re. Ps. 68; L. Mariès, *Etudes préliminaires à l'édition de Diodore de
Tarse 'Sur les Psaumes,'* Paris 1933, p. 136; quoted by P. Ternant, "La
theōria," p. 144f.

[69]For a detailed discussion of types of Christ, see J. Daniélou, *'Sacra-
mentum Futuri,' Les figures du Christ dans l'Ancien Testament,* Paris 1950.

[70]Praef. in pss. 8:23ff.

theōria could avoid the one-sidedness of Alexandrian interpretation while discerning in Scripture a double sense, literal
and spiritual. Thereby it preserved both the original meaning
of the text itself and the revelatory character of sacred history.

The exegetes of Antioch were united in their single-
minded concern to preserve the integrity of history. The task
of exegesis, they held, is to distinguish purely historical passages from those which reveal a deeper meaning through the
use of *theōria*.[71] In the case of Theodore of Mopsuestia, however, determination to observe this distinction led to a historical literalism which in great measure obscured the revelatory prophetic aspect of Old Testament events.

Born in Antioch around 350, Theodore was recognized
during his lifetime as a pillar of orthodoxy. His condemnation at the fifth Council of Constantinople represented above
all a post-Chalcedonian reaction against his christology. A
faithful disciple of Diodore, Theodore accentuated the dualistic tendencies in the thought of his teacher and thereby
prefigured the hypostatic dualism of Nestorius. Aside from
his exegetic works, Theodore expounded his christology most
fully in the *De incarnatione*.[72] An important and illuminating
summary of his thought can be found in his catechetical
homilies on the Nicene Creed.[73]

To grasp Theodore's teaching on the person of the incarnate Christ, we must recall that the theological perspective
of the Antiochians had been influenced by the Aristotelian
theory of forms. In Alexandria, Platonic idealism had given
rise to a christology which can be described as "anabatic":
Christ's humanity tended to be elevated and absorbed by His
divinity. Antiochian christology, on the other hand, was
basically "katabatic": the divine Word descended upon the

---

[71]Cf. Isidore of Pelusium, Ep. 203 (PG 78:1289), and Severian of Gabala,
de mundi creat. 4:2 (note 66 above).

[72]The de Incarnatione exists only in Greek, Latin and Syriac fragments;
see Quasten III, p. 410f.

[73]Published by A. Mingana, *Commentary of Theodore of Mopsuestia on
the Nicene Creed*, Woodbrook Studies 5, Cambridge 1932 (Syriac text with
Eng. tr.). See esp. chs. 4-5.

man Jesus to dwell with Him in a moral but non-hypostatic union (thus Diodore and Theodore). In effect, the heavenly Word (*verbum assumens*) was conceived as the "form" or "universal" which dwelt within the earthly Jesus (*homo assumptus*). This teaching, elaborated especially by Theodore, scrupulously preserved the humanity of Jesus; but its effect was to demolish the Nicene faith which it sought to defend. Its weakness was to affirm a hypostatic duality within the person of Christ by maintaining that the man Jesus was "assumed" by the divine Word. While avoiding Alexandrian docetism, it nevertheless perpetuated the heretical dualism of Cerinthus. Nestorianism was merely its logical and inevitable consequence.

Like Diodore his teacher, Theodore was the double victim of his language and his historical situation. As to language, the terminology of the Nicene formula remained somewhat hazy until the time of the Cappadocian synthesis. And in the period between 325 and 381, it was far from being accepted as the definitive expression of orthodox belief. With this in mind, we can well understand the lack of precision in the thought of Theodore and his contemporaries regarding technical terms such as "person" and "nature." Still more problematic was the historical context in which Theodore found himself. On the one hand, he felt obliged to refute Alexandrian christology which seriously threatened the human aspect of Christ's life; and on the other, he was forced to combat the subordinationist tendencies of Arius and Eunomius. His chief problem was to preserve the absolute transcendence of God and the Word while unequivocally affirming the historical reality of Jesus as Christ. The solution which he settled upon was rooted in Antiochian tradition and perhaps originated with Cerinthus himself. In a more radical fashion than Diodore, Theodore maintained that the union between the two natures of Christ (Jesus and the Word, conceived virtually as two persons) was *moral* rather than hypostatic or ontological. J. Quasten, among others, has questioned this judgment on the basis of the eighth catechetical homily. Theodore, he maintains, "teaches beyond cavil the unity of two natures in one person."[74] Taken together, however, the homilies make it quite clear that Theodore had never really grasped the distinction between *persona* (*hypostasis*) and *natura* (*ousia*). True, he does affirm the unity of humanity and divinity in Christ. But that affirmation scarcely conceals his inability to fathom and express the mystery of one person in two natures.[75]

Theodore's exegetical method was also conditioned by the Aristotelian theory of forms. We have already noted that Diodore used *theōria* to perceive the spiritual meaning of an event as revealed by typology. To the allegorists, the ultimate meaning of an event is given by an anabatic or ascending movement: as a symbol of divine reality, the event is, so to speak, elevated to the celestial plane. To the Antiochians, on the other hand, the heavenly reality descends (*katabasis*) to the plane of human history as the universal which dwells within, shapes and gives meaning to the event. We may recall their basic hermeneutic principle: every event, like every word of Scripture, possesses its own historical or literal meaning; but not every event is a vehicle of revelation. This perspective explains Theodore's tendency to stress the historical-literal sense of the text, often at the expense of its spiritual message.

Theodore employed tools of the profane sciences for his exegesis even more than did the bishop of Tarsus. Attentive to vocabulary, etymology and grammar, he made liberal use of the findings of archaeology, geography and even psychology. He took pains to determine the historical situation and the precise intent of the author, not hesitating to explain an obscure passage in the light of another whose meaning was unambiguous. Although he knew little Hebrew, he nevertheless compared Hebrew, Greek and Syriac versions of Old Testament writings in an effort to establish the primitive text. His work was guided by a number of characteristically

[74]Quasten III, p. 415, who quotes the passage. Cf. Mingana, op. cit., p. 89, quoting Theodore: "We should also be mindful of that inseparable union through which that form of man can never and under no circumstances be separated from the Divine nature which put it on."

[75]See, e.g., Hom. cat. 5; Mingana, op. cit., p. 53. Also Kelly, *Doctrines*, p. 303-309; and R. Devreesse, "Les instructions catéchétiques de Théodore de Mopsuèste," Rech Sc Rel 12 (1933), p. 425f.

Antiochian principles, of which the following are the most important: 1. Scripture is uniformly inspired by the Holy Spirit. 2. Certain passages of Scripture possess a double meaning: the literal sense, fulfilled within the historical limits of the Old Testament (down to the Maccabean age, ca. 165 B.C.); and the spiritual sense, which for Theodore meant the prophetic promise fulfilled in the incarnate Christ and in the Church. 3. The essential task of the exegete is to discern the intention of the biblical author and to elucidate the message which he seeks to impart.[76]

We should note two of Theodore's more important contributions which illustrate both the strengths and weaknesses of *theōria* in Antiochian hermeneutics: his use of typology, and his understanding of inspiration by the Holy Spirit.

To discern an authentic type in the Old Testament text, Theodore uses three interrelated criteria. First, a resemblance (*mimēsis*) must exist between the two poles or images, type and antitype. Second, the relationship between these two images (persons or events) must be in the order of promise and fulfillment, so that the type is realized or actualized in the antitype. This presupposes that history is neither static nor cyclical, but that it is in constant movement or progress from the present age to the age to come. This fundamentally biblical notion is crystalized in Theodore's teaching on the "two *katastaseis*," which emphasizes the continuity that exists between the historical present and the eschatological future.[77] And third, the transcendent reality of the antitype must actually participate in the type, thereby transforming the historical event into a vehicle of revelation. Whereas allegory views the type as "assumed" by the antitype, theoretic typology discovers the antitype *within* the type. Thus the spiritual sense is seen to be embedded within the literal sense, and the historical event itself becomes the visible expression of a

[76]A key work by Theodore, adversus alliegoricos, is lost. On the principles of his exegesis, see L. Pirot, *L'oeuvre exégétique*, p. 174f; R. Greer, *Theodore of Mopsuestia*, p. 86ff; E. Schweizer, art. cit., p. 71f; H. Kihn, *Die Bedeutung der antiochenischen Schule auf exegetischem Gebiet*, Weissenburg 1866, p. 137-148; and esp. R. Devreesse, "La méthode exégétique de Theodore de Mopsueste," RB 53 (1946), p. 207-241.

[77]See the beginning of his comm. on Jonah (PG 66:317).

celestial reality or truth. Accordingly, Theodore's eucharistic theology affirms both the eschatological character of Christ's sacrifice and His "real presence" which makes of bread and wine a "spiritual and immortal nourishment."[78]

Application of these criteria eliminates all but a few genuine types from the Old Testament. Theodore accepts the aspersion of the Israelites' doorways with the blood of the paschal lamb as a type of the outpouring of Jesus' own blood on the cross. The former sacrifice prophetically foretells liberation from sin and death, and the latter fulfills that prophecy. The brazen serpent represents a type of Christ's death and resurrection. And Jonah incarnates a typological prophecy which points forward both to the burial and resurrection of Christ, and to the universal call to conversion and salvation.[79]

The rigorousness with which Theodore applied these criteria, however, led him to reject the long accepted messianic character of a great majority of psalms and prophecies. Only Psalms 2, 8, 45, and 110 can be properly interpreted as referring to the coming Messiah. And even here Theodore seems to reject a true typology by maintaining that they are "christological" rather than "messianic," in that they depict Christ alone rather than the Messiah awaited by the people of Israel. In fact, it seems that he regarded as truly "typical" only Psalm 15, in which the image of the servant who did not meet with corruption is fulfilled in the person of the risen Christ.[80]

This reluctance to admit the presence of a spiritual meaning in traditionally accepted "Christian texts" of the Old Testament can be explained by Theodore's concern for the historical situation of the biblical author and, consequently, for the literal meaning of the passage in question. With Diodore, he believed that exegesis should discover and eluci-

---

[78]Hom. cat. 15; quoted by Quasten III, p. 421. For Theodore's criteria of types, see R. Devreesse, "La Méthode exégétique," p. 238, who gives the Greek texts; and L. Pirot, *L'oeuvre exégétique*, p. 210.

[79]Devreesse, ibid., p. 239, gives key passages from the Comm. on the Twelve Minor Prophets (PG 66:123ff).

[80]Devreesse, ibid., p. 221f, who notes that this is Theodore's sole use of tropology.

date the sense actually intended by the author: his own message as communicated to his contemporaries. It is important to
realize, however, that Theodore never rejected the principle
of "spiritual" interpretation. He is quite clear in his insistence
that authentic Old Testament types do indeed express and
prefigure the highest truth which is embodied in Christ and
the Church.[81] What he unequivocally rejects is the Alexandrian quest for two distinct meanings juxtaposed in every
event. For him, as for the Antiochians in general, an event
has only one meaning—but a meaning which, to the discerning eye of the "theoretic" exegete, is both literal and spiritual,
historical and typological. The Psalms, for example, were all
realized in the Old Testament period. Each possesses its own
literal sense which, viewed historically, applies only to its own
time and place, and not to any future epoch. Just how, then,
does the exegete discern within the Psalm a spiritual sense
which refers to the age of the Church? For Diodore, the
answer lay in the hyperbolic character of the Old Testament
passage. Theodore, on the other hand, finds the answer in
"analogy": the Psalms possess spiritual value for Christians
who find themselves in an historical situation which is analo-
gous to that of the people whom the Psalmist addresses.[82]

The historical context of an Old Testament passage
remains absolutely definitive. For it is precisely within that
context that the interpreter discerns by means of *theōria* an
authentic spiritual meaning. Thus for Theodore, Psalm 2
prophesies Christ's suffering, while Psalm 8 announces His
victory over death. Psalm 45, on the other hand, alludes to
the mystery of union between Christ and the Church. As with
Diodore, the psalm or prophecy[83] does not possess two juxtaposed yet independent meanings; rather, it possesses a "double
meaning." The literal sense is given by the historical context;
the spiritual sense is perceived by the biblical author (and,
as we shall see, by the exegete) through the inspiration of
the Holy Spirit. The entire prophecy refers equally to both

[81]In Zachar. 9:8f (PG 66:557).

[82]Devreesse, "La Methode exégétique," p. 222f.

[83]According to Theodore, the christological psalms are true prophecies.
He attributes to David (the sole author of the psalms) the role of a prophetic
visionary.

meanings. It would be quite wrong to compartmentalize the prophecy, as if one part referred to the contemporary situation of the author while the other part referred to Christ. For it is in the "shadow" (*skia*) of the event itself that both the author and the interpreter discern the revelation of divine truth.[84]

Like others of the Antiochian school, Theodore attempted to use a scientific method of exegesis to discern the true meaning of Scripture: its spiritual or soteriological message revealed by typology. Systematic in its application, yet problematic in its conclusions, his method led him inevitably to certain doctrinal positions which the Church was obliged to condemn. To his mind, the Suffering Servant of Isaiah 53 is not a true type of Christ; the Song of Solomon represents nothing more than an epithalamium composed by the Israelite king for his Egyptian bride; and the Book of Job is to be rejected as filled with "idolatry" and "pagan mythology." To the theological and liturgical tradition of the Church, however, Job and the Servant represent authentic images or icons of Christ; and the Song of Songs, whatever its historical origins, depicts the ineffable love of Christ for members of His mystical Body. To Theodore, this is sheer allegory; but to orthodox Christian tradition it represents thoroughly valid typology.

Finally we should recall that Theodore's exegetical method served to reinforce typically Antiochian tendencies toward a christological dualism. Attempting to preserve the historicity of the incarnation, he effectively separated the man Jesus from the divine Word. And by so doing, he endangered every bit as much as certain Alexandrians the Church's doctrine of the Word made flesh. It was this above all that led his successors to reject his teachings as heretical. We would be in error, however, to minimize his important contributions to exegesis, and in particular his emphasis upon the role of the Holy Spirit in scriptural interpretation.

Like Diodore before him, Theodore applies the term *theōria* both to the inspiration of the biblical author and to

[84]Devreese, "La Methode exégétique," p. 236f; cf. Theodore, comm. on Micah 5:1f (PG 66:372f).

the perception of the spiritual meaning of Scripture by the exegete. As regards the various kinds of biblical writings, there are two orders of inspiration: one proper to prophecy and the other to wisdom literature. The latter is inferior to the former and represents a mere "grace of prudence" accorded to its author, Solomon. Seized by the Spirit of God, the prophets first "saw" the content of the revelation in the form of diverse images. In a state of ecstasy (*ekstasei*), they received knowledge (*gnōsin*) of ineffable mysteries (*aporrētoteron*) through a unique vision (*theōria monē*) of the divine message.[85] This vision was given by the Spirit and contemplated by the prophet. The fruit of this contemplation was the message which he uttered in the form of a proclamation, parable or prediction.

It is important to recall that the apostles, as well as the prophets, were objects of the inspirational activity of the Holy Spirit (e.g., St Peter at Joppa, St Paul on the road to Damascus). Theodore is in full agreement with the tradition which holds that both the literal and the spiritual meanings of Scripture—New Testament as well as Old—are inspired by God.[86] Through the Spirit, the apostolic writers were able to discern (*theōrein*) and interpret the meaning of the various types revealed to prophets of the Old Covnant. In other words, they interpreted the Old Testament in the light of *theōria*: perception or divination of eschatological realities hidden within the facts of history. Now this is precisely the function of *theōria* as employed by the Christian exegete. Although the Antiochians never spell it out, there exists a direct correspondence between the *theōria* or hermeneutic vision practiced by the apostles on the one hand and by post-apostolic interpreters on the other. In the following chapter we shall discuss this correspondence and its relation to the inspirational activity of the Holy Spirit. But first we should note briefly certain important aspects of Antiochian exegesis

---

[85]In Nah. (prologue), (PG 66:401ff), quoted by Devreesse, ibid., p. 228. For the difference between prophetic and sapiential grace, Comm. on Job (PG 66:697).

[86]Theodore, In Ionam praef. (PG 66:317ff); cf. Augustine, De doctrina christiana 3:27:38 (PL 34:80) and Gregory of Nyssa, c. Eunom. 7 (PG 45:744).

which appear in the works of St John Chrysostom (ca. 347-407) and Theodoret of Cyrus (ca. 393-458).

With Chrysostom, the golden tongued orator, exegesis is placed primarily in the service of Christian proclamation. His pastoral concern led him to modify the rigid historicism of Theodore while nonetheless preserving the historical basis of *theōria*. Venerating the Bible as a "divine medication" which heals the sores of sin and death, St John Chrysostom sought with impressive ardor and profound faith to lay bare and proclaim the "divine sense" of sacred Scripture.[87]

In his commentary on the Psalms (9:4), Chrysostom distinguishes three kinds of biblical statements: those which represent only figures or symbolic images and reveal a theoretic or spiritual sense; those which possess only a literal meaning; and those which are genuinely typological, in which the divine meaning comes to expression in the historical event (*theōria* proper).[88] As an example of the first kind, which admits only a figurative interpretation, he offers Proverbs 5:19, "rejoice in the wife of your youth, a lovely hind, a graceful doe . . ." (RSV). Among those passages which can only be interpreted by the letter, he includes the affirmation of Genesis 1:1, "In the beginning, God created the heavens and the earth." Dogmatic statements of this kind, he believes, are eviscerated by allegorical exegesis. Finally, John 3:14 offers an example of authentic typology: "as Moses lifted up the serpent in the wilderness, so must the Son of Man be lifted up. . . ." In this passage, he says, the interpreter is obliged to see both an event which actually happened and a symbolic figure which designates Christ Himself.[89]

In *de poenit. hom.* (6:4), Chrysostom further distinguishes between figurative and verbal prophecies. The former are

[87]See G. Florovsky, *The Eastern Fathers*, p. 217ff (Russian).

[88]Kelly, *Doctrines*, p. 76, confuses typology and allegory in his discussion of St Chrysostom.

[89]Chrysostom, as fully as Theodore, insisted that a true resemblance must exist between type and antitype in order to preserve the historical framework of revelation: In epist. ad Gal. 4:24 (PG 61:662); cf. In Mat. hom. 52:1 (PG 57:519) and In Jo hom. 85:1 (PG 59:461).

expressed by facts or things (*hē dia pragmatōn prophēteia*) and serve to open the eyes of the ignorant, while the latter enlighten the spiritually knowledgeable. An example of a verbal prophecy is Isaiah 53:7, where Christ is prefigured as a "lamb that is led to the slaughter." Christ is also the object of a figurative prophecy such as that of the ram which Abraham offered up in place of his only son. "This sacrifice," Chrysostom says, "was a figure of the one by which Jesus Christ saved us."

St Chrysostom expounded *theōria* not merely as an exegetical method, but, like Theodore and Diodore, as an inspired perception or contemplation of revealed heavenly realities. In his treatise on the "Incomprehensibility of God," for example, he underscores the ascetic dimension of genuine prophecy. Having fasted for three weeks, Daniel experienced a revelation "when his soul was more fit (*epitēdeiotera,* "better disposed") to receive such a vision (*theōrias*), having become by fasting both lighter and more spiritual (*kouphotera kai pneumatikotera*)."[90] This Hellenistic terminology, rooted as it is in Platonic thought,[91] might seem to allign Chrysostom with the Alexandrians and their mystical, allegorical interpretation of Scripture. In fact, it merely emphasizes the essential *contemplative* aspect of *theōria*. Further on, he speaks of a vision granted to the prophet Ezechiel.[92] Whenever God offers such a revelation to His servants, Chrysostom says, He leads them into places of calm, so that their soul, untroubled by spectacles or noises, might dwell uniquely upon the divine vision. To this vision (*theōria*) accorded to the prophet there corresponds the typological interpretation (*theōria*) of the apostles and later exegetes who detect in the prophecies the hidden image of Jesus Christ.

By the quality of his own life, St John Chrysostom bore eloquent testimony to this ascetic, mystical dimension of *theōria* which, as we shall point out below, is essential to a true discernment of the spiritual meaning of Holy Scripture.

[90]On the Incomprehensibility of God, III:205-210. (*Sources chr* 28 *bis*).
[91]For a discussion of the Platonic character of such terms, see J. Daniélou, *Platonisme et Théologie mystique.* Paris 1944-53, p. 57f.
[92]III:277-286.

The last of the great exegetes and theologians of the Antiochian school was Theodoret, bishop of Cyrus. During his lifetime, Theodoret was denounced by Dioscorus, bishop of Alexandria, for his defense of Nestorius. In his Epistle 83, however, he clearly asserts his faith in the unity of two natures in Jesus Christ while accepting the title of "Theo-tokos" as attributed to Mary. At the Council of Chalcedon in 451, Theodoret was obliged to pronounce "anathema to Nestorius, and to all who do not confess that the Blessed Virgin Mary is the Mother of God and divide into two the only Son, the only-Begotten."[93] More moderate in his christo-logical views than Theodore, Theodoret was nevertheless forced to accentuate the humanity of Christ against a kind of neo-Apollinarianism which he detected in the teachings of Cyril of Alexandria. His critique of Cyril led to the con-demnation of certain of his writings at the fifth council of Constantinople in 553.

A master in virtually every area of biblical science, Theo-doret attempted to develop a hermeneutic which could eluci-date the deepest meaning of Scripture. Rejecting the excesses of allegory, he held that the literal sense preserves and reveals the spiritual sense of the text. In his exegetical studies, he reversed certain conclusions drawn by his predecessor (and perhaps teacher) Theodore. The Song of Songs, he affirmed, is a *biblion pneumatikon* that depicts the mystery of love between Christ and His Church.[94] The preface to his com-mentary on the Psalms, by the way, contains critiques of both allegorists and those who regard "predictions of the future as realities of the past,"[95] an implicit criticism of the bishop of Mopsuestia. Finally, he sees in the paschal lamb the image of the Lamb of God, pure and spotless, who takes away the sin of the world.[96]

[93]Quasten III, p. 537. For the christological controversy between Dioscorus and Theodoret, see O. Bardenhewer, *Geschichte der Altkirchlichen Literatur,* Freiburg im B. 1924, Band IV, p. 222ff.

[94]Prologue In cant. (PG 81:29).

[95]Prologue In pss. (PG 80:860). Cf. G. Bardy, "Commentaires patris-tiques de la Bible," Supp Dict Bib II, 100-102.

[96]Quaest. in Exod. 24 (PG 80:252).

Also in the preface *In psalmos,* Theodoret states his exegetical program: "I have regarded it as my duty to avoid the one extreme as well as the other [allegory and literalism]. Whatever refers to history, I shall explain historically, but the prophecies about Christ the Lord, about the Church from the gentiles, about the Gospel and the preaching of the Apostles shall not be explained as referring to certain other things, as is customary with the Jews."[97] The purpose of exegesis is to grasp and to elucidate the message of the biblical writers who wrote under the direction of the Holy Spirit. Although he appeals to patristic tradition, Theodoret clearly states that the only canon of truth or authority for faith is Holy Scripture.[98] With Chrysostom, he adopts a scientific method of exegesis in order to reveal the *soteriological* meaning of the Word of God.

A striking passage from his commentary on Isaiah illustrates quite clearly Theodoret's use of typology.[99] Interpreting Isaiah 60:1 concerning the glory of the Lord which illuminates the New Jerusalem, he speaks of the prophet's prediction as a "figure in shadow" (*skiographia*) that foretells the reconstruction of Jerusalem in the time of Cyrus and Darius. Like a multi-colored painting, the figure manifests "superior types of the truth," namely, the splendor of the Holy Church. It even reveals the "archetype" of the painting, which is the future life in the heavenly City. These predictions, he continues, refer in a certain sense to the old Jerusalem; but in a superior fashion they refer also to the Church of God "which received the light of divine knowledge and is enrobed in the glory of the Lord."

This passage offers a concise example of *theōria* as it was conceived and used by the exegetes of Antioch. The foundation of the prophecy is the historical reality of Jerusalem, the Jewish city which was under reconstruction following the period of Babylonian captivity. The literal sense of the passage refers to it alone. Inspired by the Spirit, the prophet

[97]Quasten III, p. 540.

[98]See his anti-monophysite work, Eranistes I (PG 83:48): *Egō gar monē peithomai tē theia graphē* (Ego enim in sola divina Scriptura acquiesco).

[99]On Isa. 60:1; *Theodoret von Kyros Kommentar zu Jesaiah,* ed. A. Möhle, Berlin 1932, p. 233f; cf. Chrysostom (PG 51:247).

announces the rebirth of the city by using a hidden "shadow-figure." *Theōria* discerns the literal meaning of the passage which is the prophet's inspired vision of this earthly reality. But at another level, this same historical reality reveals itself to be a "superior type of the truth": to the Christian interpreter, the earthly city is actually a type or figure of a higher reality, that of the Church. Allegory would pass directly from this earthly image to that of the ultimate reality which is the heavenly Jerusalem, the future eschatological City or Kingdom of God. In this case, the earthly city would be a mere metaphor or sign, devoid of any spiritual significance. Typological *theōria*, however, beholds precisely *within* the earthly city (the old Jerusalem), as well as *within* the anti-type which is the Church, the presence of the *archetype* or heavenly Jerusalem. It is this celestial archetype, located at the very heart of the historical reality, that bestows upon both the old Jerusalem and the Church their spiritual meaning. Not only does the historical fact participate in transcendent reality; this transcendent reality or truth is actually rooted in the fact itself, in such a way that the revelation is fully historical and real rather than a-temporal and ideal.[100]

By preserving the historical framework of revelation, *theōria* does far more justice to biblical eschatology than does allegory. For *theōria* gives full expression to the paradox of the future realized within the present. Only this perspective, this "contemplative vision," can comprehend and express the double movement which characterizes both the incarnation of Christ and the sacraments of the Church: a vertical and horizontal movement by which transcendent eschatological realities englobe and transfigure the present life of the Christian community. To schematize somewhat, we might say that for allegory this movement is in a single

---

[100] It is interesting to note that John Cassian (+ ca. 435), a contemporary of Theodoret, distinguished four senses of Scripture and also illustrated them by reference to the multiple significance of Jerusalem. The Holy City is an earthly Jewish city (literal or historical sense); it represents the Church of Christ (allegorical or christological sense); it is an image of the human soul (tropological or moral sense); and it represents the Heavenly Kingdom (eschatological sense). See the comprehensive art. on "Hermeneutics," by Raymond Brown, Jerome Bib. Comm. 71; and on Cassian 71:41.

direction: from the present to the future and from earth to heaven. *Theōria,* on the other hand, perceives this movement in two directions: the future is proleptically realized in the present, just as heavenly reality manifests itself upon earth and throughout all of creation.[101]

[101]The remark of the eminent patristics scholar H. Wolfson is surprising: "Nothing new happened [after Origen] among the Fathers with regard to scriptural interpretation," *The Philosophy of the Church Fathers,* Cambridge 1965, p. 64. Wolfson confuses allegory and typology, supposing that the allegorical method was universally employed.

CHAPTER III

Theoria: An Orthodox Hermeneutic

In the previous chapter we noticed a striking correspondence between the christology and the hermeneutic method of the schools of Alexandria and Antioch. The Platonic idealism which influenced the Alexandrians' doctrine of Christ gave equal impetus to their use of allegory. A hermeneutic that seeks ultimate meaning in celestial archetypes, at the expense of the historical event, tends consequently to de-emphasize the humanity of Christ while exalting His divinity. In a similar way, the empirical rationalism of Aristotle left its imprint not only upon the dualistic christology of the Antiochians, but also upon their typological method of interpretation. Where hermeneutics focuses upon the literal meaning of a historical fact, there too exegesis sets in relief the concrete reality of Jesus as a flesh and blood human being.

It is often maintained that the Antiochians safeguard better than the Alexandrians the doctrine of Christ's incarnation. We have found ample evidence, however, that certain representatives of both schools seriously jeopardize that doctrine: the Alexandrians tending towards a monophysitic docetism, and the Antiochians towards a hypostatic dualism which in effect separates the two natures into two ontologically distinct beings.[1]

[1]See R. V. Sellers, *The Council of Chalcedon*, p. 162f, who notes that the Antiochian tendency to underscore the distinction between God the Creator and man the creature goes back at least to Theophilus, ad Autol. 2:10. This emphasis seems to explain the inability of Theodore and Nestorius to conceive of a hypostatic union of two natures, divine and human, in one person. The importance attributed today to the empirical sciences and their

Do these diverse hermeneutic methods necessarily lead to heresy or distortions of faith, so that the Church is obliged to reject them in favor of other approaches to Holy Scripture? The opinion of most Protestant and many Roman Catholic biblical scholars today is that neither allegory nor typology can faithfully and fruitfully serve the task of exegesis. Theology has become a science, and consequently it demands scientific methodology, in particular the historical-critical approach developed especially in Germany since the mid-19th century and taken up by most present-day exegetes. To the great majority of these scholars, allegory and even typology are decidedly unscientific, and for this reason they are inappropriate as hermeneutic tools.

With regard to allegory, such a judgment is certainly justified. The specificity of Christian faith—which distinguishes it from all mystery religions—is its radically *historical* character: revelation and fulfillment of the divine economy occur within the context of creation itself. By treating historical events as parabolic symbols, allegory threatens the historical basis of faith.[2]

But must we pass the same negative judgment upon typology? As we have seen, typological *theōria* does preserve the historical nature of revelation. The works of Chrysostom and Theodoret offer lucid examples of the way in which *theōria* as a hermeneutic principle is compatible with a proper authentic divine or spiritual meaning. God reveals Himself within history. Therefore the exegete is obliged to employ a method of interpretation which corresponds to the historical framework of that revelation. By judicious use of *theōria*, the Fathers could demonstrate the typological realtionship between a prophetic image and its fulfillment, while explaining the spiritual significance of that relationship for the interior life of the believer.

methodology helps to explain the neo-Nestorian and neo-Arian (adoptionist and subordinationist) christologies which characterize modern theological circles. See G. Florovsky, "The Lost Scriptural Mind," in *Bible, Church, Tradition*, p. 14f.

[2]L. Pirot, *L'oeuvre exégétique*, p. 185ff., gives striking examples of Cyril's allegorization, paralleling his commentaries with those of Theodore on the same passages. Often Cyril totally neglected the literal sense in his concern to discover a subjective, personal message for himself or his contemporaries.

If the method was effective during the patristic age, is it realistic to argue for its usefulness within the life of the Church today? To answer affirmatively, we must show that *theoria* as a hermeneutic principle is compatible with a proper historical-critical methodology and that it complements that methodology by supplying to theology a spiritual dimension which would otherwise be lacking.

A typical definition of *theōria* appears in the *Jerome Biblical Commentary*[3]: "for all practical purposes [*theōria is*] a close equivalent of Alexandrian *allēgoria. Theōria* was an intuition or vision by which the prophet could see the future through the medium of his present circumstances. After such a vision it was possible for him to phrase his writing in such a way as to describe both the contemporary meaning of the events as well as their future fulfillment." This definition needs to be corrected for two reasons. Typological *theōria* is, as we have seen, a very different method of interpretation from allegory; and the "intuition or vision" to which it refers is proper not only to the prophet, but also to the later apostolic or post-apostolic interpreter who perceives the fulfillment of Old Testament types within the experience of the Church.

As a hermeneutic method, *theōria* was based upon two fundamental presuppositions: that Scripture is uniformly inspired by God, and that typology offers the key to its right interpretation. Reflecting Aristotelian influence, *theōria* understood the event itself, rather than the word (the witness to the event), to be the true vehicle of revelation. It sought the meaning of God's activity within the facts of history, discerning in certain events both a literal-historical sense and a divine or spiritual sense. The former, perceived and articulated by the prophet, could be expressed in either plain or figurative language. The literal sense, then, is limited by the religious consciousness and express intent of the human witness. Antiochian theologians were vague as to the degree to which the prophet had to perceive a spiritual sense within the event itself. Against allegory they unanimously insisted that one cannot speak of two distinct meanings proper to the

[3] Jerome Bib Comm 71:39.

event, one literal and the other spiritual. Rather, those historical facts which are bearers of revelation possess a "double
sense": the spiritual sense (realized in the antitype or archetype) being firmly embedded within the literal sense (expressed by the type).

In the extant works of Diodore and Theodore we find
two approaches to the problem of the spiritual sense and its
relation to the literal sense. Diodore holds that the spiritual
sense is expressed by the prophet through "hyperbole." That
is, the prophet consciously and purposefully adapted his
oracles to two epochs: his own and the future age of the
Church. To his contemporaries, these oracles seemed hyperbolic or exaggerated; but to later interpreters, who viewed
them as fulfilled, they appeared to be in perfect harmony
with the events they described. Type and antitype were thus
seen to be logically related to one another in the economy
of God. Although he never spells it out, Theodore seems
to have held a similar view of the prophet's conscious activity.
When he speaks of "analogy," however, he is describing the
way in which the later interpreter unravels the prophetic
oracle or other Old Testament fact to discern the spiritual
meaning which lies hidden within it.

The crucial question for determining the continuing validity of *theōria* is this: does *theōria* depend upon discernment
by the biblical author of the *spiritual* as well as the literal
sense of the event he is describing? The Antiochians seem
to imply that it does, for *theōria* refers primarily to that
vision or perception of spiritual truth at the heart of an historical event which the human author experienced and communicated through his writing. It is for this reason that they
place major emphasis upon the "intention of the author."

Such conscious intention, however, becomes quite unim-
portant when we consider the secondary meaning of *theōria*:
the intuitive perception of spiritual meaning not by the
author, but by the *later interpreter*. Typological fulfillment
depends upon an act of God. It is God Himself, and not the
human witness, who associates two events or facts as type and
antitype. We would argue, then, that this discernment by the
interpreter of a typological relationship within the event in

question is in fact the *primary* sense of *theōria*. What ultimately matters is not whether the prophet actually beheld in the figure of the Suffering Servant the person of Jesus Christ. What ultimately matters *for the Church* is whether in the mind of God, according to the divine economy, the Servant-figure was actually a prophetic image of salvation which was fulfilled in the person of Christ. The same holds for all Old Testament images such as Adam, Moses, the Exodus, and the manna in the wilderness. Typological *theōria* remains a valid hermeneutic principle if these types of the Old Covenant are in fact related to the saving activity of Christ in terms of promise and fulfillment. If they are not, then the concept of salvation-history is meaningless (as certain existentialist theologians hold), and consequently the work of Christ is wholly *sui generis* with no essential relationship to the history of the people of Israel.

Before we attempt to define a valid *theōria*, it would be useful to note points that the theoretic and historical-critical approaches have in common.

Historical-critical exegesis shares with *theōria* a basic concern for the literal-historical sense of biblical events and clarification of the author's intended meaning. Both methods aim to preserve the historical foundation of eschatology. Consequently, both accentuate the primacy of fact over idea, of event over interpretation, and thereby they avoid the distortions of an allegorical method which results in "eisegesis" rather than exegesis. Significantly, the accent they place upon historical literalism leads many modern scholars, as much as the most radical Antiochian, to emphasize the human nature of Christ rather than His divinity (speaking, of course, of those who profess Christian faith). As in the case of Theodore of Mopsuestia, the result is often a drastic reduction of biblical typology which issues in a general theological "minimalism." (It is by no means coincidental, for example, that Western theology envisions salvation as *koinōnia* with God or a beatific vision of the divine glory rather than as *theōsis*,

the "divinization" of man which means a real and full participation in the very life of God.)

If proponents of historical-criticism tend almost instinc-
tively to reject typology and *theōria,* it is due to presuppositions they hold rather than to any basic incompatibility
between critical analysis and spiritual vision. If, for example,
the modern critic rejects such basic elements of traditional
Christian faith as the inspiration of Scripture (i.e., if he
holds that Scripture is man's word about God rather than
God's Word addressed to the Church through human agents),
then he would logically reject as well the thought of divine
intervention in earthly affairs which both creates typological
relationships and inspires the theoretic perception of the
meaning of those relationships. We have noted that the
doctrine of the inspiration of Scripture is a basic presupposition of theoretic hermeneutics. The interpreter comes to the
text with this presupposition or without it. He may be confirmed or altered in his belief by studying the Scriptures; but
it is evident that exegesis cannot *prove* that the Scriptures
were or were not actually inspired. All it can do is confirm
that the biblical authors themselves believed that "all Scripture is inspired by God."

Other presuppositions are brought to the text by certain
proponents of historical criticism. Perhaps the most basic of
these is the notion that exegesis is essentially a historical
rather than a philosophical-theological discipline. To the
Fathers of Antioch as fully as to those of Alexandria, exegesis
properly serves the creedal, liturgical and doxological expressions of the Church. Its rightful place is within the worshiping community. In the hands of many Protestant theologians, however, exegesis has been lifted out of its ecclesial
setting and refashioned into a "science"—meaning not the
divine *gnōsis* or *sophia,* the sacred wisdom of which the
Fathers speak, but rather a systematic discipline for acquiring
objective, factual knowledge about persons and events referred to in Scripture. (Is this not due, in part at least, to
the Protestant emphasis upon the ability of each individual,
under the guidance of the Holy Spirit and quite independent
of any ecclesiastical norm or Tradition, to discern the true

meaning of God's Word?) The result is a certain estrangement between biblical and systematic theology in Protestantism, an estrangement which would be utterly incomprehensible to the patristic mind.[4]

A fallacious presupposition underlies this idea that exegesis is essentially a science in the modern sense of the term: the presupposition that history itself enshrines ultimate truth. *Theōria,* however, understands the historical event to be an essential *vehicle* of that truth, an earthen vessel that contains an eternal treasure. Yet unlike allegory, it insists that the event is indispensable as the means by which that eternal truth comes to expression. From the point of view of *theōria,* exegesis does indeed investigate the facts of history (including myths and statements of faith as well as persons and events). But it does so with the express aim of uncovering and laying bare the meaning of those events for the spiritual life of the believing community. Stated another way, an authentic *theōria* conceives the aim of biblical interpretation to be the spiritual enlightenment of God's people. The ultimate purpose of exegesis, then, is soteriological rather than scientific; and the exegete is properly a theologian rather than an historian.

Both *theōria* and historical criticism become arbitrarily limited if the exegete concerns himself solely with the "intention" of the biblical author. Clarification of that intention—what, why, and how the author speaks to his own epoch—should be, of course, the starting point of all exegesis. But hermeneutics is an interpretive discipline. Its rules should be

[4]This is not to say that Protestant theology is "unbiblical." Indeed, the starting point of all theological disciplines in churches of the Reform is Holy Scripture. Protestant systematic theology, however, tends often to slip away from its biblical foundations in an effort to reinterpret some arbitrarily chosen philosophical system, e.g., of Hegel, Heidegger or even Marx or Nietzsche. This is evident in the most influential currents of Protestant thought from Schleiermacher and Ritschl (esp. on the Kingdom of God) through Bultmann, Tillich and the "death-of-God" school. While such gleanings can be of value in "making the Gospel relevant" to our times, they often determine the outcome of exegesis in a way that plays havoc with the literal sense of Scripture.

comprehensive enough to translate the biblical witness into a relevant message for today *as part of the exegetical task itself.* This means that the exegete will properly look beyond the author's immediate intention in order to perceive the Word which God is presently speaking through the text to the Church and to the world.

Scripture itself justifies our conceiving hermeneutics in this broader sense. It is true that certain key New Testament passages affirm that the prophet was conscious of the messianic import of his message. Taking up a "word spoken by the prophet Isaiah," the Evangelist John states that "Isaiah said this because he saw [Christ's] glory and spoke of him" (12:41). Elsewhere he attributes to Jesus the affirmation, addressed to the Jews, that "Abraham rejoiced that he was to see my day; he saw it and was glad" (8:56). In the discourse of Acts 2, St Peter quotes Ps. 16:8-11 and adds that David "foresaw and spoke of the resurrection of the Christ. . . ." Finally, 1 Pet 1:10-12 describes the Spirit's activity in inspiring the prophets to foresee the fulfillment of their hope in the messianic age: "they inquired what person or time was indicated by the Spirit of Christ within them when predicting the sufferings of Christ and the subsequent glory. It was revealed to them that they were serving not themselves but you . . ." (RSV). To the Antiochians, such passages indicated that Abraham and the prophets were conscious of the precise way in which their prophecies would be realized: they "saw" Christ suffer His passion and enter into glory.

But did the New Testament authors actually attribute so concrete a vision to the prophets? Much of their message is expressed in terms of a typology of figures or images (*hypodeigma,* Heb 8:5, etc.)[5] or in terms of the fulfillment of prophecy. Although they do affirm that the prophet was conscious of a transcendent meaning hidden within the historical event, this does not mean that to their mind this transcendent meaning (spiritual sense) had been revealed to

_____
[5]Cf. Heb. 4:11 *hypodeigma*; 8:5 and 10:1 *skia*; and 9:24, where the earthly sanctuaries are *antitypa tōn alēthinōn.* Here "antitype" means simply "type." To the author, reflecting Platonic influence, the "antitype" is the image of the "archetype" or celestial reality.

the prophet in the form of a detailed image of Jesus of
Nazareth and the circumstances surrounding His life and
death. Abraham saw the day of Christ and Isaiah beheld His
glory. But their prophetic vision surely consisted of no more
than a mere aperçu or glimpse of an eternal reality which
would become incarnate in history at some future time. They
"viewed" that future incarnation in the form of a "design
in shadow" (*skiographia*), confident that God would ultimately realize their prophecy and fulfill their hope. From
their perspective, therefore, a given event bore a literal sense
either as an ordinary fact with no ultimate meaning or as a
prophetic image of some future divine act. Had they thought
in terms of a "spiritual sense," they would have attributed
it not to the event in question, but to that future, divinely
ordained antitype. In the eyes of St Paul, Christ may have
been concealed in the image of the desert rock, but He was
certainly not so perceived by the author of the Exodus narrative. This simply confirms the point made earlier, that *theōria*
is rightly understood as the vision of the interpreter rather
than of the prophet.

The "intention" of the prophet, then, is of only secondary
importance, because his own consciousness concerning the
ultimate significance of his prophecy plays no definitive role
in its fulfillment. It is the Spirit who expresses Himself in the
words of the prophet, just as it is the Spirit who fulfills the
prophecy at a future time. The exegete poses a false problem
for himself when he seeks to know "how to attribute to God
the power to include a sense in the words of His [human]
instrument when the latter is not conscious of that sense."[6]
It is quite evident that the prophet is incapable of sounding
the depths of his message to discern its full meaning for
Christian life, just as (at another level) the preacher remains
essentially unaware of the impact of his proclamation upon
the life of the individual hearer. To praphrase liturgical
language, "such is the work of the Spirit, and it is a mystery
to our eyes." To avoid an unnecessarily limited hermenuetic,
hung up, as it were, on the historical event and consequently

---

[6] J. Coppens, *Problèmes et méthode d'exégèse théologique*, Louvain 1950,
p. 16; quoted by P. Ternant, "La *theōria*," p. 154f.

fixed upon a purely literal sense, exegesis must investigate not only the meaning of an event as it was understood by the prophet (or the apostolic writer), but also its spiritual sense, i.e., its existential meaning *pro nobis,* which relates to the life of the Church. By so doing, exegesis corresponds to the method used by the apostolic authors, who sought above all the *theological meaning* of Old Testament persons and events, just as they sought to interpret the theological meaning of Christ Himself.

In their important studies of patristic hermeneutics, Henri de Lubac and Jean Daniélou have called for a re-evaluation of certain aspects of Alexandrian exegesis, suggesting that typology (if not blatant allegory) still represents a valid method of interpretation.[7] Against this view, P. Ternant, drawing upon two articles by A. Vaccari,[8] refuses to admit the presence of a "spiritual sense" for fear that allegory will result from it. Instead he argues that the spiritual and literal senses are in fact one: a *theōria* is discerned at the very core of the historical event. While we would hold the two together, seeing the event as the vehicle of the spiritual sense, we would nonetheless insist that the origin of that sense is to be found *in God Himself,* who creates a genuine typological relationship between select facts in salvation-history. By identifying the spiritual with the literal sense, Fr Ternant virtually eliminates the antitype which fulfills the original type or prophetic image.

In some way, then, the spiritual sense must be regarded as distinct, if not separate, from the literal sense. J. Coppens and P. Benoit have attempted to clarify the relationship between the two by speaking of a *sensus plenior.* By this they mean the sense which God—but not the human author— intends, and which He expresses by the *words* of Scripture

[7]H. de Lubac, *Histoire et Esprit* (1950); *Exégèse médiévale* (1959) of which important excerpts appear in *L'Ecriture dans la Tradition,* Paris 1966; J. Daniélou, *Origène* (1948).

[8]A. Vaccari, "La *theôria* nella scuola esegetica d'Antiochia," Biblica 1 (1920), p. 3-36 (see p. 15f for the four criteria of *theôria*), and "La 'teoria' esegetica antiochena," Biblica 15 (1934), p. 94-101.

as they are interpreted by the Church. A major difficulty with this view, as Raymond Brown notes,[9] occurs when the *sensus plenior* is seen to depend upon "further revelation." In this case the "fuller sense" would refer to a fuller understanding on the part of the exegete rather than to a fuller sense of Scripture. This difficulty disappears, however, if we accept that the *sensus plenior* is understood by the exegete through growth in his understanding of revelation. Yet the accent here remains on the interpretation of *words*. With the Antiochians, as with historical criticism, we should look for meaning both literal and spiritual—within the *event*. Thereby typology is preserved, and the dehistoricizing tendency of allegory is avoided.

We mean by the "spiritual sense," then, a *sensus plenior*, unperceived by the prophet but discerned by the interpreter *within the event itself* by means of *theōria*. Refusal to accept a spiritual sense in these terms often leads to a confusion of *theōria* with the exegetical method of typology.[10] To be exact, *theōria* is not a "method" at all; it is a spiritual perception or divination *inspired by the Spirit*, which discerns the existence of a typological relationship between two persons objects, institutions, or events.[11] This theoretic or spiritual sense is twofold. On the one hand, it refers to a typological association of two figures related to one another in terms of promise and fulfillment. According to this criterion, the sacrifice of Isaac is a true type of Christ's crucifixion, and the crossing of the Red Sea together with the story of Jonah prefigure His burial and resurrection. On the other hand, *theōria* discerns the existential significance of that typological relationship. It reveals its meaning *for us* as members of the Body of Christ.[12]

[9]Jerome Bib Comm 71:67.

[10]See P. Ternant, "La *theōria*," p. 156ff; also R. Greer, *Theodore of Mopsuestia*, p. 93: *theōria* is "presumably, in some sense, typology."

[11]See Th. Spidlik, *Grégoire de Nazianze, Introduction à l'étude de sa doctrine spirituelle*. Rome 1971, parts I and III on *theōria* as spiritual vision.

[12]The lack of a specifically *ecclesial* orientation limits existential hermeneutics and places in question its faithfulness to Scripture. For important discussions on this subject, see H. Cazelles, "La nouvelle herméneutique biblique," *Mededelingen* 31 (1969), p. 3-16; and *Ecriture, Parole et Esprit*, Paris 1971, esp. p. 21-44.

Fulfillment of the type by the antitype, therefore, represents not only the co-ordination of two events in the historical past. It also—and primarily—represents two constitutive moments in the *history of salvation,* a history in which we find ourselves directly and personally involved. In the divine economy, past events are actualized in the present by the work of the Holy Spirit. Just as the Jew *participates* in the Exodus event at every Passover festival, so the Christian *participates* in the crucial moments of Christ's life and ministry. In the language of Kierkegaard, the Christian becomes a "contemporaneous disciple" of Christ; the paradoxical "Moment" of the incarnation becomes "really decisive for eternity!"[13] Existentialist theology interprets this "contemporaneousness" in such a way as to eliminate salvation-history. To Orthodox Christianity, however, this experience becomes actual within *the liturgical life of the Church.* History fully retains its primal meaning as the context of God's saving activity. Through the liturgy, the Church actually participates in the saving events of the past, culminating in Holy Week, when she journeys with her Lord from suffering and death to glorified life. It is this very real liturgical participation in the saving events of history that constitutes the primary aspect of the spiritual sense. *Theōria* enables the Christian to *discern* the soteriological meaning of an event and to *participate in it* personally and in communion with the Church as a whole. Both aspects, discernment and participation, are made possible by the "anamnetic activity" of the Holy Spirit: the gift of an "inspired memory," by which the Christian grasps the revelation both on the level of intelligence and on the level of existence. It is rightly termed a "spiritual sense" because it issues from the activity of the Spirit Himself.

Thus far we have not spelled out the significant difference between the *theōria* of the biblical author and that of the later Christian exegete. Failure to do so would imply that Scripture and Tradition are equal in terms of their revelatory value and authority. This is not the case, however, as the

[13]S. Kierkegaard, *Philosophical Fragments,* Princeton 1936, ch. 4.

Church Fathers make perfectly clear. It is true that the Antiochians attributed a theoretic perception both to biblical authors and to the later interpreter. Relative to the Old Testament prophet, the New Testament writer was just such a "later interpreter." In both their cases, *theōria* can be closely associated with revelation: God's self-disclosure through historical persons and events. Yet Diodore and his disciples referred also to a *theōria* which was essential to *post-apostolic interpretation*. This order of *theōria* is more closely related to typology as an exegetical method. In fact there are three orders or degrees of *theōria*. First, there is the ecstatic vision of the prophet that precedes his auditory apprehension of the revelation he is to communicate. Then there is the perception by the inspired New Testament author of a spiritual sense revealed in the prophet's oracle by typology. Finally, the post apostolic exegete interprets the relationship between the Old and New Testaments on the basis of his own typological *theōria*.

In what sense can we say that each of these constitutes an authentic *theōria* or inspired vision of the spiritual meaning of historical facts? Raising the question obliges us to touch upon the delicate problem of inspiration. Generally speaking, "inspiration" denotes the influence which the Holy Spirit exercises upon human instruments, leading them to communicate divine revelation in a language conditioned by their particular historical and cultural milieu. More specifically, the term refers to the Spirit's guidance of biblical authors, whose writings have been proclaimed canonical or normative for Christian faith. To the Church, the Bible is the unique "canon of truth" or "rule of faith." This means that all tradition (the unfolding of biblical revelation within the life of the Church) must be measured against Scripture and judged in terms of it. For the Church recognizes that Scripture enshrines a unique quality of revelation: a plenitude and an inerrancy that are proper to it alone. (Such plenitude and inerrancy are, of course, relative; to insist that they are absolute is to stumble into a fundamentalist biblical literalism.) Consequently, it would be quite wrong to attribute an equivalent value or quality of inspiration to the New Testament author and to the patristic or modern exegete. If the Church recognizes Holy Scripture as the unique canon of faith, it does so to prevent a proliferation of doctrines claimed to be inspired but which in reality are heretical. This does not mean, however, that the inspirational activity of the Spirit is limited to Holy Scripture. All genuine tradition (*paradosis*) is in a certain sense "inspired." Fr Sergius Bulgakov spoke of tradition as "the living memory of the Church."[14] Patristic interpretation of the New Testament, for example, constitutes an essential part of that "living memory." Insofar as patristic teaching remains faithful to the norm of Scripture, the Church is free to accept it as truly inspired Tradition. The same can surely be said for the exegesis and preaching of today.

Thus we are obliged to distinguish two different orders or degrees of inspiration: that of Scripture and that of Tradition. Such a distinction has long been made to mark the difference between canonical and deutero-canonical writings of the Old Testament.[15] One may object that a book can hardly be "partially inspired." It is not a matter of "partial" or "full" inspiration, however, but rather of the *authority* granted to a particular writing by the Holy Spirit, an authority which is merely recognized and acknowledged by the Church. To distinguish Scripture and Tradition in terms of the Spirit's activity, we might speak of *revelatory inspiration* and *anamnetic inspiration*. The former signifies the inspiration of biblical authors by whom divine revelation is communicated to the Church; and the latter, the "living memory" of the Church by which she interprets that revelation in order to make it meaningful and accessible to the faithful.

This distinction between the inspirational quality of Scripture and of Tradition is suggested by Scripture itself, and in particular by the Farewell Discourses of the Gospel of St John. One passage above all, relating Jesus' teaching about

14S. Bulgakov, *The Orthodox Church*, N.Y. 1935, p. 19; and for the relationship between Scripture and Tradition, esp. p. 28f. See also the important art. of G. Florovsky, "The Function of Tradition in the Ancient Church," *Bible, Church, Tradition*, p. 73-92.

15S. Bulgakov, ibid., p. 29ff.

the work of the Spirit-Paraclete, provides the basis for all Orthodox hermeneutics:

> "I have yet many things to say to you, but you cannot bear them now. When the Spirit of truth comes, he will guide you into all the truth; for he will not speak on his own authority, but whatever he hears [or: will hear, *akousei*] he will speak, and he will declare to you the things that are to come [*ta erchomena*]. He will glorify me, for he will take what is mine and declare it to you. All that the Father has is mine; therefore I said that he will take what is mine and declare it to you." (16:12ff-RSV)

The meaning here is not that the Spirit communicates new revelations or doctrines to the Church. The "truth" into which the Spirit guides the faithful is the truth of Christ Himself. Revelation concerns primarily the *person* of Jesus Christ, and not doctrine as such. For doctrine, in the form of Tradition, is the Church's own *witness* to Jesus and to the meaning of His life, death and resurrection. It is, however, an inspired witness: a recollection (*anamnēsis*) and an interpretation (*hermeneia*), indeed an illumination (*phōtismos*)[16] of the unique Truth revealed in the incarnate person of the Word of God.

Before Christ's resurrection and the coming of the Spirit at Pentecost (Jn 20; Ac 2), the disciples were incapable of grasping the full meaning of His words. The Spirit of Truth, sent from the Father by the Son, reveals all the Truth, at first to the disciples and then to successive generations of Christians. Within the Church (by definition, the realm of the Spirit), He speaks of "the things that are to come" (*ta erchomena*), meaning eschatological events which will terminate the history of salvation. What are these eschatological events? Perhaps the judgment upon sin alluded to in the preceding verses[17]; perhaps the effective proclamation of the

---

[16]Cf. 2 Cor 4:4, "illumination (*phōtismon*) of the Gospel of the glory of Christ."

[17]C. K. Barrett, *The Gospel According to St John*, London 1960, p. 408.

Word within the believing community,[18] the interpretation
"in relation to each coming generation [of] the contemporary
significance of what Jesus had said and done."[19] From the
context, however, "the coming things" seem rather to mean
fulfillment of the plan of salvation at the eschaton, when
the sufferings of the present age are brought to an end and
Christ returns in glory to lead His own to a place prepared
for them in the Kingdom of God (14:2f).

During the present age, the glorified Christ *continues
His work of revelation* within the Church through the inspirational, "interpretive" activity (*hermeneia*) of the Holy Spirit:
"When the Spirit of Truth comes, He will declare to you the
coming things . . ." Translated into human language, this
revelation has already received its normative form in the
apostolic witness preserved in Holy Scripture. Interpretation
of that Scripture, however, constitutes another aspect of that
same revelation: the aspect of Holy Tradition. There is no
conflict between the two. In fact Scripture and Tradition
bear complementary witness to God's truth, because each has
its origin in Jesus Christ, who alone determines their ultimate
content.

The close relationship between Scripture and Tradition,
between the apostolic witness and its interpretation, may be
illustrated by comparing Tradition to the sacred image. Word
and Icon include four common elements. First, the event
itself, representable and represented, by which revelation is
imparted to the Church. Second, the inspirational work of
the Spirit, who accords to the biblical author or to the
iconographer a vision (*theōria*) of the eternal reality or truth
which lies at the heart of the event. Third, the material
expression of that truth in the human language of words or
of graphic form and color. Finally, the believer's own act
of interiorizing that truth as it reveals itself to him through
the Word or through the icon. While remaining fully normative or canonical, the Word is illuminated by the icon just as
it is by Holy Tradition. Thus the kondakion of the Feast
of the Victory of Orthodoxy concludes with the emphatic

---

[18]R. Bultmann, *Das Evangelium des Johannes*, Göttingen 1964, p. 443.
[19]R. Brown, *The Gospel According to John* II, N.Y. 1970, p. 716.

affirmation, "We confess and proclaim our salvation in word and images." This confession is possible because the icon is actually a part of Tradition—as is the Word itself. For Scripture and Tradition are not two separate sources of revelation set off one against the other; nor should they be viewed as two sides of the same coin. Rather, Tradition may be conceived as a living stream of witness to divine truth revealed in the person of Jesus Christ. It is an inspired witness, granted to the Church by the Spirit of Truth. One current, indeed the main current of that stream comprises the canonical Scriptures. Iconography and patristic theology constitute other aspects of Tradition, as do the orthodox fruits of modern exegesis.

In conclusion, we want to indicate the way in which *theōria* can creatively serve the exegete of today as well as the interpreter of an earlier, pre-critical era.

To do so, it is first necessary to define certain terms that recur in contemporary discussions of hermeneutics. The problem of the different senses of Scripture is complicated by an imprecision and lack of agreement concerning technical language. Reference is made to a multitude of meanings: literal, historical, allegorical, typological, spiritual, figurative, mystical, tropological, anagogical, and *sensus plenior*.[20] Several of these go back to St Thomas of Aquinas and medieval Catholic exegesis.[21] Without denying the value of carefully nuanced terms to express the diversity of scriptural meanings, we would nevertheless prefer to simplify and clarify certain of these usages. Above all, it would seem necessary to do away with the expressions "allegorical sense" and "typical" or "typological sense." Allegory and typology are in reality two different *methods* of exegesis which interpreters employ to discover a meaning that transcends the letter of the text.[22]

[20]Robert-Feuillet, *Introduction*, p. 189ff; J. Coppens, "Nouvelles réflexions sur les divers sens des Saintes Ecritures," NRTh 74 (1952), p. 11-15; and his work *Les harmonies des deux Testaments*, Tournai-Paris 1949.

[21]See the 3-vol. study of H. de Lubac, *Exégèse Médiéval*, Paris 1959.

[22]H. de Lubac, *L'Ecriture dans la Tradition*, p. 24-47 on the spiritual sense; also note 1, p. 29: "si l'on parle d'exégèse typologique, on aura soin d'éviter 'sens typologique': pur jargon, que n'excuse aucune nécessité."

Properly speaking, there are only two basic "senses" contained in Scripture: the literal sense and the spiritual sense.

Theōria, however, is neither a scriptural sense nor a method for doing exegesis. It cannot be simply equated with the spiritual sense, nor should it be identified with typology or allegory. For *theōria* is a "vision" of divine truth communicated by the Holy Spirit to the Church. It is an inspired vision, experienced and articulated by the human agent. Whereas the Hebrew prophet received his revelatory vision in a state of ecstacy, the Christian exegete becomes an instrument of the Spirit through *contemplation,* which we might define as openness to divine grace at the level of heart as well as of mind. This implies that the work of exegesis, like the preaching of the Word or the painting of sacred images, is in the fullest sense a divine "vocation" or calling. An atheist can do the work of an historian to uncover the literal sense of a biblical passage. But to accomplish the task of *hermeneia,* the exegete must submit himself to the guidance of the Spirit of Truth (Jn 16:13ff). For the interpretation of that Truth occurs through a *synergism* or co-operation between man and God: what Paul Evdokimov calls "theandric energy, the human act within the divine act."[23] In the profound image of Maximus the Confessor, "man has two wings to reach the heavens: freedom, and with it, grace."[24] Applied to biblical hermeneutics, this means that scientific research stands in perfect harmony with *theōria* or contemplative vision, so long as the exegete does in fact submit himself to the grace and purpose of God.

Such a view of the aim and method of exegesis is only possible where Scripture and Tradition are understood to be "theandric" or divine-human realities. If certain schools of modern interpretation tend to place faith in crisis, it is due in large part to the fact that numerous influential commentators have lost sight of the divine character of Holy Scripture and approach it as they would any historical document. Where the New Testament is viewed, for example, as an expression of

---

[23]P. Evdokimov, *L'Orthodoxie,* Neuchâtel 1965, p. 102.
[24]Ad Thal. 254 (PG 90:512), quoted by P. Evdokimov; ibid., p. 101-102 on synergism.

the faith of the primitive Church rather than as an inspired witness to divine activity within history, its unique character as God's Word addressed to man is thrown into question. Certainly we can no longer accept a crude biblical literalism which holds that the words of Scripture were dictated by the Holy Spirit. Nevertheless, the enduring value of *theōria* lies in its awareness of an authentic *co-operation* between the Spirit and the biblical author which issues in the genuinely inspired witness of the Gospel.

The exegetes of Antioch overcame the historical positivism of Aristotle by their recognition that the Bible is indeed a sacred book of divine origin. Submitting themselves to the revelatory-interpretive activity of the Spirit, they were able to go beyond the limits of history without denying it. But once again, such a hermeneutic was possible only because they shared an unshakable conviction that the glorified Christ, in the age of the Church and by the economy of the Spirit, pursues His work of revelation through Scripture and through Tradition.

Theōria or contemplative vision, then, is as essential to the exegete as it was to the biblical authors. It would be a mistake, however, to think that *theōria* is separate from exegesis *per se*, as a subjective interpretation which merely complements the objective findings of critical analysis. As we have indicated, *theōria* includes both the inspired vision by which the exegete discerns the spiritual sense of a text, and the attitude of contemplation which is an essential condition for receiving that vision. *Theōria* thus informs and guides every aspect of exegesis. It begins with scientific research of the passage in question, in order to understand and clarify its literal sense: the historical situation of the author and his community; the various motives which led to composition of the text; the origin and nature of independent sources and their kerygmatic, liturgical or catechetical use (the sciences of literary criticism, Redaktions- and Formgeschichte, etc.). Once he has determined the literal sense of the passage (the sense the author himself understood and intended to communicate), the exegete moves to the question of the spiritual sense which the passage reveals for the present life of the community of faith. These two stages in the work of interpretation are distinct, but they are by no means separate. They do not involve pure scientific research on the one hand and pure spiritual interpretation on the other. For *both the literal and the spiritual sense derive from divine activity within history.* Therefore both senses are discerned by the Spirit-given grace of *theōria.*

When one understands and accepts the divine origin of *theōria* and its hermeneutic function, one sees that *theōria* embraces every aspect of biblical interpretation: from rigorously scientific exegesis to liturgical hymnography. It is *theōria* that unifies and places in the service of faith such diverse expressions of interpretation as modern biblical commentaries and the spiritual hymns of Romanus or Symeon the New Theologian. And it is *theōria* that enables the Church to practice an authentic *orthodoxia* by the use of liturgical poetry such as the dialogue between Gabriel and Mary at the Feast of the Annunciation.

This it does, not by rejecting or ignoring the absolute authority of canonical Scripture, nor by refusing to build faith upon the rock of history. To the contrary, *theōria* has no meaning apart from historical revelation. But like the apostolic witness to that revelation, *theōria* knows that divine reality (*alētheia*), which discloses itself within the historical event, is not confined to that event but speaks as well to each succeeding generation. Thus *theōria* offers a vision of invisible reality, a reality that forever eludes the probing inquiry of the empirical sciences. This vision into the hidden depths of divine revelation is granted to the interpreter who consciously and faithfully assumes an attitude of contemplation or prayer. The true theologian, as the Fathers remind us, is the man who prays. The same is surely true for the genuine exegete.

Recovery of the contemplative aspect of *theōria* would do much to restore to exegesis its *doxological* quality. Interpretation of the Word of God is properly a function of the worshiping Church. It is as closely united to sacramental grace and to spiritual warfare as it is to preaching of the Word. Like the sacraments and ascetic struggle, its sole purpose is to guide the Church into ever deeper union with her glorified Lord. Accepted as such, the arduous task of exegesis can be transformed by the interpreter into an offering of praise. It can discover its proper place within the believing community, in order to devote itself unambiguously to proclamation of "all the truth."[25]

[25]Other evaluations of patristic *theōria* have recently appeared, of which the most important and interesting is perhaps the first volume of a three-part study by B. de Margerie, *Introduction à l'Histoire de l'Exégèse. I: Les Pères Grecs et Orientaux,* Paris (Cerf) 1980. The author offers sound analyses of the exegetical methods employed by representatives of the school of Antioch, as well as by other major interpreters among the Fathers. Like the vast majority of modern scholars, however, Fr de Margerie tends to confuse *theōria* with typology (although he does recognize that the two are not identical and that *theōria* cannot be equated with a "sensus plenior"). From an Orthodox point of view, his work suffers primarily from a failure to relate adequately the *theōria* of the biblical author (prophet—apostle) with that of the later interpreter (apostle—exegete). As we have tried to demonstrate in this present study, *theōria* as conceived and employed by the Fathers, especially those of the Antiochian school, includes "both the inspired vision by which the exegete discerns the spiritual sense of a text, and the attitude of contemplation which is an essential condition for receiving that vision." As our earlier chapter on "Exegesis and Interpretation" indicates, *theōria* is ultimately the work of the Holy Spirit acting within the Church, to reveal the full sense of Biblical revelation: its original literal and spiritual meaning in a given historical context, and its significance as the Word of God for today.

PART II

LIVING THE WORD

CHAPTER IV

Confessing the Faith in Liturgical Celebration

An intimate relationship, often misunderstood and generally neglected, exists between the act of *confession* and the act of *celebration.* For belief to become a living and life-giving faith, it must be "confessed": publicly proclaimed both as a witness to one's personal conviction and as an affirmation of the universal, divine truth that alone has the power to save the world. If I confess my faith, I do so not only to articulate and reinforce my own belief, but also to elicit and confirm the belief of other people. Confession by its very nature is a communal, public act, performed in concert with others for the mutual enrichment of all. Such confession, however, must not only be verbalized; it must also be "lived out," that is, celebrated as a common activity of the believing commuiity, in which the Word of God is interpreted and confessed.

In the following chapters we shall be looking at the "power of the Word" as it comes to expression in creedal formulas of the New Testament and the Church's eucharistic liturgy. The question we want to consider here concerns the interrelationship between confession of faith and liturgical celebration: what role do confessional statements play in the liturgy, and in what sense can we affirm that the liturgy itself functions as a confession of faith?

Faith is usually understood to be a precondition of liturgical action, the liturgy being conceived as a re-enactment of

117

previously acquired theological and spiritual convictions. This image is faulty for two reasons. In the first place, it ignores both the pedagogical-catechetical character of the liturgy and the dynamic quality of faith. For faith grows and deepens insofar as it is nourished by the "liturgical Word." Secondly, this view distorts the true function of ritual, whose purpose is not primarily to *preserve* tradition, to conserve the deposit of faith, but to *re-actualize* the content of faith within the life and experience of the Church.

To treat this topic even superficially, it is important to understand just what we mean when we speak of a "confession of faith." What indeed is the "faith" we confess: its origin, content and impact upon the believer? What does it mean to "confess" faith? Does the act itself have a particular significance and effect other than to recall and to repeat certain dogmatic affirmations? Finally we should ask how confession takes form in the Church's liturgy and whether the liturgy itself has "confessional" value. To answer such questions, we shall have to consider the problem of the relation between doctrine and worship, between the formal expression of Christian faith and the "living out" of that faith through the liturgical activity of the Christian community. While the point of view represented here is that of a priest of the Orthodox Church, the subject concerns every Christian confession that grounds its life and mission in proclamation and celebration of the divine Word.

I. *The Substance of Faith*

"By grace you have been saved through faith," declares the apostle, "and this is not your own doing, it is the gift of God" (Eph 2:8). What is the meaning of the qualifying phrase "through faith"? Is the faith that saves essentially an act of intellectual assent or of existential commitment? Or must we say that faith is not an "act" at all, but rather an "openness" to divine grace, "the lack of resistance to what we hope to receive," as it has been popularly defined? Are members of Christ's Body called "faithful" because of their doctrinal belief, or their trusting obedience to the divine will, or their (passive) receptivity of justification and salvation?

To St Thomas Aquinas, faith "is an act of the intellect assenting to divine truth under the influence of the will moved by divine grace" (Sum. Th. II.II. 2, 9). The medieval scholastic mind conceived of faith as a rational process by which the soul seeks to apprehend divine truth, such "truth" being identified with official Church doctrine. Attempting to return to a more biblical, and particularly Pauline, understanding of faith, the Protestant Reformers stressed the existential character of man's relationship to God. "Faith" in reformed thinking came to mean essentially "trust" or "confidence" in the divine promises articulated by the prophets and fulfilled in the person of Jesus Christ. Protestant theology consciously de-emphasized the doctrinal, catechetical content of faith until the term no longer signified—as it had since the apostolic period—"right belief" as opposed to "heresy" (1 Tim 1:3-4; 4:1; 1 Jn 4:1-3; Ign Pol 3:1; Ign Eph 6:2; etc.).[1] Instead, it came to designate personal acceptance of the proclaimed Word of God, a subjective response of loving obedience to the divine will revealed through Scripture.

To Orthodox thought and experience, however, "intellectual assent," "existential commitment," and "openness to grace" are by no means mutually exclusive. The "faith" confessed by the Church entails by its very nature a personal commitment to divinely revealed truth. "I am the Way, the Truth, and the Life"; and faith is in the first instance a response of loving submission to that truth (*alētheia*: ultimate reality), embodied in Christ and revealed by Him. Such truth, however, has specific limits and a precise content. Divine life has revealed itself in a particular way through a particular Person. To "open itself" to that life, faith must necessarily conform to the content of revelation. Therefore doctrines—authoritative formulations of revealed truth—are

---

[1]The term *haireseis* in 1 Cor 11:19 (cf. Gal 5:20) may refer to "factions," persons condemned for their divisiveness rather than for their doctrinal beliefs. The context, however, juxtaposing *schismata* with *haireseis*, suggests that the latter refers to "heretics," false teachers who will arise within the community before the parousia. This passage would then be the oldest extant reference to "heresy" as "false doctrine."

necessary for the structure of faith as well as for its proclamation and its transmission from generation to generation.
"Faith" without formal content that corresponds to divine
revelation becomes subjective opinion, the definition of
heresy. But dogma without personal commitment remains
sterile; appealing only to the mind, it is incapable of moving
the heart. As the Reformers rightly insisted, however, faith
must never be confused with a meritorious work. It is rather
an "openness," an emphatic "yes!" pronounced in response
to the divine initiative. "By grace you have been saved," but
only through faith that eagerly seeks and joyfully receives
the gift of life.

From this point of view, faith my be described as personal commitment to revealed truth, or more precisely, to the
divine Person who incarnates and reveals the truth. "*I am*
the truth*," Jesus affirms. Such an identification means that
truth is more than the sum total of dogmatic formulations.
As the self-expression of divine Being, truth is nothing less
than life itself, and the unique "way" that leads toward that
life. As such, truth is both the content and the fulfillment
of faith.

The intimate relationship between truth and faith, between divine initiative and human response, was clearly perceived under the Old Covenant. In the language of the people
of Israel, "faith" signifies "knowledge of God" (e.g., Isa
43:10). As all knowledge, however, it is grounded in *experience*; in this case, experience of the living God, the Creator
and universal Ruler who loves and chastens His people while
guiding them toward fulfillment of their sacred history. It is
a personal and communal experience that elicits trust, prac-
tically a synonym of hope (cf. Ps 26:13 LXX). Its opposite
is not "unbelief" in the sense of an agnostic indifference to
truth or a dogmatic "a-theism." It is rather a conscious rejection of the source of truth, an open and violent rebellion
against the divine will and, therefore, against the very Person
of God. In the Hebrew tongue, "to hear is to obey"; the
two actions are expressed by the same verb, *shamea* (Gen
22:18; Ex 5:2; Jer 7:23; etc.). The opposite of belief, dis-
belief or unfaithfulness, means a refusal "to hear," a volun-

tary rejection of the divine will or revealed truth. In the first instance, then, "infidelity" is not a moral category; it is deception or error, a spiritual and theological deviation from the way that leads to union with God.

The New Testament takes up and deepens the Hebrew concept of faith by stressing its dynamic, creative character. Faith is a *dynamis*, a power capable of moving mountains or receiving healing and saving grace. Here too its basic meaning is "confidence," an unqualified trust in divine claims and divine authority embodied in the person of Jesus Christ. Such confidence necessarily presupposes a true and precise conception of who Jesus is and of the origin of His redemptive works. Faith, then, is essentially faith in the *kerygma* and in Tradition, the latter being simply interpretation of the *kerygma* within the Church under the guidance and inspiration of the Holy Spirit. This, however, means more than mere intellectual assent to doctrinal formulations. For the paradox—more accurately, the antinomy—of faith lies in its acceptance of the rationally incomprehensible and unacceptable affirmation of God-become-man, of death and resurrection, of the sanctification and divinization of fallen human nature. Initially, then, faith presupposes a "Kierkegaardian leap," a rationally untenable acceptance of the "Word of the Cross," folly to the Greeks, a scandal to Jews, and irrelevant supersition to the modern mind. But as our experience makes painfully clear, faith at this initial stage will weaken and disappear if it is not confirmed and deepend by an authentic and transforming experience of God within our daily existence. It is for this reason—to provide just such a living experience and thereby to render the believer truly "faithful" —that faith is confessed liturgically within the Body of Christ.

II. *The Confession of Faith*

The very act of confessing personal and corporate belief effects the transformation of faith from an incipient or inchoate stage to one that is fuller, deeper, and more mature. A child raised in a Christian context will grow in his faith progressively by continually hearing the Word of God and by regularly participating in the Church's liturgical worship. The incipient faith of a former agnostic or atheist, however, normally rests upon a temporary suspension of the cognitive faculty because the content of the Church's proclamation cannot be directly verified by empirical evidence. His commitment is based upon a conviction of the heart rather than of the mind. "Blind faith," though, cannot endure. The object of faith must become the object of knowledge, a personal spiritual knowledge that includes yet goes beyond rational apprehension. Acquisition of such knowledge requires direct, personal, and intimate experience of the One in whom faith is invested. A major function of the Church's liturgical practice is to offer such experience to the worshiping community: through eucharistic participation, through adoration and intercession, but also through the act of confession.

"The Word is near you, on your lips and in your heart (that is, the Word of faith which we preach); because if you confess [homologeseis] with your lips that Jesus is Lord and believe [pisteuseis] in your heart that God raised Him from the dead, you will be saved" (Rom 10:8-9). The earliest Christian kerygma affirmed the resurrection of Jesus from the dead and His exaltation as Lord of the created universe (cf. Phil 2:9-11). From the very beginning, proclamation of the kerygma presupposed a fundamental commitment to its content: not merely an intellectual acceptance of its claims, but a response of personal devotion, an act of love. The risen Lord asks Peter not if he believes in Him, but rather if he loves Him (Jn 21:15-17). This is not because love is prior to faith, but because in the final analysis faith and love are indistinguishable. The Word of faith must be expressed "in the heart" as well as "on the lips." Otherwise it has no meaning. It is the very opposite of "faith," which, like the opposite of love, is hypocrisy, a sheer lie.

Confession of faith forms an integral and indispensable part of the Church's worship. It shares with hymns of praise and litanies of supplication an essential pedagogical character. Specialists in the field of advertising know all too well that a frequently repeated word or phrase imprints itself indelibly upon the unconscious mind. From a Christian point of view, this principle finds its most positive expression in the repetition of doctrinal hymns and universal petitions: addressed to God, they simultaneously instruct and inspire the believer, leading him toward a deeper, more knowledgeable faith, while increasing his sensitivity to the needs of the fallen world in which he lives.

Confessions of faith, however, whether in the form of creedal affirmations such as the Nicene Creed or of hymns of praise such as the festal troparia of Orthodox tradition, possess a quality unique to liturgical formulas. Like the Word of Scripture, a confession of faith not only instructs; it also *communicates* the truth it expresses by enabling the believer to participate directly and personally in that truth. A confession of faith in Orthodox tradition is known as a "symbol." According to patristic teaching, this means that the confession, by virtue of its symbolic character, "re-presents" or re-actualizes within the experience of the confessing community the divine-human events that it relates. Confession of Christ's incarnation, crucifixion and resurrection, for example, constitute a "recital" in the technical, biblical sense of the term: not merely a recounting, a verbal repetition of past events, but a *re-presentation* or *re-actualization* of the events such that the one who confesses the event truly participates in it. While enabling the believer to affirm a common faith with the whole of the universal Church, the confession renders present within the confessing community the reality which it proclaims. Like the Word of Scripture, the confession of faith is a divinely inspired witness to God's redemptive activity within history. And like Scripture, it not only recalls the past; it also makes of the past salvation-event a present reality within the life of the Church. While Scripture retains a unique quality as the canon or norm of faith, the ultimate *regula veritatis,* traditional confessional symbols serve to actualize and to deepen faith thanks to the quasi-sacramental character they share with the biblical Word. It is this sacramental character that enables the act of confessing faith within a liturgical framework to transform the liturgy from a mechanical rite, extrinsic to the Church's life and mission, into an authentic salvation-event. What would otherwise be vain repetition and meaningless gesture, becomes a life-giving witness to truth. By virtue of this transformation, liturgy becomes something other than mere ritualism; it makes possible a real participation in the ongoing redemptive activity of the Holy Trinity within the Church and for the salvation of the world.

An important qualification needs to be added, however. A confession of faith possesses this life-giving, sacramental quality only insofar as it faithfully conforms to the divinely inspired content of Holy Tradition. "Confess with your lips and believe in your heart," exhorts the apostle. As his appeal to the *kerygma* confirms, faith and its confession are authentic only when they are grounded in the apostolic witness to revealed truth. Deprived of that ground, faith has no content, for there is no real object to which the believer can relate. Heresy is destructive, in other words, because it is based upon illusion.

The faith confessed by the Church is thus both a gift and a response: "By grace you have been saved through faith . . . the gift of God." In the context of the Ephesians letter, this divine gift (*theou to dōron*) refers not to faith as such, but to the redemptive economy by which God brings about man's salvation. Faith itself is a gift, however, insofar as it springs from a personal response to the transforming experience of divine love. In its initial stage, it is seldom perceived as other than belief in the promises of God, belief which reposes upon purely human initiative. Mature faith, however, is the fruit of an ever-growing, personal relationship with the three Persons of the Holy Trinity, who bestow every spiritual gift, including the gift of faith. From an initial "acceptance of the improbable," faith becomes progressively transformed, by the indwelling power of the Spirit, into an attitude of humble and joyful trust before the self-disclosing mystery of divine compassion. Finally, where Christian existence is brought to perfection, faith and love merge in total receptivity to the divine "energies" or power that brings about a union in grace between God and man.

True faith seeks constantly to transcend itself, to rise

above mere belief by attaining union with divine life. The purpose of the liturgy, then, is not only to extend and to participate in the cultus continually offered to the Father by Christ, our High Priest.[2] Its principal function, for which Christ lived, died, and rose again to be exalted above the created world, is to achieve the transfiguration of the world and the divinization (*theōsis*) of human life.

III. *The 'Anamnetic' (Christological) Dimension of the Liturgy*

According to popular conception, the Church's liturgy is composed of two dimensions, the one horizontal or historical, the other vertical or transcendent. This cruciform image needs to be corrected insofar as it gives the impression that the temporal and eternal aspects of liturgical action are distinct and basically unrelated. To stress the essential unity and continuity between the two, we would prefer to speak of the *anamnetic* and *epikletic* dimensions of the liturgy. The former "paschal" aspect refers to the recapitulation of salvation history within the worshiping Church, an "actualizing" recital of God's redemptive activity throughout Israel's history that culminates in the victory over sin and death accomplished by the death and resurrection of Christ. The latter "pentecostal" aspect designates the work of the Spirit, who gives access to the fruits of this redemptive activity within the context of liturgical worship, particularly, but not exclusively, in the celebration of the eucharist.

The act of confession within Israel normally took the form of a recital that reactualized a past event in the present experience of the people, such as recital of the exodus tradition at the Passover festival. Confession of sin also consisted of a recollection and recitation of the sinful act (e.g., 2 Sam 12) or sinful state (Ps 50:1-5, LXX)—not to repeat it, but to awaken the individual and collective moral consciousness to its destructive effects. The aim of such recollection

---

[2]As liturgical action is often defined. See, for example, the editorial introduction to *Concilium,* no. 82, Feb. 1973.

was to prepare the heart for forgiveness. Similarly, proclamation of God's mighty acts (Ex 15:1-18), together with praise and thanksgiving for His saving work (Ex 15:21; Ps 148-150), served to render those acts present and actual. Both kinds of confession, penance and proclamation, occurred within a *cultic setting* and constituted a vital part of Israel's worship. Occasionally the Old Testament describes other cultic confessions that proclaim "who God is" in Himself and for His people. These primitive formulations, such as the *Shema* (Dt 6:4, "Hear, O Israel, the Lord our God, the Lord is one"; cf. Num 15:41), are revealed to Israel by God Himself as a form of direct self-disclosure. Known to Jesus (Mk 12:29) and practiced as a required observance in rabbinic Judaism (Berakoth 2), the *Shema* is actually an early "credo": the Israelite "hears" (*shamea*) the divine revelation and accepts it as a true statement of his own belief. Its repetition within the framework of cultic worship serves to unite the confessor with the One whom he confesses as well as with the whole of the Israelite community that shares the confession. The "credo" thus serves to renew and to reactualize the covenant relationship between Yahweh and His chosen people.

As numerous psalms attest, proclamation and praise are inseparable components of Israel's confessional statements (Psalms 25:7; 99:4-5; 116; 144; and 148-150 included in the Church's service of laudes). To adore the Name of the Lord is to confess His unique power and authority while publicly recounting the blessings of His covenant-love (*hesed*). A similar merging of confession and adoration characterized the worship of the early Church. Here again the confessional statement finds its natural setting in the cultus. John the Baptist, as will Jesus Himself, calls for repentance and "confession of sin" before baptism (cf. Ac 19:18; Jas 5:16; 1 Jn 1:9; 2:1). Even the missionary *kerygma* is first articulated in the context of communal prayer (Ac 2-3). And if Peter's confession occurs "in the district of Caesarea Philippi" (Mt 16), its full significance will only be grasped and experienced in the liturgical life of the apostolic Church.

Whereas Israel praised God by recounting His glorious

deeds accomplished for the people's salvation, early Christians were especially concerned to confess the personal identity of Jesus. The most primitive formulas appear to be those that relate *what God did* through His Son (e.g., Ac 3:14-16, 26), while later confessions were built upon christological titles that express *who Jesus was* as Son of God, Christ (Messiah), High Priest, eschatological Prophet, Advocate (*parakletos*, 1 Jn 2:1; Jn 14:16), etc. Such a "development" cannot be pressed too far, though, for even the earliest confessional hymns and formulas include distinctly christological titles (Ac 3:15, "the Author of life"; Ph 2:11, "Lord" or *Kyrios*, the divine Name in the OT). Early christological hymns, such as Phil 2:6-11, Col 1:15-20 and 1 Tim 3:16, show that confession of Jesus as Lord and Christ formed an integral part of Christian worship in the first decades after the resurrection. The word of Jesus concerning reciprocal confession ("Everyone who acknowledges [*homologesei*] me before men, I will acknowledge before my Father who is in heaven," Mt 10:32; cf. Lk 12:8) made of that confession an absolute condition for entering into eternal life. Faithfulness to Christ in the face of persecution soon became recognized as a supreme, if not unique, pathway toward salvation: "If we endure, we shall also reign with Him; if we deny Him, He will also deny us" (2 Tim 2:12). As a consequence, saintliness came to be recognized in the "confessors" and "martyrs" of the Church, those who suffered even unto death in order to defend "the good confession" of faith, that is, to bear witness to divine truth in imitation of Jesus' own confession before Pilate (1 Tim 6:12-13).

From earliest times the Church's liturgical life served to reactualize the events proclaimed by these primitive Christian confessions. The Baptist's witness to Jesus as the expiatory Lamb of God found liturgical expression in the Agnus Dei, as Isaiah's vision of the thrice-holy divine presence did in the Sanctus. Other scriptural affirmations, concerning the reality of Christ's incarnation (1 Jn 4:2; Jn 1:14), His fulfillment of the law and the prophets (Mt *passim*; Ac 24:14), His resurrection from the dead (Rom 10:9f; 1 Cor 15:3-5), and His exaltation and glorification as Lord and High Priest

(Phil 2; Heb 3-4; 9-10) who intercedes for His people by the offering of His own sacrificial blood (1 Jn 2:2; Heb 9:19; Rev 7:4), were progressively woven into the several anaphoras or consecratory prayers of the eucharistic liturgy. The most complete and theologically most profound of these is without doubt the anaphora of the Byzantine Liturgy of St Basil. These long prayers, together with the intercessions that follow them, do more than simply recall or remember past events. By the power of the Spirit, who dwells within the Church to bestow His sanctifying grace through Word and Sacrament, the liturgical action that includes a recital of sacred history has the effect of rendering the fruits of that history present and accessible: the worshiper actually *participates in the redemptive event* proclaimed by the liturgical Word and its corresponding gestures.

Consciousness of this real and present participation in the salvation event is one of the most important and striking aspects of Orthodox liturgical worship. Again and again the Church recalls and relives the past, in order to take part *now* in the eschatological grace of the future. This telescoping of time, the actualization of past and future in the *hic et nunc* of ecclesial experience, occurs with the confession of human sin as it does with the confession of divine redemptive activity. The Canon of St Andrew of Crete, for example, sung during the first and fifth weeks of Great Lent, is a solemnly beautiful and vivid recital of the history of human corruption met and transfigured by the irresistible power of God's forgiving grace.

> I have sinned, O Lord, I have sinned against Thee.
> Be merciful to me, for there is no one who has sinned
> in this world whom I have not surpassed in iniquity . . .
> (5th week, Ode 3)

There follows a recital of the rebellious deeds of various Old Testament figures; then the penitent, individual and community, proclaims:

> I cried with my whole heart to the God of mercy, and

from the depths of hell He has heard me, and He
raised my life out of corruption!

(Irmos, Ode 6)

A similar note of contrition (as distinct from "guilt") is
heard in the sacrament of penance, whose prayer of absolution also refers to our common history of sin and to the forgiveness that reconciles and unites the penitent to Christ's
Holy Church.

The term "liturgy" in Orthodox usage refers primarily
to the eucharistic celebration, and it is there that the recitation
of sacred history in the form of confessional statements attains its most complete and sublime expression. At the heart
of the eucharist stands the Nicene-Constantinopolitan Creed
(an essential element as well of the baptismal liturgy). This
universal confession of the One, Holy, Catholic, and Apostolic
Church recounts in lapidary phrases the whole of the divine
economy, from creation, through redemption and resurrection, to eternal life. At the same time that it symbolically
actualizes God's saving activity within the ecclesial community, the Credo offers praise, "all glory, honor and adoration,"
to the three Persons of the Holy Trinity. A similar fusion of
praise and doctrinal confession is found in the hymn "Monogenēs" ("Only-begotten Son of God and Immortal Word . . .")
that completes the second antiphon of the Liturgy of the
Catechumens.[3]

Liturgical recitation of sacred history is itself a "salvation
event" insofar as it enables the confessing community to participate in the redemptive events of that history. It is an
"eschatological event," for through the Church's confession,
the Word is both proclaimed and fulfilled. Proclamation of
the Kingdom, on the lips of Jesus or of future generations
of believers, renders the Kingdom proleptically present: not
merely "by anticipation," but as a transcendent reality that
continually breaks into the historical order to bring about the
ultimate transfiguration of man and the cosmos.

[3]The Liturgy of the Catechumens corresponds to the Liturgy of the Word
in Western rites and is so called because in the early Church catechumens
could only participate in this first, catechetical portion of the eucharist service.
For a detailed discussion of the "Monogenēs," see chapter 6 below.

The "anamnetic" dimension of the liturgy, then, involves not only a recital and reactualization of past events. It embraces the future as well. In the liturgy we "remember the future," thereby rendering present in the experience of the earthly Church the future eschatological fulfillment, which is the object of our deepest hope and longing. This seemingly paradoxical aspect of liturgical worship is clearly expressed in the anamnesis or eucharistic memorial of the Liturgy of St John Chrysostom. Following the Words of Institution, the priest intones:

> *Remembering* this saving commandment [to consume the Body and Blood of Christ for the remission of sins] and all those things which have come to pass for us: the Cross, the Tomb, the Resurrection on the third day, the Ascension into heaven, the Sitting at the right hand, and *the second and glorious Coming* . . .

The community thus commemorates, "remembers" in the sense of making present and accessible, both the saving events accomplished by Christ during His earthly ministry and the eschatological fulfillment of those events when He will come in the glory of His Parousia to judge the living and the dead.

He who is, and was, is also He who is to come. The coming of the Son of God, however, is a continuous reality that is actualized, known and celebrated in liturgical worship. The Ascension did not create a separation between the Lord and His disciples. The faithful are not abandoned as "orphans" in the midst of a hostile, unbelieving world (Jn 14:18). For the "economy of the Son" is one with the "economy of the Spirit," the Paraclete or Spirit of Truth who descends ever again upon the Church in a pentecostal outpouring of divine power and grace. Consequently, the "anamnetic" dimension of the liturgy is complemented and fulfilled by its "epikletic" dimension: it is the Spirit who bestows upon liturgical confessions, as upon Scripture itself, the symbolic quality that makes of the Word a present reality to those who receive it by faith.

IV. The 'Epikletic' (Pneumatological) Dimension of the Liturgy

We have already distinguished incipient or inchoate faith, the first tentative steps toward acceptance of the Church's dogmatic claims, from mature faith, a personal and intimate commitment to the God of love who is the object of the Church's proclamation. These two stages of faith in fact represent two moments in an ongoing inner process that leads toward a final transfiguration of human into divine life.

Orthodox anthropology is rooted in the Genesis affirmation that man is created in the *image of God*, that by his very nature he is a *bearer of divine life*. Obscured by the personal rebellion that we call sin, the divine image nonetheless survives intact; constantly threatened with annihilation, it remains—by grace—ultimately inviolable. Simply stated, patristic teaching holds that man's very nature is shaped in the image of divinity. Because of sin, however, man is alienated from God, a fact that hinders him from manifesting within his personal existence the moral and spiritual "likeness" of the divine Being. Christian vocation, whether lived out in the monastery or in urban society, has one principal aim: to restore and renew the divine image within the life of the believer, so that his every action and his very being might reflect the divine "likeness" in all its glory and compassion.

This vocation or invitation to participate in the fullness of divine life is received within the Church: the theandric or divine-human communion that unites the living and the dead in the glorified Body of Christ. The Church is not, in the first instance, an institution; it is before all a *celebration of divine mystery* (*mysterion*: sacramental reality) within the created order. We may even affirm that the *essence* of the Church is "liturgy," the "work of the people" (*leitourgia*) who act in concert (*synergia*) with the Holy Trinity to achieve the redemption of all things. This liturgical action, which determines Christian existence at its most fundamental level, is essentially *epikletic*. Ceaselessly invoking the presence and power of the Holy Spirit upon itself and upon material "symbols," the worshiping community experiences through the liturgy an inexhaustible outpouring of divine grace, the grace of Pentecost that Jesus describes as "power from on high" (Lk 24:49; Ac 1:8).

The epikletic dimension of the liturgy is both initiated and fulfilled by the Spirit. He is at one and the same time what in Aristotelian terms are called the "efficient" and the "final" causes, the source and the end of liturgical action. As such, His role parallels and complements the role of Christ who is High Priest of the eucharistic mystery, both Celebrant and Sacrifice, the One who offers and the One who is offered in the liturgical celebration. The Spirit complements this high priestly function by "descending" upon the community and upon the eucharistic gifts to sanctify and transform them (the people as well as the bread and wine!) into the glorified Body of Christ, and by uniting the community and its celebration to the unique transcendent and universal Eucharist offered to the Father by the Son within the heavenly sanctuary (Heb 4-10).

Orthodox eucharistic theology refuses to specify the mode or the moment of this sacramental transformation. It recognizes in the *epiklesis,* however, the culmination of both human and divine initiative. The preceding liturgical action, including repetition of the Words of Institution, prepares for this ultimate invocation of "power from on high," to consummate the eucharistic mystery. Through the priest, the community makes a self-offering of praise and supplication in the form of bread and wine, common earthly elements with no intrinsic sacramental value. Only by the transfiguring power of the Spirit does this humble offering become a divine gift: what the Church offers to God, God transforms into spiritual nourishment, "the true Bread from heaven that gives life to the world" (Jn 6:32f). "Thine own of Thine own we offer unto Thee . . .," declares the celebrant in the name of the gathered assembly. Receiving bread from the earth, we offer it to the Creator as a sacrifice of praise and thanksgiving. Yet what we offer, He transforms and offers to us in return in the form of life-giving, divine gifts. The power to change these Holy Gifts into the Body and Blood of Christ belongs to God alone. It is for this reason that Orthodox eucharistic tradition places the *epiklesis* after rather than before the Words of Institution. While the Institution grounds the liturgical action in Christ's celebration of the Last Supper, it is the Spirit, in response to the invocation of the people, who unites the community and its offering to the eternal celebration of our High Priest. This is why the *epiklesis* also calls for an actual transformation of earthly elements into heavenly realities. Through the visible, material substances of bread and wine, we truly partake of invisible, spiritual food. This is not a metaphor; it is a metaphysical reality that permits the Spirit to accomplish the still greater transformation of our own flesh and blood into the divine Body of the glorified Lord.

The whole of the Orthodox eucharistic liturgy, the Divine Liturgy as it is so appropriately called, constitutes a "confession" of this reciprocal activity between the Son and the Spirit, by which the Church both offers and becomes an offering to the Father. From the opening benediction ("Blessed is the Kingdom of the Father, the Son and the Holy Spirit . . .") through the anaphora and the concluding "prayer before the *ambon*," the community expresses its praise in the form of a trinitarian confession that seeks to receive "every good and perfect gift from above, coming down from the Father of Lights." Yet this confession on the part of the faithful is itself inspired, elicited as it were, by the presence of the Spirit who dwells within the Church to unite the confessing community to the Father through the Son.

Liturgical action, then, especially as it culminates in eucharistic celebration, is characterized by a double movement: "anabatic" and "catabatic," ascending and descending. Often this double movement is understood in an overly simplified way, as if the "anabatic" aspect referred to the elevation of the people (the *sursum corda*), while the "catabatic" aspect consisted in the divine response. In reality, both human and divine action in the liturgy include each aspect of this double movement. On the one hand, the people "lift up their hearts" in praise, supplication and invocation of divine power. In response, the Spirit descends to effect the transfiguration or

"metamorphosis" of the people and the eucharistic offerings
into the glorified Body (understood as both "Church" and
"Eucharist"—1 Cor 10-11). The *epiklesis* of the Liturgy of
St John Chrysostom expresses this reciprocal movement in
the following terms:

> Again *we offer unto Thee* this reasonable and blood-
> less sacrifice [worship], and ask Thee, and pray Thee,
> and supplicate Thee: *Send down* Thy Holy Spirit *upon
> us* and *upon these Gifts* here offered . . . Making the
> change by Thy Holy Spirit.

The litany after the consecration, however, invites our prayer:

> That our God, who loves mankind, *receiving* [the
> "offered and sanctified" Gifts] upon His holy, heavenly,
> and ideal altar for an odor of spiritual fragrance, will
> *send down* upon us in return His divine grace and the
> gift of the Holy Spirit.

This is an appeal for a continuing outpouring of the Spirit
upon the gathered Church. For the transformation of bread
and wine into the Body and Blood of Christ has already been
accomplished by this same Spirit who "elevates" both the
community and the gifts so that the earthly sacrifice might
unfold upon the heavenly altar. "Grant us to stand blameless
and without condemnation before Thy holy altar," the priest
implores in the "mystical prayer" preceding the Cherubikon.
Although the Spirit "descends" upon the historical community, the eucharistic metamorphosis of both the people and
the Holy Gifts is accomplished by the *ascension* of the Spirit,
by the "transferal" of the people and the Gifts to the heavenly
sanctuary, so that their celebration becomes one with the
unique and eternal Eucharist of Christ. (Accordingly, the
expression "real presence" means the presence of the eucharistic community before the celestial altar, as much as it does
the presence of Christ within the earthly Church.) Finally,
the people themselves "descend" once again in the Spirit to
assume their eucharistic mission within the world, a mission

that includes intercession and witness as well as *diakonia.*
As the disciples descended from Mt Tabor after the Transfiguration, so the earthly Church must leave the heavenly
sanctuary to assume its vocation of witness to the world, a
witness exercised by "power from on high," the pentecostal
dynamis of the Holy Spirit.

To what extent can we maintain that the epikletic aspect
of the liturgy is also confessional? As a recital of sacred
history, the anamnetic aspect of liturgical worship is clearly
dogmatic, constituting a credo in the true sense of the term:
recital of God's redemptive acts has meaning only insofar as
the believer affirms those acts in his own life through "faith
worked out in love." The same, however, may be said of the
invocational aspect of liturgical celebration. For divine activity depends directly upon human cooperation, that "openness" to grace that the Fathers call *synergia.* In order for the
Spirit to accomplish the eucharistic mystery "for the life of
the world and its salvation," there must be an affirmative
human response. The very act of pronouncing traditional
liturgical formulas presupposes that the community *confesses*
(that is, accepts as its own and identifies with) the truth
expressed by those formulas. The Donatist question—whether
an "unworthy" priest or, by implication, an unbelieving
community can truly perform liturgical action—poses no
problem here. For a local community *is* the universal Church
to the dgree that it affirms *through its confession* its adherence to Holy Tradition. If a given local community refuses
to affirm that revealed truth, it *ipso facto* severs its tie with
the Church and becomes heretical (not merely schismatic).
As for individual members of the community, their faith, confessed in word and deed, is the indispensable criterion for
their membership in the Body of Christ. If they refuse to
make and to live out that confession, they too cut themselves
off from the whole. In neither instance, however, is the
ecclesiastical reality as such deformed or diminished.

This means that the Church is founded upon a reciprocal
action between its divine and human elements. There where

one bishop (represented, perhaps, by the priest) celebrates
with one member of the faithful, the Church is present in all
of its fullness. There the Spirit descends upon the Church
and *upon the world* to work out the economy of salvation.
Without this human presence, the notion of the descending-
ascending activity of the Spirit becomes meaningless. With
characteristic compassion, the divine Wisdom has granted to
created and fallen humanity an indispensable role in accom-
plishing its own salvation. There is nothing "Pelagian" in
such an affirmation. For the power and the initiative remain
wholly in the hands of God. As for man, his role is to offer
a response that consists in giving free expression to the deep
inner longing that seeks union with the divine source of his
existence. This longing, progressively articulated over the
centuries in creedal statements as well as in prayers of invocation, constitutes the heart, the living center of the liturgy.
Yet like the movement of the liturgy itself, this longing is
reciprocal: the ascent of fallen man towards the uncreated,
transfiguring Light is possible only because of the prior
descent of the Son and the Spirit, the "two hands" of the
Father (St Irenaeus), who embrace the world with the ardent
love that seeks to "make all things new."

V.   *Confessions in the Liturgy and the Liturgy as Confession*

By confessing his faith in unison with the whole Church,
the believer explicitly or implicitly invokes upon himself and
upon his ecclesial community the transforming power of the
Holy Spirit. At the initial stage, faith is elicited by the Spirit
through the preached Word, the apostolic witness to God's
redemptive activity in human history. Hearing the Word
(*akouein*), the catechumen comes progressively to obey it
(*hypakouein*), to interiorize it, and to make it the cornerstone
of all intellectual and practical activity. It is the Word itself
that effects this change. For the Word possesses its own inherent power, the divine power of the Spirit who "indwells"
and animates the Word, using traditional verbal expressions
to communicate the truth embodied in the divine Logos.

Proclamation of the Word—contained in Scripture, but also in liturgy—is consequently an eschatological salvation-event, rendering present in the life and experience of the Church the historical events of sacred history and the transcendent, sanctifying power of divine grace. Thus the Word comes to expression through two essential and complementary forms: the apostolic witness, and the liturgical celebration that interprets and reactualizes that witness from generation to generation.

Confessions of faith within the liturgy take a variety of forms: formal dogmatic statements (e.g., the Nicene Creed, the Monogenēs, confession of the Trinity "one in essence and undivided"); trinitarian prayers of supplication and praise (the Trisagion, the Cherubikon, ekphoneses); doctrinal affirmations contained in the eucharistic canon, the festal canon of matins, the stichera of vespers and laudes and so on. In fact every liturgical formula is in essence a "confession of faith," even the petitions of the various litanies. To pray for "the peace of the whole world" and "the salvation of our souls," is at once to confess faith in the creative power and authority of God, in the eschatological gift of peace bestowed by the risen Christ, and, generally, in the revealed divine economy that seeks to save the world.

On the other hand, liturgical formulas that are devoid of traditional dogmatic elements are a contradiction. For the very purpose of liturgy is to transform human life by exposing it to a constant affirmation and actualization of truth. By its very nature, liturgical action *communicates* what it proclaims. Unless its content is faithful to apostolic tradition, it will inevitably distort that tradition and lead the Church into *planē*, error or deception.

The liturgy, however, is not merely a vehicle for the expression of divine truth. (Otherwise the divine economy could be accomplished solely by proclamation of the apostolic message—a notion utterly foreign to Orthodox-Catholic conviction and experience.) For the liturgy possesses a dynamic quality, a self-realizing inner movement that we have characterized by the terms "anamnetic" and "epikletic." While recapitulating the events that constitute its history of salvation, liturgical celebration also makes that history a present reality, one in which the believer directly and personally participates to become a "contemporary" of Christ as truly as were the twelve disciples. At the same time, and by a complementary movement, the earthly community participates in the transcendent realm of the Kingdom, celebrating its mysteries (sacraments) upon the heavenly altar while bearing witness to the world that by the indwelling of the Spirit, "the Kingdom of God is within you" (cf. Lk 17:21; Jn 14:23; 2 Cor 1:22; 5:5).

Comprising a multitude of creedal affirmations, the liturgy is itself a "confession of faith," an offering of praise, supplication and intercession that unites the believer in common worship with Christ, the High Priest of our sacrifice. Traditionally, Orthodox mission in the world takes liturgical celebration as its point of departure and as its conclusion. This is because the hymns, prayers, gestures and ornaments of the ritual possess a symbolic character of their own. Integrated into a harmonious, dramatic re-enactment, these various elements touch even the most objective onlooker with a message, a witness that has the power to convert unbelief into saving faith. Such a "conversion," however, is equally necessary in the life of the committed believer. Therefore the liturgy exists to "sanctify the time" of every year, week and day. Ideally, this sanctifying activity, accomplished through the liturgy by the operation of the Spirit, leads to a thorough-going conversion of such proportions that time and eternity merge in the experience of the faithful to form a new world, a new creation that anticipates and gives immediate access to the New Jerusalem of apocalyptic vision. Through the liturgy, then, more than through any other aspect of their earthly life, members of Christ's Body undergo a continuous inner conversion that leads from faith to faith, from glory to glory.

Seen in this perspective, the distinction commonly made between liturgy and doctrine, between *theologia prima* and *theologia secunda,* becomes irrelevant, even false. For theology —insofar as it is undertaken in consonance with scriptural and patristic reflection—is essentially "mystical," interpreting divine revelation while evoking a response of faith to that revelation. Theology, like the liturgy, is a divine-human enterprise whose proper context is the worshiping Church. To paraphrase the late Fr Sergius Bulgakov, "theology must be drawn from the depths of the eucharistic chalice." This means that the liturgy must enshrine and give expression to theology, just as theology must reflect and interpret the divine activity that reveals itself in liturgical practice. Thereby theology can retain its true character as "contemplation of the divine Word," an inspired perception and faithful witness to truth. And thereby liturgical celebration, far from being mere "ritual," a mechanical and ultimately pointless adherence to rubrics, can become in the life of faith the clearest and most eloquent expression of the affirmation, "I believe . . ."

CHAPTER V

Trinitarian Liturgical Formulas
in the New Testament

The liturgical worship of Orthodoxy has been chiefly shaped by the Church's faith in the triune God. Worship is essentially trinitarian, offering adoration and supplication to God as a tri-unity of divine Persons. Together with the study and meditation of Holy Scripture, the liturgy is the principal means by which God and man encounter one another in an intimate and self-giving *personal* relationship. Through the prayer of the gathered community, the Spirit unites worshipers to Christ, who in turn introduces them into a filial relationship with the Father.

Yet the movement of prayer is two dimensional: the Father Himself *seeks* worshipers in Spirit and in Truth. As *Archē*, the origin and principle of all temporal and transcendent life, He engages in a personal quest, as a shepherd seeks a lost sheep or a father a lost son, by sending His own Son in the power of the Spirit to redeem and save fallen humanity, reuniting the human person to the Godhead through the divine "energies" or sanctifying grace.

Such is the experience of the Church, elaborated by the Greek Fathers in their teaching on salvation as *theōsis*: an actual "divinization" or ontological participation (κοινωνία/ μέθεξις) in the very life of God, a union-by-grace between divine and human existence.

As we saw in the preceding chapter, this operation or "economy" of salvation through divinization is accomplished

141

above all by the Church's liturgical worship. In the prayer of the gathered community, "Person meets person" to form a union of mutual devotion, fidelity and love. Therefore the liturgy can be nothing other than trinitarian. For what transforms worshipers into authentic "persons" (and they become such in the fullest sense only through worship) is their acquisition of the transfiguring grace communicated by the three divine Hypostases.

In what way and to what degree is this "liturgical experience" of the Church grounded in biblical revelation? As Orthodox, we often content ourselves with quoting the late and problematic affirmation of 2 Peter 1:4, to show that the doctrine of *theōsis* is, in fact, taught by Holy Scripture. But this is hardly adequate. The Fathers, after all, never held that we become participants of the divine φύσεως (nature), taken in the sense of οὐσία (essence). A better approach would be to examine tripartite liturgical statements of the New Testament to determine whether they originally functioned as true liturgical formulas, that is, as fixed symbols in the Church's ritual; and whether they in fact serve to ground the Church's trinitarian teaching in biblical revelation. In this way we can lay the groundwork for further investigation of the biblical teaching on salvation and the way in which we are called to participate in divine Life.

The New Testament contains only two passages that seem indisputably to be trinitarian liturgical formulas: the baptismal commission of Matthew 28:19b, and the closing benediction of St Paul's second letter to the Corinthians, 13:13 (RSV, NEB = 13:14).

Nevertheless, the New Testament is rife with tripartite statements, often liturgical in character, that associate God, Jesus and the Spirit in terms of their hypostatic interrelationships as well as their *economia,* their saving work on behalf of the Church and the world. Our purpose in this chapter is to show how the early Church thought about relationships between the three divine Persons and how it incorporated that reflection into its liturgical worship. We shall pay special attention to Jesus' baptismal commission and to St Paul's three-fold benediction, in an effort to determine both their original significance and their kerygmatic value within the Church's cultus.

I.

In his well-known study of early Christian confessions of faith,[1] Oscar Cullmann argued that the New Testament contains no trinitarian or tripartite creedal formulas. "The trinitarian statements that we find in the New Testament (particularly 1 Corinthians 13:13)," he maintained, "do have a liturgical character, but they are not confessions of faith."[2] While he does detect bipartite confessions referring to Christ and God, the vast majority of true confessional formulas contain a single christological element, affirmations such as "Kyrios Iēsous," "Jesus is Lord/Messiah/Son of God." He concludes that tripartite confessions represent a later development, appearing for the first time in the mid-second century.

This widely accepted position[3] needs to be amended for two reasons. In the first place, Professor Cullmann makes too sharp a distinction between confessions of faith and liturgical formulas. Can we really maintain that the benediction of 2 Corinthians 13:13, for example, or the baptismal commission of Matthew 28:19, has a "liturgical" but not a "confessional" character? To do so is to categorize New Testament affirmations in an artificial way and thereby to obscure the fact, essential to early Christian faith and worship, that *confession* and *celebration* are complementary aspects of the same "theandric" or divine-human activity.[4] Confession of the Word is essentially a liturgical act, just as celebration of the Word serves to bear witness to the truth that the Word enshrines.

[1]"Les premières confessions de foi chrétiennes," in *La Foi et le Culte de l'Eglise Primitive,* Neuchâtel (Switzerland), 1963, p. 49-87.

[2]*Ibid.,* p. 68, n.1.

[3]For a comprehensive treatment that bases its approach on Cullmann's analysis, see A. W. Wainwright, *The Trinity in the NT,* SPCK, London, 1962/77.

[4]The confessional aspect of liturgical celebration and its "theandric" character are discussed in ch. 4 above.

To the apostolic mind, no clear-cut distinction existed between confession and celebration, a fact evident from the development of creeds in conjunction with baptism.[5] This does not, of course, mean that the *Sitz im Leben* or "life setting" of all creedal statements was the liturgy. Confessions of apostolic faith took shape as well in polemical contexts to defend the *depositum fidei* against Gnostic or Judaizing heresies (e.g., 1 Jn 4:2). They developed particularly in the context of catechetical instruction prior to baptism (Ac 8:35f; 17:2f) and proved indispensable for apologetic argument (Rom 1:3f) and kerygmatic preaching (1 Cor 15:3-5). It appears likely that they also took form in relation to rites of exorcism (cf. Mk 9:38; Ac 19:13f, "by the name of the Lord Jesus"). This does not alter the fact, however, that the basic function of creedal statements was to instruct the candidate in preparation for baptism and to offer members of the Body of Christ an inclusive and concise summary of their belief in God's redemptive work on their behalf. In both cases, this faith was expressed and deepened particularly in the framework of liturgical celebration.

Secondly, we must insist that no sharp distinction existed between single, double and triple member formulas referring to God, Jesus and the Spirit. Prof. Cullmann's observation that creedal statements developed in linear fashion, from one-member to bipartite and only later to tripartite formulas, thus also needs to be corrected. Recent exegetical analysis of bipartite units such as the Christ-hymn of Philippians 2 and the introduction to Romans has shown beyond doubt that such complex formulas developed *simultaneously* with simpler one-member "christological" affirmations.[6] And, as we shall see, there is sound reason to regard Romans 1:1-4 as an early

[5] See J. N. D. Kelly, *Early Christian Creeds,* Longman's, NY-London, 1960; ch. 2, "creeds and baptism."

[6] The "linear development" theory of creedal formulation was first worked out by R. Seeberg, "Zur Geschichte der Entstehung der apostolischen Symbole," in *Zeitschrift für Kirchengeschichte* (NF) III, 1922, p. 1ff. As Prof. Cullmann points out, Seeberg overstated his case. For the primitive character of Phil 2:6-11 and Rom 1:1-4, see, in addition to the critical commentaries, R. P. Martin and A. Feuillet (works cited in the following chapter on the "Monogenēs," note 29); also J. N. D. Kelly, *Creeds,* p. 27f; and C. H. Dodd, *The Apostolic Preaching and its Developments,* London 1936/44.

tripartite formula that unites Father, Son and Spirit in a confession of praise for God's redemptive activity "among all the nations."

New Testament form-criticism has detected in the apostolic witness a large number and variety of liturgical elements, most of which can be grouped under the headings of acclamations, doxologies and hymnic confessional statements.

Single article acclamations (cries of praise or supplication) include the "Hallelujah" and "Amen" of Jewish origin; the familiar term "Abba" ("dear father") used by Jesus and Christians in addressing God (Mk 14:36; Rom 8:15; Gal 4:6); the christological titles "Kyrios" and "Son of God" attributed to Jesus, often in a baptismal context (Mk 1:11; Col 1:13f, 15-20; Phil 2:11; cf. the interpolated confession of Ac 8:37); the quality "axios" (worthy) attributed in a titular fashion to God as Creator (Rev 4:9-11) or to Christ as the sacrificial Lamb (Rev 5:9-12); and the supplication "Marana tha," "Our Lord Come!" This last acclamation, referring to the "parousia" of Christ in glory, is an ancient liturgical element that could be called a "Christ-epiklesis," uttered most likely in a eucharistic context (cf. Rev 22:20; 1 Cor 16:22; Did 10:6).[7]

Two observations should be made at this point. First, while such acclamations refer to God and to Jesus, significantly none is addressed to the Spirit. This suggests that to the earliest Christians the Spirit, however His relation to the Father and the Son might have been understood, could not properly be addressed by terms of praise or swayed by cries of supplication. His personal identity is not yet clearly perceived, as it will be in a later age, and He remains to the Christian mind "the Spirit of God" or "the Spirit of Christ" (Rom 8:9-11). While the Spirit may be "personified," as we shall see later on, God and Christ alone are truly "per-

[7]For a thorough, sound evaluation of these various elements, see K. Wengst, *Christologische Formeln und Lieder des Urchristentums*, Gutersloh, 1972.

sonal" and thus appropriately addressed as the objects of worship.[8]

The second observation concerns the meaning of these and other single member creedal statements. While they may contain only one article, they should not be considered to be "christological" as opposed to "trinitarian." To affirm "Jesus is Lord" is to acknowledge the intimate relationship that exists between Jesus Christ and God the Father, who has bestowed upon His glorified servant the title "Kyrios," the very name by which God revealed Himself to Moses on Mt Horeb (Ex 3:14; Phil 2:9-11). In similar fashion, the title "Prophet," attributed to Jesus especially by Johannine tradition, signifies His role as the eschatological bearer of the Spirit who fulfills the prophecy of Joel 2:28f, by communicating to His disciples the gift of His own Spirit.[9] Like all christological titles, acclamations addressed to Jesus express the belief that an intimate and personal relationship exists between the Father and the Son (as the christological title "Son of God" and the epithet "Abba" clearly confirm). The conviction that a similar relationship unites the Spirit to God and Jesus is suggested by statements such as Romans 5:5, 1 Corinthians 2:10, 2 Corinthians 3:17, and the Paraclete-sayings of the Farewell Discourses.[10] Titles and acclamations,

[8]Throughout the history of the Church, even after recognition by the second Ecumenical Council (Constantinople I, 381) of the full divinity of the Spirit, few liturgical prayers have been addressed to the Third Person of the Trinity. The most well known of those in common use are probably the *Veni (Spiritus) Creator* (9th cent.) of Latin tradition and the "O Heavenly King" (4th cent.; St Basil?) that introduces the divine office in Orthodox worship. The most ancient Orthodox formulas address themselves to Christ or God the Father and refer to "thy Holy Spirit." Epikleses that invoke the gift of the Spirit upon the eucharistic gifts and baptismal waters, as well as at specific moments in daily life (e.g., the prayer before study), are invariably addressed to God the Father, the source of divine life. Even the liturgical texts of the feast of Pentecost tend to speak of the Spirit in the third person, while stichera and troparia are addressed to God or Christ. Notable exceptions do occur, however, such as the Canon of Lesser Compline celebrated in the evening of Pentecost Sunday (preserved only in Slavonic service books) and the exapostilarion of the matins of Pentecost: "O Holy Spirit, who procedes from the Father and was sent by the Son upon the unlettered apostles, save and sanctify those who acknowledge thee to be God!"

[9]Joel 2:28f; cf. Jn 6:14; 7:40 with 1:33; 15:26; 16:7; and 19:30; 20:22.
[10]Jn 14:16f, 26; 15:26; 16:7-11; cf 16:13-15.

while consisting of single elements, presuppose both inter-personal and economic relationships between God, Jesus and the Spirit, and should therefore not be considered to be purely christocentric. At this early stage, needless to say, perception of such relationships was grounded in revelation and experi-ence rather than in metaphysical reflection.

The doxological elements of the New Testament fall generally into the following categories:

1. *Epistolary greetings* include starkly simple statements (1 Thess 1:1) as well as complex kerygmatic proclamations (Gal 1:1-5). Nearly all such formulas in the New Testament are bipartite, linking Jesus (Christ) and God (the Father) in a single liturgical salutation addressed to the eucharistic assembly (cf. Phil 1:1; Col 1:1-2; 4:15f). The tripartite greetings of Romans and 1 Peter are exceptions to be noted further on.[11]

2. To these formulas of salutation may be added *closing benedictions* which, like the opening formula "grace and peace be with you," also bear the stamp of liturgical usage. Most of these contain a single article such as "the grace of the Lord Jesus Christ be with your spirit" (Rom 16:20; 1 Cor 16:23; Gal 6:18; Phil 4:23; 1 Thess 5:28; 2 Thess 3:18; Phm 25), although occasionally we do encounter bipartite formulas such as Romans 16:27 (part of a later interpola-tion?), Ephesians 6:23f, and the elaborate benediction of Jude 24-25. The unique occurrence of a tripartite blessing at the close of 2 Corinthians will be discussed in detail below.[12]

3. *Thanksgiving formulas*, while addressing thanks to God, associate the Lord Jesus Christ in the work of liberation from sin and salvation to eternal life (Rom 7:25; 1 Cor 15:57; 2 Cor 9:13-15; cf. Phil 1:3-6; Col 1:3f; 1 Thess 1:2-4 . . .).

[11]III John is a different sort of exception in that it makes no mention of a divine name in its greeting. This is probably to be explained by its purpose: a personal note rather than an epistle addressed to a church community, it is unique among canonical writings, including Philemon.

[12]It would be tempting to see a linear development in these epistolary benedictions from a primitive one-element to a later two-element formula. The fact that the relatively late epistles Col (4:18), I Tim (6:21) and Tit (3:15) invoke no divine name but conclude simply with "Grace be with you," however, warns against such a deduction.

4. *Praises* concluding with "Amen!" tend to be addressed to God alone (Rom 11:36; Gal 1:5; Eph 3:20f; Heb 13:21; 1 Pet 5:11; Rev 7:12 . . .), but once again the doxology is uttered in gratitude for the victorious, saving work of God in Jesus Christ.

Among the most important liturgical elements in the New Testament are confessional statements in the form of hymns. Such elements can be detected and distinguished from other kerygmatic and catechetical material by their grammatical structure,[13] poetic rhythm, and christocentric content. As Ephesians 5:18-20 demonstrates, however, confessional and doxological hymns were understood to be inspired by the Spirit and addressed chiefly to God: "Be filled with the Spirit, addressing one another in psalms and hymns and spiritual songs, singing and making melody to the Lord with all your heart, always and for everything giving thanks in the name of our Lord Jesus Christ to God the Father."

These early Christian hymns, of which numerous fragments are preserved in the New Testament, Didache, and other contemporaneous writings,[14] had, like all liturgical elements, a double purpose: to *praise* God for his redemptive activity in Christ and to *instruct* the Christian community in the faith. Adoration and edification were intimately intertwined in the early Church's celebration, as St Paul makes clear in a parallel passage: "Let the word of Christ [ὁ λόγος τοῦ Χριστοῦ] dwell in you in all of its richness, teaching and instructing yourselves in all wisdom, with psalms, hymns and spiritual songs, with thankfulness singing in your hearts to God" (Col 3:16). Once again we see that confession of faith and liturgical celebration are inseparable. Devoid of doctrinal content, liturgical expression has no meaning; it is, in fact, inconceivable. On the other hand, doctrine can only become a living word and a source of genu-

[13]Such as introductory pronouns followed by participial clauses (Phil 2:6; Col 1:15; Eph 2:14; Heb 1:3).

[14]See esp. R. Deichgräber, *Gotteshymnus und Christushymnus in der frühen Christenheit*, Göttingen 1967; R. P. Martin, *Worship in the Early Church*, Cambridge 1975; K. Wengst, op. cit.; and for a recent analysis of certain fragments (Phil 2:6-11; Heb 1:2-14), O. Hofius, *Der Christushymnus Philipper 2, 6-11*, Tübingen 1976..

ine knowledge insofar as it points beyond itself and enables the Church to celebrate "with all its heart" the glory and mercy of God.

What remains to be determined, however, is the relationship expressed by these hymnic confessions between God, Jesus and the Spirit. Form-criticism has tended to stress the christocentric character of most of these primitive Christian hymns: they celebrate above all Christ's twofold existence[15] "in the flesh" and "in the Spirit" (Rom 1:3f; 1 Tim 3:16; 1 Pet 3:18), or His redeeming work accomplished by a descending-ascending movement denoted by the terms "incarnation" (kenosis) and "glorification" (Phil 2:6-11; Heb 1:3; 1 Tim 3:16; 1 Pet 3:18f, all based more or less directly on the image of the humiliated and exalted Suffering Servant of Deutero-Isaiah). A similar motif, but with a different accent, is found in the Christ-hymns of Colossians 1:15-20 and Ephesians 2:14-16. These and numerous other fragmentary hymnic confessions might seem to confirm Prof. Cullmann's contention that the New Testament contains no triadic confessions as such and that the confessional material we do find is essentially christological. This view can be maintained, however, only if we overlook the considerable number of *triadic formulas*, both liturgical and kerygmatic, scattered throughout the Gospels, the Letters, and other apostolic writings.

We have already seen that epistolary formulas, doxologies, and certain liturgical hymns bear witness to particular *rela-*

[15] "Existence" is preferable to "nature" when speaking of NT christology. The technical term *ousia* never occurs in canonical writings (its sole use in Lk 15:12f refers to material goods); and *physis* has a "metaphysical" sense only in the late passage II Pet 1:4, where a distinction is made between the corruption of earthly life and participation (*koinōnia*) in "the divine nature." The closest the NT comes to distinguishing divine from human "nature" is Phil 2:6f, where *morphē theou* and *morphē doulou* signify differing "modes of existence" rather than distinct "essences." The absence of metaphysical terminology in Scripture, however, by no means invalidates its use by the Church Fathers, any more than modern existential and ethical categories ("choice," "being," "decision," freedom as "liberation," etc.) are a priori invalid for interpreting the biblical message in our own day. In both instances, the criterion is fidelity to the *meaning* of Scripture rather than to its specific terminology.

tionships between God, Jesus and the Spirit. These relationships can be expressed by titles such as "Father," "Son" and
"Lord," or by grammatical elements such as prepositions and
possessive forms ("the Spirit *of* God/Christ," Rom 8:9; "the
grace of God given *in* Christ Jesus," 1 Cor 1:4) as well as
conjunctions ("grace and peace from God our Father *and*
the Lord Jesus Christ," 2 Cor 1:2; cf. 13:13). Must we conclude that such combinations are haphazard or that they
function "liturgically" but not "confessionally"? Or can we
detect in their structure and through their context a clear
doctrinal purpose that obliged the apostolic authors to form-
ulate them in this and in no other way? And if so, what do
these formulas reveal about the nature of the relationship
between those whom the Church would subsequently proclaim to be three divine Persons united in a single, undivided
essence?

Before turning to the tripartite affirmations of the New
Testament, however, it is important to specify what we mean
when we speak of "trinitarian formulas." If by "trinitarian"
we mean a formal statement that seeks to define the inter-
personal relationships of the three divine Persons in terms
of the classical formula μία οὐσία, τρεῖς ὑποστάσεις,
then the word is used anachronistically when applied to
apostolic writings. The Semitic mind—including the mind of
Christ—simply did not speculate on ontological relationships
between Father, Son and Spirit, as the Church Fathers were
obliged to do in a later Hellenistic context. This does not
mean, however, that we must make an absolute distinction
between *theologia* and *economia*, and conclude that Scripture
bears witness only to the latter. Such is a common error of
modern biblical scholarship, an error based on the unwarranted supposition that the Bible concentrates uniquely upon
God's "mighty acts" (Ac 2:11) and has no interest in speaking of the conditions that unite Father, Son and Spirit in a
common divine being and existence as well as in a common
activity. Consider, for example, statements such as Jn 10:30,
"I and the Father are one"; Phil 2:6, "[Jesus Christ] was
in the form of God"; 2 Cor 3:17, "the Lord is the Spirit";
1 Cor 2:10, "the Spirit searches . . . even the depths of God";

Jn 15:26, "I shall send [the Spirit] to you from the Father, the Spirit of Truth who proceeds from the Father"; as well as confessions of faith such as 1 Cor 8:6, affirming the unity of God the Father and the Lord Jesus Christ as the common ground of human existence; and Jn 20:28, where Thomas declares that Jesus is both Lord and God. Taken in their respective contexts, these and many similar statements confirm at the very least that the apostolic writers were concerned not only with God's saving activity within the world, but also with the reciprocal and interpersonal activity of the individual identities within the Godhead in working out the divine economy. This is true despite the fact that the biblical authors used relational rather than ontological categories. If Father, Son and Spirit are not united in a common divine life, then the message of incarnation and resurrection, as well as the titles "Son of God" and "Lord," lose all meaning. In fact, a title is truly "christological" only insofar as it affirms, explicitly or implicitly, a relationship of "unity-in-being" between God, Jesus and the Spirit. Consequently, when biblical tradition speaks of divine redemptive activity, it necessarily presupposes "trinitarian" relationships that the Church, at a later date, would qualify as "consubstantial and undivided."

With this in mind, we can turn our attention to the most important tripartite statements in the New Testament to determine how they express and reveal the being and activity of the three divine Persons. This survey, we should add, by no means intends to be exhaustive. Its aim is merely to indicate a direction that should prove useful for further, more intensive exegetical work: to study the operations of God within human life in order to penetrate, as far as a necessarily apophatic approach will allow, into the mystery of divine life. Such an approach should in addition help to overcome an artificial separation between *theologia* and *economia* as well as between doctrinal confession and liturgical celebration.

II.

The annunciation and birth narratives of Matthew and

Luke have few elements in common and represent two originally independent traditions.[16] Comparing Mt 1:18-25 with Lk 1:26-38; 2:1-7, we find the activity of the Spirit described in significantly different ways. In the former, an "angel of the Lord" tells Joseph in a dream that "what is in [Mary] is conceived [γέννηθεν—'has been begotten'] by the Holy Spirit." The voice continues with the promise that she will bear a son, whose name "Jesus" signifies His saving mission on behalf of the people of Israel. Here Mary is "found to be with child of the Holy Spirit" (ἐκ πνεύματος ἁγίου), the aim of the statement being to affirm the miraculous conception and birth of the Messiah in fulfillment of prophecy (Isa 7:14). In St Luke's Gospel, however, a far more explicit association is made between the three divine Persons, and the evangelist indirectly announces the succeeding stage in salvation history by linking the conception of Jesus with the "conception" of the Church through the divine power (δύναμις) of the Spirit at Pentecost:

— "The Holy Spirit will come upon you and the power of the Most High will overshadow you . . ." (Lk 1:35).
— "I shall send the promise [ἐπαγγελία = the Holy Spirit] of my Father upon you . . . [you shall be] clothed with power from on high" (Lk 24:49).
— "Wait for the promise of the Father . . . you shall receive power by the coming of the Holy Spirit upon you" (Ac 1:4, 8).[17]

The annunciation constitutes a "Marian Pentecost," a quasi-epikletic pronouncement in which the voice of the Father (through his angelic messenger) proclaims the incarnation of the Son by the power of the Holy Spirit. Correspondingly, the "promise of the Father" uttered by the Son

[16]In addition to the critical commentaries, see R.E. Brown, *The Birth of the Messiah*, NY 1977; esp. p. 311-316.

[17]The aorist participle *epelthontos* has instrumental value ("you shall receive power by virtue of the coming of the Holy Spirit upon you") and is correctly translated by E. Haenschen, *Die Apostelgeschichte* (Meyer), Göttingen 1968, p. 104: "indem der hl. Geist auf euch kommt."

is realized when the Son sends the Spirit upon the Church to empower the disciples to assume and to broaden the scope of Jesus' own ministry by preaching the Gospel "to the ends of the earth" (Ac 1:8). St Luke thus bears witness, albeit implicitly, to the "trinitarian" relationship between Father, Son and Spirit by designating the Father as the source or origin from whom spring both the Son of God (Lk 1:35) and the Spirit, who is Himself "sent" by the Son (Lk 24:49). This relationship is conceived in the same way, although expressed in more precise language, in the Gospel of St John, where the "only-begotten Son, sent by the Father" (1:14; 5:23) in turn "sends" upon the Church the Holy Spirit, who Himself "proceeds" from the Father.

These terms "to send" (ἐξαποστέλλειν, πέμπειν) and "to proceed" (ἐκπορεύειν), long the focal point in the centuries-old "filioque" controversy, can only be correctly understood in the light of the total Gospel witness. Without doubt the evangelists employed them to depict a hierarchical relationship between the three divine Persons and to differentiate between the "sending" of the Son and the Spirit on the one hand, and the "procession" of the Spirit from the Father on the other. What should not be obscured, however, either in exegetical work or in ecumenical discussion, is the fact that the evangelists show no interest whatsoever in delving into the inner mystery of the divine being *apart from His saving activity* within the Church and the world. To their minds, no distinction is conceivable between *theologia* and *economia*. Accordingly, verbs that specify the relation between Father, Son and Spirit are verbs of action that express the movement of God towards his fallen creation.

If Scripture reveals the divine origin of the Son, who is "begotten" of the Father, and of the Spirit, who "proceeds" from the Father, it does so to affirm that the work of redemption is not the result of any human initiative but is accomplished by God Himself. Every bit as important to the biblical witness as the verbs of generation and procession, therefore, are the various verbs that express the *sending* of the Son and the Spirit, by whom the Father realizes His saving work. This means that no interpretation of the ontological relationships between the three divine hypostases can claim to represent the biblical witness faithfully if it is not based upon the revelation of God's activity within human history. And conversely, no interpretation of the divine economy—or of the Church's mission within the world—can claim validity or authority if it ignores God's self-revelation as a trinity of Persons with a common divine essence as well as a common divine will. Stated in other terms, neither a purely "metaphysical" nor a purely "social" Gospel can do justice to biblical revelation.

Two other events in the life of Christ, celebrated in the Church as major liturgical feasts, further affirm the inseparable relationship between *theologia* and *economia* in New Testament revelation. The Synoptic scenes of the *baptism* and *transfiguration* are strikingly similar in their portrayal of Father, Son and Spirit. In each scene, Jesus is accompanied by witnesses who can attest to the event; He is revealed as the "beloved Son" ("chosen Son," Lk 9:35) by the Father's heavenly voice (cf. Ex 40:34-38; Isa 42:1; Ps 2:7); and He is shown to be the bearer of the Spirit who appears in symbolic form as a dove or as divine light.[18] The purpose in each is to proclaim that Jesus is the Son of God, not merely by adoption, but as the "only-begotten," engendered by the Father and incarnate by the Holy Spirit.[19] As the Son will "send" the Spirit following His resurrection and glorification, so the Spirit "sends" the Son, first by incarnating divine life within the womb of the Virgin, then by indwelling the Son and investing Him with full divine authority to reveal the person and will of the Father (cf. Jn 1:33; 3:34).

Orthodox trinitarian doctrine, grounded in the witness of Scripture and expressed in liturgical hymnography, formu-

[18]In the Johannine parallel to the Baptism (1:32-34), the Baptist rather than the Father is made to testify "that this is the Son of God": an alteration of the Synoptic tradition for polemical reasons. The fourth evangelist records the Father's voice only in 12:27-30, the Johannine parallel to the Synoptic Gethsemane scene.

[19]Such is the meaning not only of the birth narratives, but also of Mk 1:1-11.

lates these reciprocal relationships and revelatory activity in the following terms:

> At Thy baptism in the Jordan, O Lord, was revealed the worship of the Trinity. For the voice of the Father bore witness to Thee by calling Thee His beloved Son, and the Spirit in the form of a dove confirmed the truth of His words. O Christ our God, who hast appeared to us and enlightened the world, Glory to Thee!
>
> (Baptism Troparion, tone 1)

Trinitarian relations are never revealed for their own sake, abstracted from the reciprocal redemptive activity of the three divine Persons. The heavenly voice at Christ's baptism proclaims that in Him all messianic prophecy of the Old Testament has come to fulfillment: the new age of salvation has dawned and a new creation is at hand, symbolized by Christ's entering the baptismal waters. As the Word of God called forth order out of chaos by separating the firmament from the primeval waters (Gen 1:9-10), so that same divine Word descends into the waters of fallen creation in order to restore the original harmony between heaven and earth, between man and God, through a new creative act to be perpetuated in the Church through the sacrament of baptism (cf. Jn 3:5-8 and St Ignatius, Eph 18:2, where we find the earliest interpretation of Christ's baptism as a cosmological event "to purify the waters by His passion"). The descent of the Spirit "confirms" the eternal filial relation of Jesus of Nazareth to the God of Israel, not by His physical presence only, but by His revelatory activity as Spirit of Truth within the life and mission of the Church (cf. Jn 14:26; 16:13-15). Such a threefold revelation of divine being and activity calls forth not only faith, but also adoration: "O Christ our God, who has appeared to us and enlightened the world, Glory to Thee!" Faith itself can become a saving response to divine activity on man's behalf insofar as it issues in *leitourgia*, a genuine "service" of praise and thanksgiving addressed to the Author of life (Ac 3:15). Revelation of triune relationships, therefore, serves the purpose of salvation both by communicating knowledge of the divine economy and by eliciting a response of *eucharistia* or thanksgiving on the part of the believer.

To many exegetes today, such an interpretation of the baptismal scene would be dismissed as extravagant extrapolation upon the original biblical witness. Scriptural language, however, was in large measure molded in the context of liturgical celebration, especially by preaching within the eucharistic assembly. The Matthean tradition of the institution of the Lord's Supper, for example, has been modified even more than that of Mark and Luke by liturgical practice in the early Church. Similarly, the account of Jesus' baptism both shaped and was itself shaped by the Church's baptismal services. We can no more interpret the biblical witness to Jesus' baptism in isolation from the Church's own practice than we can explain the meaning of Jesus' words and actions in the Upper Room apart from the eucharistic celebration of local Christian communities in which the New Testament took written form and to which it was addressed. If much modern exegesis attempts to do so as a matter of principle, it is due to a persistent tendency, dating from the Reform, to minimize liturgical influences upon the shaping of Scripture by exaggerating the importance of kerygmatic proclamation. As we have seen, however, many of the most primitive kerygmatic formulas and acclamations were integrally woven into the Church's liturgical worship.

It is this close interrelationship between kerygma and worship, between proclamation and confession of faith on the one hand and the liturgical celebration of that faith on the other, that permitted and encouraged early Christian hymnographers to interpret biblical passages with the aim of revealing their "spiritual" and not merely their "literal" (historical) sense. Thus the exapostilarion of the matins service at the feast of the transfiguration proclaims that the visible light radiating from Christ upon the mountain was the divine, uncreated Light of both the Father and the Spirit:

Unaltered light of the light of the unbegotten Father,

in Thy brilliant light, O Word, we have beheld today
on Mount Tabor the light of the Father and of the
Spirit, the uncreated light that enlightens all creation.

Here, as in the troparion of the baptism of Christ, the Church
proclaims its experience of a veritable *theophany* in which
Father, Son and Spirit reveal Themselves to the eyes of
human witnesses. In each case, revelation of the Trinity has
an essentially economic purpose: the divine glory manifested
in the incarnate Son "has appeared to enlighten the world."

Numerous other passages in the Gospel tradition, although
not of liturgical origin, contain bipartite or tripartite formulas
and allusions that confirm the point that revelation of the
divine Persons is inseparable from revelation of their mutual
saving activity. Immediately following His baptism, for example, Jesus is "led up" (ἀνήχθη, Mt 4:1) or "cast out"
(ἐκβάλλει, Mk 1:12) into the desert *by the Spirit* in order
to overcome Satanic temptation and confirm His role as the
one who reveals and accomplishes the Father's will for the
salvation of the world. In all three Synoptic Gospels, Satan
or unclean spirits confess Jesus to be "Son of God" (Mt 4:3;
Lk 4:3; Mk 3:11; 5:7), unwittingly manifesting His authority and power over the "ruler of this world" (Jn 12:31). A
similar confession on the lips of Peter (Mt 16:16) marks
the turning point in St Matthew's Gospel by affirming that
this revelation, accorded by the "Father who is in heaven,"
constitutes the foundation of the Kingdom in the form of
the messianic community. If Christ declares that it is by the
Spirit of God that He casts out demons (Mt 12:28; but cf.
Lk 11:20), the purpose of the exorcisms is to reveal and confirm "that the Kingdom of God has come upon you." Again,
in Luke's version of the famous "Johannine passage" (10:22;
cf. Mt 11:27), the evangelist notes expressly that Jesus "rejoiced in the Holy Spirit" as He declared that the reciprocal
knowledge between the Father and the Son is revealed by
the Son to those whom He chooses, that is, to the disciples
and, through them, to the Church (Lk 10:23f).

In the Fourth Gospel, the relationship between revelatory and soteriological activity is still more evident. The Spirit descends from the Father to abide in Jesus at the baptism (1:33), thereby investing Him with full divine authority to reveal and accomplish the Father's will (3:34; cf. Lk 4:18). Through the revelatory activity of the Son, the Father seeks worshipers "in Spirit and in truth," that is, through the inspiration of the Spirit of Truth (4:23f). Jesus' own words are "spirit and life," for the Spirit acting through the words of the Son is τὸ ζῳοποιοῦν, the "giver of life" (6:63). This same Spirit, welling up within the heart of Jesus (or the believer) is again identified as the source of eternal life in 7:37-39. After several chapters in which no further mention is made of the Spirit, He appears again in the Farewell Discourses, where He is revealed to be a personal, divine being who "proceeds from the Father" and is "sent by the Son" into the world. Here once again, revelation of inner trinitarian relationships has as its primary aim revelation of the divine economy of salvation: "the Paraclete, the Holy Spirit, whom the Father will send in my name, will teach you all things and bring to your remembrance all that I have said to you" (14:26; cf. 16:13-15). This "hermeneutic function" of the Spirit,[20] His continuing revelation and actualization of the divine economy in the life of the Church, is possible only because of the intimate relationship that exists between Himself and the Son, a relationship of unity in being and will. As Jesus declares His oneness with the Father (10:30; cf. 5:18) and manifests that oneness by word and act, so He manifests a similar oneness with the Spirit: "He breathed upon (the disciples) and said: Receive the Holy Spirit" (20:22). And just as Jesus' own embodiment of the Spirit serves to accomplish the Father's saving will, so also the disciples, newly filled with charismatic power and authority, are sent into the world to fulfill the will of their risen Master by proclaiming forgiveness and reconciliation (20:21, 23).

In the Gospel tradition, as such passages make abundantly clear, revelation serves above all the work of salvation.

---

[20]See chapter one above.

Further evidence of the soteriological purpose of revelation is furnished by the much discussed concluding pericope of the first Gospel, Mt 28:16-20.[21] Verse 19b, βαπτίζοντες αὐτοὺς εἰς τὸ ὄνομα τοῦ πατρὸς καὶ τοῦ υἱοῦ καὶ τοῦ ἁγίου πνεύματος, "Baptizing them in the name of the Father and of the Son and of the Holy Spirit," is the only element of Gospel tradition that unites God, Jesus and the Spirit in a formula that appears to be of unquestionably liturgical origin. Before we can accept such a conclusion, however, we should consider the following questions: 1. What is the relation between tradition and redaction in this pericope: can we reasonably attribute the command to Jesus Himself; or must we ascribe it either to primitive oral tradi-

[21]Recent exegetical literature on this passage is voluminous. For a complete bibliography up to 1973, see J. Lange, *Das Erscheinen des Auferstandenen im Evangelium nach Mattäus.* Würzburg, 1973, p. 513-556. The following studies have been particularly useful for this present article: Bornkamm, G., "Der Auferstandene und der Irdische, Mt 28:16-20," in Bornkamm, Barth, Held, *Überlieferung und Auslegung im Matthäusevangelium,* Neukirchen (1975) 287-310; Brooks, O. S., "Matthew XXVIII 16-20 and the design of the First Gospel," *Journal for the Study of the NT* 10 (1981) 2-18; Conybeare, F. C., "The Eusebian Form of the Text Matth 28:19," *Zeitschrift für neutestamentliche Wissenschaft* 2 (1901) 275-288; von Dobschütz, E., "Zwei- und dreigliedrige Formeln," *Journal of Biblical Literature* 50 (1931) 117-145; Hubbard, B., *The Matthean Redaction of a Primitive Apostolic Commissioning: an Exegesis of Mt 28:16-20.* Missoula Scholars Press, 1974; Kingsbury, J. D., "The Composition and Christology of Matt 28:16-20," *JBL* 93 (1974) 573-584; Lohmeyer, E., " 'Mir ist gegeben alle Gewalt.' Eine Exegese von Mt 28:16-20," in *In Memoriam Ernst Lohmeyer,* Stuttgart (1951) 22-49; Martin, J. P., "The Church in Matthew," *Interpretation* 29 (1975) 41-56; Meier, J. P., "Two Disputed Questions in Matt 28:16-20," *JBL* 96 (1977) 404-424; Michel, O., "Der Abschluss des Matthäusevangeliums," *Evangelische Theologie* 10 (1950-51) 16-26; Molina, B. J., "The Literary Structure and Form of Matt 28:16-20," *New Testament Studies* 17 (1970-71) 87-103; Rigaux, B., *Dieu l'a ressuscité: Exégèse et théologie biblique.* Duculot Gembloux (Belgique) 1973, esp. 254-258; Schieber, H., "Konzentrik im Matthäusschluss. Ein form- und gattungskritischer Versuch zu Mt 28, 16-20," *Kairos* NF 19 (1977) 286-307; Schneider, J., "Der historische Jesus und die urchristliche Taufe," in *Der historische Jesus und die kerygmatische Christus,* Berlin (1960) 530-542; Strecker, G., *Der Weg der Gerechtigkeit,* Göttingen, 1962; Trilling, W., "De toutes les nations faites des disciples (Mt 28, 16-20)," *Assemblées du Seigneur* 28 (1969) 24-37; Trilling, W., "Die Auferstehung Jesu, Anfang der neuen Weltzeit (Mt 28, 1-8)," in *Christusverkündigung in der synoptischen Evangelien,* Munich (1969) 212-243; Vögtle, A., "Das christologische und ekklesiologische Anliegen von Mt 28, 18-20," *Studia Evangelica* II (1964) 266-294.

tion[22] or to the evangelist Matthew?[23] 2. Is the formula explicitly "trinitarian," affirming an ontological relationship between Father, Son and Holy Spirit; or does it express exclusively the activity or economy of God within history? 3. Is the command properly classed as a "liturgical formula," or is the label anachronistic; that is, does its inclusion at the close of the first Gospel mean that it functioned as a fixed baptismal formula within a liturgical framework in the Matthean community; or was it originally subordinated to the command to "make disciples of all nations," and only later transformed into a ritual formula to serve the sacramental practice of the post-apostolic Church?

To the post-Nicene Fathers, the baptismal commission was unquestionably pronounced by Jesus Himself as a central element in His revelation of the mystery of the Holy Trinity. Their interest in the formula, however, is less liturgical than doctrinal and polemical. Gregory of Nazianzus refers to Matthew 28:19 in an effort to prove the divinity of the Holy Spirit, who is shown to be of divine nature by virtue of the fact that He divinizes those who are baptized: "If the Spirit is not to be adored [as divine], how then can He divinize me by baptism?"[24] The chief accent here is upon the operation of the Spirit; His full divinity is manifested and confirmed by His saving activity. The long series of attributes ascribed to the Spirit that Gregory takes from Scripture likewise confirms that the divinity of the third Person is revealed by His work of regeneration.

Cyril of Alexandria, in his "Dialogues on the Trinity,"[25] quotes Matthew 28:19 four times to defend the divinity of the Son against persistent Arian attacks. Quoting the same passage, Athanasius had already denounced Arian baptism as supposedly effected by a creature as well as by the Creator.[26] Cyril takes up this argument to show that the glory of the Son is not simply added to His humanity but constitutes a

[22]As E. Lohmeyer, *op. cit,* (note 21).

[23]See J. D. Kingsbury, *op cit,* (note 21).

[24]*Pōs eme theoi dia tou baptismatos?,* Theological Discourses 31:28-29 (Sources Chrétiennes 250).

[25]S.C. 231, 237, 246.

[26]Athanasius, Oratio II Contra Arianos (41, 42); ed. Montfaucon, 1853.

divine attribute that originates with the Father [οὐσιώδη καὶ ἐκ Πατρός; IV.505, 29-31]. And elsewhere he declares, "we have been baptized into the unique divinity and lordship [θεότητά τε καὶ κυριότητα μίαν; VII.633, 11-14] of a Father, a Son and a Holy Spirit: not into several numerically distinguishable gods, nor do we worship a [mere] creature."

If the Eastern Fathers draw upon Matthew 28:19 to affirm the full divinity of the Son and Spirit, as well as the efficacy of trinitarian baptism, St Jerome sees in vs. 18-20 the essential transmission of evangelical doctrine from Jesus to His apostles [*vocatis apostolis doctrinam evangelicam tradidit; In Mat IV.25, 14f*]. In both traditions the orthodox position takes for granted that the baptismal commission represents the *ipsissima verba Jesu* and confirms the Nicene-Constantino-politan dogma of the consubstantiality of the three Persons of the Godhead.

This traditional view was first brought into question dur-ing the Enlightenment, when historical-critical exegesis ar-gued, on the basis of primitive apostolic preaching preserved in the Acts, that the earliest baptismal formula was "in the name of Jesus (Christ)" or "in the name of the Lord Jesus" (Ac 2:38; 8:14-19). Working on the principle of increasing complexity as evidence of later tradition, Protestant biblical scholars on the whole rejected the authenticity of Mt 28:19b and declared it to be a liturgical formula expressing the doc-trinal convictions of the "post-Easter Church." Further study, however, showed conclusively that the formula was ancient and perhaps as primitive as those found in the Acts, and that it circulated in pre-Gospel oral tradition simultaneously with those that command baptism in the name of Jesus only.[27]

But are the commands to baptize "in the name of Jesus" and "in the name of the Father, the Son and the Holy Spirit,"

---

[27]E. Lohmeyer, *op cit,* defended this theory in detail in the mid-1940's, locating the one-member formula in Jerusalem tradition while attributing the three-member Mt formula to Galilean origin (p. 32f). See also J. P. Meier, *op cit,* p. 410: "the triadic baptismal formula in v. 19b is probably not redactional, since it never appears elsewhere in Mt and since Mt would not likely introduce a new baptismal formula into his church." For a defense of the authenticity of the formula, see J. Lebreton, *Les Origines du Dogma de la Trinité,* Paris 1910, esp. 257-259, 478-489.

in fact "baptismal formulas"? If we compare the relevant Acts passages, taking into consideration their respective contexts, then it appears highly doubtful that the expression "in the name of (the Lord) Jesus (Christ)" reproduces a liturgical formula used in the earliest baptismal rite. The following four passages from Acts speak of baptism "in the name":

— 2:38, "Peter (said) to them: Repent, and be baptized each of you in [ἐπί] the name of Jesus Christ for the forgiveness of your sins, and you shall receive the gift of the Holy Spirit."
— 8:16, "[the Samaritans had not yet received the Holy Spirit] but they had only been baptized in [εἰς] the name of the Lord Jesus."
— 10:48, "[Peter] commanded them to be baptized in [ἐν] the name of Jesus Christ."
— 19:5, "[the Ephesian disciples] were baptized in [εἰς] the name of the Lord Jesus."

In 2:38, Peter begins his Pentecostal address by quoting from the prophecy of Joel, a passage that ends with an implicit call to repentance (v.21, "whoever calls upon the name of the Lord shall be saved"). Peter accuses his hearers of responsibility for the death of Jesus ("whom you crucified," vs. 23, 36; cf. 4:10). Yet because His passion and resurrection were according to the "plan and foreknowledge of God," He has been exalted to the right hand of God, from whom He sends the promised Holy Spirit (2:33). Peter concludes with the affirmation, addressed to "the house of Israel," that "God has made Him both Lord and Christ, this Jesus whom you crucified." In response to the kerygma, that typically demands repentance together with an act of faith (3:19; 4:10-12; 5:31f; 10:43; 13:38f; cf. Rom 10:8f), the Jews ask, "What shall we do?" Peter's reply in v. 38 constitutes a summary of the kerygma that includes the elements of repentance, baptism and reception of the Spirit. The phrase "be baptized . . . in the name of Jesus Christ" is an appeal to unite themselves to Jesus as the true Messiah (Christ) of Israel, through the sacramental rite of baptism. It is not presented as a ritual formula in and of itself, but rather signifies that baptism accomplishes union with Christ. For "in the name" means "to become the possession of," to "participate in" the life of the one whose powerful name is invoked.[28]

That the expression "in the name of (the Lord) Jesus (Christ)" is not as such a fixed baptismal formula is further shown by the variety of prepositions employed (ἐπί, ἐν, εἰς), together with the variant forms of the "name": "Jesus Christ" or "the Lord Jesus." It should be further noted that other references to baptism in Acts contain no mention of Jesus or of the "name" (8:38; 9:18; 16:15, 33; 18:8), although such an argument from silence has little weight. Nevertheless, Acts 8:12f shows that "the name of Jesus Christ" defined the *content of the kerygma*. If Peter commands Cornelius and his household to be baptized "in the name of Jesus Christ," it is because this name alone bestows forgiveness of sins and the gift of the Spirit (10:43-48). And if Paul baptizes the Ephesian disciples "in the name of the Lord Jesus" (19:1-7), he does so to contrast the baptism of Jesus from that of John: Apollos and the other "Jews" had been baptized "into John" (18:25; 19:3) but not "into Jesus." These expressions no more imply the use of a ritual baptismal formula than does 1 Cor 10:2, which affirms that the Old Testament "fathers" were "baptized into Moses" (cf. 1 Cor 1:13-15). Finally, it is significant that in Acts 22:16 Paul is exhorted by Ananias to "rise up and be baptized, and wash away your sins, calling upon His name." Here the one baptized—and not the performer of the rite—invokes the name of Jesus.

As in Rom 6:3 and Gal 3:27, we should see in the expression "baptized into Christ" or "into the name" of Jesus, not a liturgical formula employed systematically by the celebrant of the rite, but rather a *kerygmatic proclamation* that affirms the meaning of baptism: incorporation into the eschatological community that bears the name of Jesus Christ and worships Him as Lord and Savior. For it is "in the name of Jesus" that

---

[28]The supernatural power of the divine name is well attested throughout the Ancient Near East as well as in the NT; cf Ac 3:6; 4:12; Mk 16:17; Lk 10:17, etc. Salvation is only "in the name" of Jesus: Ac 4:12; 10:43; cf. I Cor 6:11 (just as in the OT, Yahweh grants deliverance to those who invoke his name, Ps 53:1, LXX).

the Word is preached (Ac 5:40), and forgiveness of sins is
assured (1 Jn 2:12), just as it is "in the name of the Lord
Jesus Christ and in the Spirit of our God" that baptism
accords purification, sanctification and justification (1 Cor
6:11).

What must we conclude, then, regarding the "trinitarian"
formula of Mt 28:19? Is it too a kerygmatic proclamation
that expresses the meaning and content of baptism? Or do
we have here a true liturgical formula pronounced by the
celebrant of the baptismal rite? Finally, can the formula be
attributed to Jesus Himself, or, as the vast majority of modern exegetes contend, must we see here a spurious command,
placed on the lips of Jesus by the "post-Easter Church"?

Formulated in this way, the question is false and mislead-
ing. As W. Trilling has pointed out, there is another "her-
meneutical option" to the alternative "authentic tradition
stemming from Jesus, or kerygmatic creation of the Christian
community."[29] The question should rather be posed in terms
of "legitimate" or "illegitimate" tradition. For reasons other
than Trilling's, we would assert that the Matthew formula
is part of "legitimate" tradition, even if it could be proven
that Jesus did not pronounce the formula in its extant form
before His ascension. As St John makes clear in the Farewell
Discourses, the risen and ascended Lord continues His revelatory activity within the Church through the person and
presence of the Spirit of Truth (14:26; 16:13-15). The
question of the "historicity" of the Matthean formula thus
becomes wholly secondary insofar as we are willing to grant
that the risen Lord continues to address His Church through
the indwelling Spirit. If this appears to be begging the question, we should remember that the formula in Matthew
forms part of the tradition attributed to Jesus after His
resurrection, when the question of "historicity" becomes ultimately insoluble and the Church is obliged to rest its knowledge of the Lord's teachings upon faith grounded in the
apostolic witness.

According to that witness, the risen Christ issued to His
disciples a missionary command that included: 1) proclama-

[29]W. Trilling, "Die toutes les nations," p. 26.

tion of the kerygma (that later developed into pre-baptismal catechesis); 2) baptism for the remission of sins and reception of the Holy Spirit (interpreted by St Paul in a Hellenistic milieu as incorporation into Christ and sacramental participation in His death and resurrection); and 3) post-baptismal instruction.[30] That this threefold commission is not an invention of the first evangelist is shown by the secondary ending of Mark (16:15f); by Lk 24:44-48/Ac 2:22-42; and by passages such as Gal 1:6-9; Col 2:6-15; 3:1-17; and 1 Thess 1:5-7, that confirm the witness of Acts 2, according to which the apostles practiced baptism from the very beginning, immediately after Pentecost, and associated with it not only kerygmatic proclamation and a call to repentance, but also post-baptismal instruction that included both doctrine and parenesis.[31]

The question that concerns us here has to do with the authenticity and meaning of the triadic formula in Matthew 28:19b. Did the risen Lord Himself command His disciples to baptize? And if so, did He specify use of the triadic formula? Or must we attribute the injunction to baptize to the early Church and conclude that Jesus only commanded the Eleven to "make disciples (of all nations)"?

Christian baptism was patterned after Jesus' own reception of baptism at the hands of John. Whereas the multitude accepted John's baptism as a sign of repentance for entry into the eschatological Kingdom (Mk 1:4, par.), Jesus submitted to the rite in order to inaugurate His earthly ministry which would establish the Kingdom, and to manifest His messianic role as the Coming One, anointed by God with the Holy Spirit. Possessing the Spirit throughout His ministry, Jesus communicated or "baptized with" the Spirit only after His death and resurrection. If, as John 4:1-3 suggests, Jesus, or His disciples in His name, baptized prior to His crucifixion, such a baptism was merely a continuation of the Baptist's own ministry: baptism in water for the forgiveness of sins. Jesus' "baptism with the Spirit," prophesied by John, was only

---

[30]On this third aspect, see C. H. Dodd, "The Primitive Catechism and the Sayings of Jesus," in *More New Testament Studies,* Eerdmans 1968, 11-29.

[31]R. Bultmann, *Theology of the New Testament* II, NY, 1955, 218ff.

accomplished after the resurrection, when the Risen One appeared to the Eleven on Easter Sunday (Jn 20:19-23), or at the feast of Pentecost, when the ascended Lord sent the Spirit upon the reconstituted group of the Twelve (Ac 2:1-4).[32]

Nothing whatever indicates that the Spirit-filled apostles were themselves baptized (with the exception of those who, as former disciples of John, had previously undergone a water baptism). Yet despite the arguments of some scholars who attempt to distinguish between the "water baptism" of John and the "Spirit baptism" of Jesus on the grounds of Ac 1:5; 11:16 and Mk 1:8,[33] the close association of water baptism with reception of the Spirit throughout Acts shows clearly that Christian baptism was instituted at Pentecost and conferred the Spirit *through* the sacramental medium of water. As Jesus was manifested to be *pneumatophore* by His own baptism in the Jordan, so the Christian initiate unites himself to the eschatological community and to its Head through the rite of immersion while simultaneously receiving the gift of the Spirit.

Apparent exceptions such as Ac 10:44-48; 8:14-17 and 19:2-5, are to be explained on theological grounds. Acts 10 marks the "Gentile Pentecost" that parallels the "Jewish Pentecost" of ch. 2, when the Spirit first came upon the apostles in fulfillment of the Joel prophecy that speaks only of an outpouring of the Spirit. Acts 8 depicts a similar "Samaritan Pentecost" in which it is shown that apostolic authority alone can "fulfill" baptism in the name of Jesus by conferring the Spirit. And Acts 19, which, with Acts 8, seems to show that the Spirit is bestowed through the laying

[32]An important, if not wholly convincing contribution to this theme has been made by Bp. Cassian (Besobrasoff), *La Pentecôte Johannique*, Valence-sur-Rhone, 1939.

[33]J. Schneider, *op cit* (note 21), speaks of a discontinuity between the Spirit baptism of the Messiah and the water baptism practiced by the apostles at Pentecost. With most modern biblical critics, he eliminates passages such as Jn 3:5 and Mt 28:19 as redactional. The question of the relation between water and Spirit baptism is well treated by C. S. C. Williams, *A Commentary on the Acts of the Apostles,* London 1964, p. 287-293. See also the valuable study by J. D. G. Dunn, *Baptism in the Holy Spirit,* London 1970, that treats in detail all relevant NT passages.

on of hands rather than through baptism, once again intends to demonstrate the indispensable role of the apostles in transmitting the gift of the Spirit to the newly "illumined" initiates.

From this evidence we may conclude that the eschatological outpouring of the Holy Spirit was accomplished by Jesus after His resurrection; that the apostles were the immediate recipients of this gift, and as such had no need to submit themselves to water baptism; and that they perpetuated the effusion of the Spirit through the water rite that was modeled upon Jesus' own baptism in the Jordan. This water rite was a "mystery" or sacrament in the full sense of the term, communicating a spiritual gift through a material medium. In continuity with the preaching and baptism of both John and Jesus (Mk 1:4, 15), administration of the rite presupposed repentance and faith in the person of Jesus as the One in whom the Kingdom is inaugurated. And in the "distinction/association" between baptism and the outpouring of the Spirit in certain passages of the Acts, we find the origin of the Church's sacramental practice that unites *baptism* with *chrismation*, the former constituting incorporation into the eschatological community through sacramental identification with the death and resurrection of Christ, and the latter actualizing in the life of the initiate the Pentecostal outpouring of the Spirit.

Such evidence gives considerable support to the traditional view that Jesus Himself included in His missionary commission a command to baptize. For there is no other way that the eschatological "baptism in the Spirit" could be actualized in the life of the individual believer and in succeeding generations of the Church. The risen Lord alone confers the Spirit. If apostolic mediation is essential (perpetuated in the Church through the priestly ministry), it is only to administer the rite. As with the eucharistic mystery, Christ alone remains the true celebrant of the rite, both subject and object of the sacrament.

While the triadic formula of Matthew 28:19b most likely circulated in the oral tradition of the early Church well before Matthew composed his Gospel, the internal evidence

does not permit us to affirm unequivocally that the formula
stems from Jesus Himself. On the grounds of the above discussion, we may conclude that in the early Church the phrase
"in the name of (the Lord) Jesus (Christ)" was *not a
baptismal formula as such,* pronounced by the celebrant during the sacramental rite. Rather, it was used as *a verbal
symbol* to designate the sacrament and to describe its purpose
(incorporation into the eschatological community of which
Christ is Head), much as the expression *"klan arton"* designated the sacrament of the Lord's Supper or Eucharist (Ac
2:42). Didachē 7:1 (cf. Justin, Apol. I:61, 3; but Dial. 39:2)
shows that by the early second century the triadic formula of
Matthew 28:19b had inded become a fixed liturgical element
of the baptismal rite. And the antiquity of the Didachē
witness, reflecting first century practice, gives considerable
weight to the argument that the formula was also so used in
the early Matthean community.[34] The unresolved—and ultimately unresolvable—question is whether the triadic formula
originated with Jesus Himself.

If in fact Jesus did instruct His disciples to baptize using
the triadic formula of v. 19b, then the meaning of the
formula (unique in the New Testament) can perhaps be in-
ferred by analogy with the institution of the Lord's Supper.
The words "This is my body/This is my blood" constitute
a liturgical formula insofar as they were intended by Jesus
to be repeated in the Church's eucharistic celebration ("Do
this in remembrance of me," 1 Cor 11:23-26). The meaning
of those words, however, is summed up by the Synoptic
formula "poured out for many" (which Matthew interprets
as "for the forgiveness of sins," 26:28), as well as by the
Pauline reference to "the new covenant in my blood." These
diverse formulas faithfully represent the teaching of Jesus
concerning the redemptive significance of His passion and

---

[34]W. Rordorf and A. Tuilier, *La Doctrine des Douze Apôtres—Didachē*,
S.C. 248, Paris 1978, p. 170, n. 4, maintain that "La formule baptismale
trinitaire était d'usage dans la mission pagano-chrétienne; dans la mission
judéo-chrétienne, on baptisait au nom de Jésus." This is disproved by Ac
10:44ff. Did 9:5, "those baptized in the name of the Lord," simply shows
that "baptism in the name" was, so to speak, a generic term to designate the
rite and did not as such constitute a liturgical formula.

death: participation in the sacred meal offers the communicant, as a member of the Body of Christ, participation in the victory achieved by His death and resurrection. *Liturgical in form, they are soteriological in meaning.*

If Jesus thus established a liturgical rite to communicate salvation to His disciples, is it not probable that He instituted a similar rite for those who responded to the call to "become disciples"? In other words, the analogy between baptism and eucharist, both of which communicate forgiveness of sins and incorporation into the glorified Body of Christ, suggests that Jesus not only gave His disciples the command to baptize, but that He also provided them with the ritual formula by which the rite should be effected. As for the content of that formula, we have seen that it most likely was not "in my name," transformed by the apostles into the third person, "in the name of Jesus." The fourth Gospel is not alone in showing that the Son "does only what He sees the Father doing" (5:19). Although Jesus has received full authority as the eschatological prophet and judge (Jn 3:34f; 5:26f; Mt 28:18), He nevertheless can "do nothing" on His own authority but seeks only to accomplish the will of the Father who sent Him (Jn 5:30; 7:16-18). It would thus be wholly consistent with His overall mission and teaching for Jesus to command His disciples to baptize not only in His own name, but also in the name of the Father, by whom all authority is granted and to whom the Son entrusts those who believe in Him as their unique mediator; and in the name of the Spirit, who fulfills the mission of Jesus in the Church, chiefly through baptismal regeneration and sanctification.[35]

While such a line of reasoning remains conjectural, certain conclusions can be drawn regarding the use and meaning of the formula within the early Church. Because the three Persons are called "Father," "Son" and "Holy Spirit," this verse has traditionally been regarded as the New Testament cornerstone of the doctrine of the Trinity. The original meaning of Jesus' commission would be distorted, however,

---

[35]H. Schieber, *op cit* (note 21), draws a rather similar conclusion but emphasizes the role of individual "acceptance" of the three Persons in faith at the expense of the "mystical" or sacramental dimension of baptism.

if we failed to take account of its context within the Gospel and particularly of the missionary charge that accompanies it. Whatever the ultimate origin of the baptismal commission (whether it represents the *ipsissima verba Jesu* or an element of pre-Gospel oral tradition), Matthew's purpose in vss. 16-20 is not to express a "trinitarian truth" concerning relations between the three hypostases of the Godhead. His aim is rather to express an "economic truth," affirming the authority of the risen Lord to bring about universal salvation through His abiding presence within the Church and within the Church's mission. Here again, the decisive emphasis is upon the saving activity of the three divine Persons. To St Matthew, this activity presupposes a "synergism," defined as the apostolic mission to "make disciples of all nations," incorporating converts into the Church community by baptizing them in the threefold divine Name and by teaching them the revealed doctrinal truths and moral injunctions necessary for salvation.

We have seen that the baptismal commission of Matthew 28:19b was employed as a trinitarian liturgical formula in the context of Christian initiation no later than the early second century, and probably well before. In the context of Matthew's Gospel, however, it is subordinated to the primary command to "make disciples of all nations." This is evident from the grammatical structure of the commission: three participles (πορευθέντες, βαπτίζοντες and διδάσκοντες) governed by the finite imperative μαθητεύσατε, a verb proper to Matthew that occurs elsewhere only in Acts 14:21. The baptismal commission, then, must not be isolated from its context and treated as a free-floating liturgical formula whose meaning is determined by the sacrament rather than by the overall message of the first Gospel. Here once again, *theologia* is inseparable from *economia*. Baptism in the name of the Holy Trinity has meaning only insofar as it serves to unite the initiate to divine life and to render him an *onomaphore*, a bearer of the divine Name. This inner, sacramental transformation, however, must be complemented by the *didache*, instruction in apostolic tradition and in the new Torah of which Christ Himself is both bearer and revealer. The baptismal rite, then, is neither more nor less "liturgical" than post-baptismal catechetical instruction in revealed divine truth. Both are necessary to render the initiate a true "disciple" of the risen Lord, one whose discipleship comes to expression both in liturgical worship and in active witness before the world.

III.

An examination of tripartite formulas and triadic references outside the Gospels confirms the foregoing conclusion: insofar as they can be detected in the New Testament, liturgical elements are invariably *kerygmatic* or *catechetical* in character, revealing and teaching divine truth for the salvation of newly illumined members of the Body of Christ. Celebration and confession thus constitute a unified response to the complementary redemptive activity of the three divine Persons within the Church and "for the life of the world."

The opening verses of writings as disparate as the Acts and Romans, for example, leave no doubt that to the apostolic mind Father, Son and Spirit are united in a common being as well as a common will. Once again, it would be anachronistic to speak of "trinitarian doctrine" in the New Testament. But the groundwork for reflection that will lead to later conciliar dogmas is clearly laid in the earliest Pauline letters as well as in the Gospels and later catholic epistles such as 1 Peter and Jude. To be sure, Romans 8:9-11, 2 Corinthians 3:17f, and similar passages show that Paul neither works out nor feels the need for a systematic doctrine concerning inner trinitarian relations. Because his chief aim is proclamation of divine, saving *activity* within the Church and the world, he can freely affirm that "the Lord is the Spirit," just as he can virtually identify Christ, the Spirit of Christ, and the Spirit of God. As passages such as Rom 1:1-4; 5:1-5; 8:2-11, 12-17, 26f; 14:17f; 15:7-13, 14-21 and 30 demonstrate, however, in a single epistle Paul is capable of distinguishing with precision the respective roles of Father, Son and Spirit within the divine economy. While the Father is the ultimate author of salvation, the inaccessible fountain of both divine and

human existence, He reveals and renders Himself accessible
by sending the Son as a humble Servant, to assume in kenotic
obedience the full weight of human life and death. It is the
Son who redeems, justifies, and glorifies fallen humanity by
His incarnation, death and exaltation. The "economy of the
Father and the Son," however, is fulfilled and actualized ever
anew in the life of the Church by the Spirit. As Spirit of God
and Spirit of Christ, He prepares the redemptive ministry of
the Son by "speaking through the prophets" of the former
Covenant. As the One who alone "searches the very depths of
God" (1 Cor 2:10), He grants participation in the life of
the inaccessible Godhead by sanctifying the faithful, so that
they might penetrate into the awesome realm of divine holiness. Through the Holy Spirit given in baptism the Father
pours out His love into the hearts of those who hope to
share in the divine glory (Rom 5:5). Finally, it is the Spirit
who unites believers to God in prayer, enabling them as
adopted brethren of Christ to address their common Father
by the tender and affectionate name "Abba!"

Considering other tripartite phrases and passages that
have a clearly liturgical origin, we find the chief emphasis
placed once again upon the threefold saving activity of God.
Suffice it to mention the following: 1 Cor 6:11, "You have
been washed, you have been sanctified, you have been justified
in the name of the Lord Jesus Christ and by the Spirit of our
God." This verse is taken up in modified form in the Orthodox
office of chrismation. In its Pauline context, however, it refers
to the experience of baptismal renewal. As in Mt 28:19,
purifying, sanctifying and justifying activity is accomplished
through the divine Name, that is, through the concerted
economy of the three divine Persons. Similar trinitarian
affirmations appear in Tit 3:4f; Heb 6:4-6 and 1 Jn 4:13f,
where the possibility of "abiding" in God (the Father) is
accorded by the Spirit of Christ. Trinitarian baptismal allusions are probably to be found as well in 2 Cor 1:20-22,
where χρίσας, like σφραγισάμενος, refers either to the
baptismal rite or to charismatic gifts,[36] and not to the apostolic

---

[36]J. Héring, *La seconde épitre de Saint Paul aux Corinthiens,* Neuchâtel-
Paris 1958, p. 27f.

commission (as interpreted by the RSV; cf. 1 Jn 2:20, 27);
Gal 4:6; Rom 5:5; Eph 1:11-14; 4:3-6; 1 Pet 1:2 (a possible
allusion to both baptism and eucharist); 1 Jn 3:24 and 5:6-8
(excluding the 4th cent. "comma Johanneum").

As these passages demonstrate, there where the New
Testament suggests "ontological" relationships, it refers not
to inner trinitarian relations, but to the "unity of being"
made possible between God and His human creatures through
baptism, a unity expressed by terms such as παλιγγενεσίας
("regeneration," "rebirth"; cf. Jn 3:3-5; Rom 6:4); μέτοχος
("partaker" or "participant"; cf. Heb 3:1, 14: "partakers
of Christ"; 6:4: "partakers of the Holy Spirit"); and μένειν
("indwell," "abide": the Johannine equivalent of μετέχειν).

Still other tripartite formulas and allusions appear in
kerygmatic and catechetical rather than liturgical contexts:

Acts 1:1-4; 1:8; 2:32f; 7:54f; (cf. 9:31); 10:38; 20:28 (if
αἵματος τοῦ ἰδίου means Christ as Son of God).

Romans 1:1-4; 5:1-5 (perhaps an allusion to baptism, developed in ch. 6); 8:2-11 (cf. Phil 1:19; 1 Cor 15:45);
8:12-17; Gal 4:6 (cf. 1 Pet 1:11); 8:26f (cf. 8:34 and the
respective intercessory roles of Christ Jesus and the Spirit);
14:17f; 15:7-13 (a passage that sounds "liturgical" but is
probably a free composition inspired by Pss 18; 117; Dt 32;
Isa 11, etc.); 15:14-21, 30.

1 Corinthians 2:8-10a; 2:10b-16 (cf. Eph 3:1-6); 12:3, 4-5
(αὐτὸ πνεῦμα, αὐτὸς κύριος, αὐτὸς θεός, to whom
are attributed respectively χαρίσματα, διακονίαι and
ἐνεργήματα, once again stressing the distinctive functions
of each divine Person while attributing absolute power and
authority to God: if "all authority" has been given to the
Son, Mt 28:18, the ultimate origin and wielder of that
authority remains God the Father; cf. Phil 2:9-11; Jn 5:19-23;
17:2).[37]

[37]For various interpretations of the "trinitarian" character of I Cor 12:3-5,
see esp. H. Conzelmann, *Der erste Brief an die Korinther,* Göttingen, 1969,
244f; F. Martin, "Pauline Trinitarian Formulas and Church Unity," *Catholic*

Galatians 3:11-14; 4:6 (cf. Rom 5:5, a possible baptismal reference fulfilling Ezek 36:26); 5:16-25 (whereas the "gifts" of the Spirit confer unity within the Church, the "fruits" of the Spirit confer the moral rectitude necessary for inheriting the Kingdom of God; cf. 2 Tim 1:6f).

Ephesians 2:18-22 (through Christ, both Jews and Gentiles have access in one Spirit to the Father; the Church is defined as a "holy temple in the Lord," a "dwelling place of God in the Spirit"); 3:14-19 (recalling Gal 3:11-14); 5:18-20 ("be filled with the Spirit . . . making melody to the Lord . . . giving thanks in the name of our Lord Jesus Christ to God the Father": liturgical worship is not only addressed to God, it is actually accomplished by the reciprocal activity of the three Persons; cf. Rom 8:15c-16, 26-27).

Philippians 2:1 (see below); 3:3 (reading Θεοῦ rather than Θεῷ: we worship "by the Spirit of God," as Eph 5:18-20; cf. Jn 4:24).

Colossians 1:6-8 ("grace of God . . . minister of Christ . . . love in the Spirit"; see re. 2 Cor 13:13, below).

1 Thessalonians 1:2-6; 5:18f.

2 Thessalonians 2:13f (the election of God the Father leads to acquisition of the "glory of our Lord Jesus Christ" through the sanctifying work of the Spirit; cf. 1 Pet 1:2).

Hebrews 2:3-4; 9:14 (very likely an illusion to the actualization of Christ's sacrifice in the eucharistic celebration); cf. 10:29.

1 Peter 3:18-22 (reading πνεύματι as "the Spirit," contrasting the death of Christ in the flesh with His resurrected life

Biblical Quarterly XXX/2 (1968) 199-219 (important also for II Cor 13:13); T. Holtz, "Das Kennzeichen des Geistes (I Kor XII 1-3)," *New Testament Studies* 18/3 (1972) 365-376; and J. M. Bassler, "I Cor 12/3—Curse and Confession in Context," *JBL* 101 (1982) 415-418.

in the Spirit, as Rom 1:3f and 1 Tim 3:16. For the same theme concerning the new life in Christ, see Jn 6:63, the Spirit is the "giver of life"; and 1 Pet 4:6—the Gospel is preached to the dead so that they might live "like God by the Spirit." That πνεύματι here refers to the divine Spirit is shown by the flesh-Spirit antithesis of 3:18); 4:13f (a probable baptismal allusion: "the Spirit of glory and of God rests upon you," a rewording of Isa 11:2, to express the transferal of messianic "anointing by the Spirit" from Christ to the believer).

1 John 2:18-27 (another baptismal reference to anointing by the χρῖσμα or Spirit, that empowers the believer to confess the Father and the Son; cf. 3:24; 4:13f; and 5:6-8).

The most explicit trinitarian formula outside the Gospels is the well-known closing benediction of 2 Corinthians: Ἡ χάρις τοῦ κυρίου Ἰησοῦ Χριστοῦ καὶ ἡ ἀγάπη τοῦ Θεοῦ καὶ ἡ κοινωνία τοῦ ἁγίου πνεύματος μετὰ πάντων ὑμῶν, "The grace of the Lord Jesus Christ and the love of God and the communion of the Holy Spirit (be) with all of you" (13:13). As with the baptismal commission of Matthew 28:19b, we should first determine whether this formula served a specifically liturgical function in Paul's letter and in the practice of the Corinthian church.

Byzantine eucharistic liturgies took up and modified this benediction by reading *"our* Lord Jesus Christ" and "God *the Father*,"[38] thereby rendering it both personal and unambiguously trinitarian. Apart from 2 Cor 13:13, however, the New Testament contains no tripartite benedictions that can be unreservedly classified as stereotyped liturgical formulas. Where such benedictions appear, they seem rather to be free compositions by the author, whose concern is to associate God, Jesus and the Spirit in a context that, once more, affirms their respective roles in the divine economy. This is as true

[38]*Hē charis tou Kyriou hēmōn Iēsou Christou kai hē agapē tou Theou kai Patros kai hē koinōnia tou hagiou Pneumatos, meta pantōn hymōn,* preceding the *sursum corda* at the beginning of the anaphora.

of the primitive "pre-trinitarian" formula of Rev 1:4f as it
is of the later (ca. 80?) passage Jude 20b-21, which is both
a blessing and an exhortation:

— Rev 1:4f: "Grace to you and peace from Him who is
    [ὁ ὤν] and who was [ὁ ἦν] and who comes [or "is
    to come," ὁ ἐρχόμενος], and from the seven spirits
    who are before His throne, and from Jesus Christ,
    the faithful witness, the first-born from the dead and
    the ruler of the kings of the earth."[39]
— Jude 20b-21: "Pray in the Holy Spirit, keep yourselves
    in the love of God; await the mercy of our Lord Jesus
    Christ by which you shall obtain [εἰς] eternal life."

Yet a careful examination of the context of 2 Cor 13:13
makes it clear that it too is a free composition by the apostle
and not a stereotyped liturgical formula, as it later became.
Chapters 10-13 represent St Paul's impassioned defense of
his apostleship. Recent criticism has attempted to show that
these four chapters constitute part of the "severe letter"
mentioned in 2:3f and 7:12, and thus pre-date chapters 1-9.[40]

[39]Patristic theology and Byzantine iconography transferred this three-fold
designation from God the Father to Christ, the Pantocrator, who is from all
eternity (*ho ōn*) and who is awaited in the glory of His parousia. Lohmeyer
op cit, p. 30f, may be correct in seeing a progression from triadic formulas
found in Jewish Apocalyptic (God/Lord of Spirits; the Elect One/Son of
Man; the Angel/angels: I Enoch 39:5-7; 51:3f; 61:8-10) to the tripartite
formulas of the NT. Mk 8:38 (Son of Man, Father, angels) and Rev 1:4f
(God, seven spirits, Jesus Christ) would thus represent intermediate steps
in the development of a triadic vision of God as "Father/Son/Spirit." While
such a development might be verifiable historically, Orthodox "theoretic"
exegesis would see in the apocalyptic and Mk-Rev triads typological images
of the self-revealing Trinity (*pace* R. H. Fuller, "On Demythologizing the
Trinity," *Anglican Theological Review* 43 (1961) 121-131).

[40]II Cor 6:14-7:1 is almost certainly an unconnected fragment, of unde-
termined date and origin, perhaps a part of the first letter addressed by Paul
to the Corinthians, alluded to in I Cor 5:9-11. On the composite character of
II Cor, see H. D. Wendland, "Die Briefe an die Korinther," in *Das Neue
Testament Deutsch* vol 3, Göttingen (1966) 7-11; G. Bornkamm, "Die
Vorgeschichte des sog. Zweiten Korintherbriefes," *Sitzungsberichten der Heidel-
berger Akademie der Wissenschaften*, 1961, p. 2ff, revised in *Geschichte und
Glaube II. Gesammelte Aufsätze IV*, 1971, p. 162ff; and W. G. Kümmel,
Einleitung in das Neue Testament (17e Auflage), Heidelberg 1973, p. 249-
255, who defends the original literary unity of II Cor.

Whatever the case may be, the conclusion 13:11-13 is clearly a literary unit that closes this polemical section with an appeal to mutual reconciliation:[41] "As for the rest, brethren, rejoice, renew and admonish yourselves, agree with one another, be at peace; and the God of love and peace will be with you. Greet one another with a holy kiss" (vss. 11-12).

Paul then concludes with the triadic benediction whose structure and content can be explained on the basis of his usual epistolary endings as well as the foregoing admonitions. The apostle habitually closes his letters with the christological formula, "The grace of the Lord Jesus Christ be with you" (1 Thess 5:28; 2 Thess 3:18; 1 Cor 16:23; cf. Rom 16:20; Gal 6:18; Phil 4:23). At the close of 2 Cor, he begins the final benediction in the same way: "The grace of our Lord Jesus Christ. . . ." In the preceding verses, however, he has exhorted the Corinthians to "think the same thing," that is, to be of one mind and one accord. The imperatives "rejoice" and "be at peace" bring to mind the "fruit of the Sipirt" that Paul elsewhere contrasts with the "works of the flesh": love, joy, peace . . . (Gal 5:22); and he assures his readers that "the God of love and peace" will be with them. In the concluding verse he takes up this theme and gives it a new significance by expanding the christological benediction into a triadic formula: "and the love of God and the communion of the Holy Spirit be with all of you."

We are led inevitably to the conclusion that *the threefold benediction of 2 Cor 13:13, like all other triadic statements of the New Testament, is not strictly speaking a "liturgical formula."* As a formal benediction, it of course has a liturgical function. And allusion to the "holy kiss" strongly suggests that Paul intended his letter to be read at the eucharistic assembly.[42] It would be an error, however, to see here, as most interpreters seem to do, a stereotyped ritual formula that had a fixed place in the cult of the Corinthian church. As with the baptismal commission of Mt 28:19b and every other

[41]S. M. Gilmour, *Interpreter's Dictionary of the Bible* vol I, 695-697, makes the common error of separating the triadic benediction from its immediate context and thus fails to perceive the inherent unity of the whole passage.

[42]See G. Dix, *The Shape of the Liturgy,* London 1945/1964, p. 105-110.

triadic statement that we have examined, 2 Cor 13:13 is essentially *kerygmatic*, constituting a proclamation of the Gospel of salvation. It is "trinitarian" insofar as it affirms and stipulates the complementary roles of God, Jesus Christ and the Holy Spirit within the divine economy, the working out of sacred history. If the law came through Moses, St Paul, like the fourth evangelist, knows and declares that redemptive and justifying grace came through Jesus Christ (cf. Gal 2:20f; Jn 1:17). Similarly, Paul, like the apostle John, knows God to be the ultimate source of *agapē* or divine love, the greatest of all spiritual gifts that defines the essential attitude of the Father toward His human children and elicits on their part a response of love for God and for one another (1 Cor 13:13; Rom 5:5; 8:28-39; 1 Jn 4:7-11).

Similar reference to the context of this benediction resolves as well the much debated question of the meaning of the expression ἡ κοινωνία τοῦ ἁγίου πνεύματος. Exegetes are divided as to whether the "Holy Spirit" is to be read as a subjective or objective genitive. In v. 11, God as subject dispenses love and peace. The first two gentives of the tripartite blessing are likewise subjective: "the grace bestowed by Christ and the love bestowed by God . . . be with you." The difficulty with the third element arises largely from a reluctance to conceive the Spirit as a Person and the consequent temptation to interpret the expression as an objective gentive: "communion in the Spirit," in the sense of communal participation in the Spirit as a divine, but impersonal, power. The question, in other words, is whether the Spirit is depicted as a Person who bestows the gift of "communion" upon the community, as Jesus Christ and God bestow grace and love; or whether the apostle conceives the Spirit Himself to be the gift, originating in God and bestowed by Him.

We have already noted that Paul's language regarding the Spirit is fluid, leading him to speak of "the Spirit," "the Holy Spirit," "the Spirit of holiness" (Rom 1:4), "the Spirit of Christ" and "the Spirit of God" (Rom 8:9-11; cf. 1 Thess 4:8; 1 Cor 2:12; Gal 4:6). To many exegetes, this proves that to the apostle's mind, the Spirit was thought of as a divine power and a principle of mediation between God and man, rather than as an independent hypostasis, a Person within the essentially undivided Godhead.[43]

Steeped in Old Testament tradition, Paul quite naturally envisioned the Spirit as a charismatic power, a *dynamis* intimately associated with the Person of God and, as such, transferable to the Person of the risen Jesus as Kyrios. Nowhere does he present the Spirit as an independent, personal entity to the degree that Jesus does, for example, in the Farewell Discourses of the fourth Gospel. We have nevertheless seen that Paul attributes to the Spirit a prophetic and sanctifying activity proper to Him alone. In addition, Paul ascribes to the Spirit various attributes and attitudes that are proper only to personal beings: He bears witness on behalf of the faithful and aids them both by effecting their prayer and by interceding for them (Rom 8:15f; 26f; Gal 4:6); He is subject to grief (Eph 4:30), and yet he bestows joy (Rom 14:17; Gal 5:22; 1 Thess 1:6) as the essential mark of Christian existence. Coupled with evidence from other parts of the New Testament, such characteristics allow us to speak legitimately of a "personification" of the Spirit, even if the terms *hypostasis* and *persona* rightly belong only to a later age.[44]

If the Spirit is in fact personified in Paul's thought, then a third alternative is possible for the interpretation of 2 Cor 13:13. Rather than defining *koinōnia* either as a gift mediated *by* the Spirit or as human participation *in* the Spirit, we can speak of it as the *self-giving act* of the Spirit that creates authentic communion—reconciliation and harmony—between members of the Body of Christ.

[43]See J. Hainz, *Ekklesia: Strukturen paulinischer Gemeinde-Theologie und Gemeinde-Ordnung*, Regensburg 1972, p. 326; somewhat modified in his later work, *Koinonia: "Kirche" als Gemeinschaft bei Paulus*, Regensburg 1982; although with the majority of modern critics he refuses to speak of the Spirit as a "Person" and denies that the triadic formula is "trinitarian." Similar positions are defended by E. von Dobschütz, *op cit* (note 21), and I. Hermann, *Kyrios und Pneuma. Studien zur Christologie der paulinischen Hauptbriefe*, Munich 1961, p. 135-141. For a defense of the "personal" character of the Spirit in II Cor 13:13, see P. Gaechter, "Zum Pneumabegriff des hl. Paulus," *Zeitschrift für Katholische Theologie* 53 (1928) 345-408; and E. B. Allo, *St Paul: Seconde Epitre aux Corinthiens*, Paris 1956, p. 343.

[44]The "personal" characteristics of Spirit in the NT are summarized by A. W. Wainwright, *op cit* (note 3), p. 200-204; see also H. Schlier, *Der Brief an die Epheser*, Düsseldorf 1957/1971, p. 227f.

Throughout the New Testament, *koinōnia* signifies at one and the same time a particular quality of relationship with God and with other members of the Christian community.[45] If the earliest believers "persevered in *koinōnia*" (Ac 2:42), this means far more than the fraternal bond suggested by the term "fellowship." The real import of the term is conveyed by Paul's first letter to the Corinthians. In 1 Cor 1:9 he declares: "God is faithful, by whom you were called into *koinōnia* of His Son, Jesus Christ our Lord." As 1 Cor 10:16 demonstrates, such *koinōnia* involves "participation" both in the eucharistic gifts of Christ's Body and Blood, and in the one Body of the Church. The gentive of 1:9, κοινωνία τοῦ υἱοῦ αὐτοῦ, κ.τ.λ., is thus both subjective and objective. Our communion in Christ and with one another is possible by virtue of His voluntary self-sacrifice on our behalf. He is both Subject and Object, Celebrant and Sacrifice, Giver and Gift of the eucharistic mystery. Participation in Him, however, is inseparable from "communion one with another" in the unity of the ecclesial Body. For this reason, Paul can also employ the term *koinōnia* to designate the collection of money made by the Hellenistic churches and sent to the mother church in Jerusalem as a concrete, material symbol of the unity that binds Christians, both Jews and Gentiles, in a universal, corporate "communion" (Rom 15:26; 2 Cor 8:4; 9:13; cf. Heb 13:16). It is this dual emphasis that explains how Paul can speak in the same brief epistle of *koinōnia* "in the Gospel," "in the Spirit" and "in the sufferings of Christ" (Phil 1:5; 2:1; 3:10; cf. Phm 6). As the author of 1 John insists, speaking in the name of his Church community, "we proclaim to you what we have seen and heard, so that you may have communion [*koinōnia*] with us; and our communion is with the Father and with His Son Jesus Christ" (1:3, 6-7).

The closest New Testament parallel to the closing benediction of 2 Corinthians is Paul's own plea in Phil 2:1, "If

45Ph. Menoud, *La Vie de l'Eglise naissante*, Neuchâtel 1952, p. 22f, distinguishes four related meanings of the term *koinōnia:* spiritual, material, eucharistic and ecclesiastic. While this categorization is a bit too rigid (the "spiritual" includes the "eucharistic," as the "material" includes the "ecclesiastic"), his analysis of Act 2:42 remains quite valuable.

there is any consolation in Christ, any encouragement in love, any κοινωνία πνεύματος . . . fulfill my joy by being of one mind." Here as well the theme is that of communion between members of the Body of Christ, grounded in self-giving divine love. In his exhaustive study of the term *koinōnia*, Josef Hainz has shown that the basic meaning of the term is "communion with someone through common participation in a given reality," and he rightly labels the third genitive in 2 Cor 13:13 a "gentive of origin" rather than a "genitive of possession."[46] As such, the expression "communion of the (Holy) Spirit" signifies communion between members of the Christian community, a communion that has its source solely in the Spirit Himself. For it is He who *communicates* divine grace and love to the gathered faithful, thereby rendering the Father and the Son present within the ecclesial Body. In Phil 2:1 as in 2 Cor 13:13, then, Paul exhorts the divided and disruptive community to "be of one mind," that is, to rediscover and reawaken among themselves the bond of love signified by the term *koinōnia*, a bond that is created and maintained by their common participation in the life-giving and sanctifying, personal reality of the Holy Spirit.[47]

As with Mt 28:19, the closing benediction of Paul's second letter to the Corinthians is essentially trinitarian, stressing above all the concerted saving activity of the three divine Persons. Both the baptismal and the blessing formulas name the Holy Spirit as their third term because of the Spirit's function within the framework of salvation-history. In the present, eschatological "age of the Church," the Spirit actualizes ever again, within the sacramental life of the worshiping community, the redemptive will and work of the Father, accomplished through the kenotic sacrifice of the Son. The activity of the three Persons is inseparable, constituting a

[46] J. Hainz, *Koinonia*, p. 48-50.

[47] E. Lohmeyer, *Die Briefe an die Philipper, an die Kolosser und an Philemon*, Göttingen 1964, p. 82-84, eloquently develops the parallel between Phil 2:1 and II Cor 13:13 in the light of Christian martyrdom that unites the apostle and the Philippian church in the "consolation of Christ," the "encouraging love (of God)" and the "communion of the Spirit." This last element, as always with Paul, signifies the exercise of brotherly love through common "participation in the Gospel" (Phil 1:5); Lohmeyer, p. 17.

single divine economy for the salvation of the fallen created order. Like the Father and the Son, however, the Spirit has His own specific place and role within that economy. As a self-revealing and self-communicating expression of triune life, He is essentially "personal." And it is through His distinctively personal quality that He renders Himself accessible, making it possible for members of Christ's Body to *participate* in Him while receiving from Him the charismatic gifts and fruits necessary for maintaining authentic *communion* among themselves.

IV.

On the basis of the foregoing analysis, we may conclude that the New Testament contains no triadic statements that represent stereotyped liturgical formulas used in the first Christian generation.

Mt 28:19b and 2 Cor 13:13 were taken up in the ritual of the post-apostolic Church and used respectively as a baptismal formula and as a eucharistic benediction. Their original function, however, was basically kerygmatic: they were in essence revelatory statements whose purpose was to affirm and to define, in the context of a divine commission and apostolic blessing, the reciprocal saving work of God the Father, the crucified and exalted Christ, and the Holy Spirit.

These and similar statements lent themselves to formal liturgical usage within the Christian cultus for two main reasons. In the first place, they served as lapidary confessional symbols that expressed the Church's growing consciousness of the fundamentally *triune* life and will that constitute the Godhead. In the New Testament period, theological reflection and the language used to express it remained fluid and imprecise. Yet thought and language naturally grow together. Accordingly, the tripartite, quasi-liturgical formulas of the New Testament served as vital links in the long chain of doctrinal affirmations that began with the most primitive single member acclamations ("Jesus is Lord," "Marana tha") and led to highly complex symbols such as the Apostles' and

Nicene-Constantinopolitan Creeds. And they could do so precisely because of their *revelatory* and *kerygmatic* nature.

In the second place, tripartite statements of the apostolic period were woven into the liturgical fabric of the Church's worship because they reveal and express above all the ultimate "divine service": the concerted *leitourgia* accomplished by the Father, the Son and the Spirit on behalf of fallen humanity.

This second factor has far-reaching implications for the practical life and activity of Orthodox Christians and their Church communities. As Orthodox living in the midst of a decidedly non-Orthodox Western culture, with all of its pressures and temptations, we all too often seek refuge and consolation—as well as cultural and religious identity—in the beauty of our liturgical services and the integrity of our theological tradition. All too easily we define *orthodoxia* as "right confession," rendering lip-service to dogma and canons while willfully forgetting that "Orthodoxy" means above all love, joy and peace in the Holy Spirit, giving full expression to our innermost longing for eternal communion with divine life. Yet even when we comprehend and live out our faith as "true glorification" of the Holy Trinity, we tend to obscure the "summons of the Cross." We tacitly deny the demands of our faith by refusing to accept ascetic identity with the passion of our Lord.

If, as Pascal maintained, "Christ is in agony until the end of the world," it is because the world, of which He is Creator and Lord, suffers its own self-imposed agony. For this reason, the Risen One, in His inexhaustible love for mankind, dwells among His own "until the end of the age." But this is also why, before His ascension, He renewed the original vocation of Israel by issuing to His apostles the divine commission to "go, make disciples of all nations, baptizing and teaching them. . . ." Faith in the incarnation, in the divinity of Christ and in the Holy Trinity itself, is above all faith in God's "mighty acts" on behalf of His fallen and destitute creatures. Yet in the mystery of His unfathomable will, He has chosen to save mankind through the ministry of weak and fallen human agents. With St Paul, every baptized member of the

Body is consequently called to become a "minister of reconciliation," a *leitourgos* in our common priestly service (2 Cor 5:18; Rom 15:16; cf. 1 Pet 2:5, 9) for the healing of a world that is "sick unto death." Ultimately, then, the *leitourgia* of men and the *leitourgia* of God serve a single, sublime purpose: to permit "the light of the knowledge of the glory of God in the person of Jesus Christ" (2 Cor 4:6) to enlighten and to transfigure all of creation.

It is to this end that the divine initiative seeks to evoke a twofold response on the part of Christian people: adoration offered to the Holy Trinity, and service undertaken for the world. Just as celebration is inseparable from confession, *lex orandi* from *lex credendi,* so the two are indissolubly linked to a *lex agendi,* a "rule of action." Without this third aspect of loving, self-giving service—the devoted, personal commitment that St John Chrysostom called "the sacrament of our brother"—the Church's creeds and its liturgical worship are meaningless. Confession and celebration of "the Holy Trinity, consubstantial and undivided" constitute an authentic liturgical act only insofar as they lead to a true "synergism" between God and man, a serious and total participation in the grace of Jesus Christ and the love of God for the establishment of a deep and lasting spiritual communion within the Church and within the world.

CHAPTER VI

Confessing the *Monogenes:* The Only-Begotten Son

Do ancient confessions of faith still have meaning for the life and mission of the Church today? The growing number of attempts by Protestant and Catholic Church commissions to create "an ecumenical confession of faith" suggests that for the non-Orthodox, traditional formulations of the Church's faith need to be modified or entirely recast, in order to speak directly and relevantly to the situation of Christian people within the modern world.

Solid groundwork for such a reformulation appeared in an issue of *Concilium,* published in 1978, under the title, "An Ecumenical Confession of Faith?" In their introduction, Hans Küng and Jürgen Moltmann stated: "The confessions of faith of the Ancient Church do not correspond very well at all to the needs of our day, and, what is more, they present the elements of faith in a polemical context that fails to state what is essential to Christian belief. Most important is their neglect of social and ethical concerns."[1]

Such an attitude towards traditional creeds poses a problem for the Orthodox Churches that have been active in the ecumenical movement since its beginning. They, perhaps more than others, recognize that the various Christian confessions can only be united by a common confession of faith.[2] Yet

---

[1]Page 7 of the French edition. See also the Orthodox view presented by Mgr Damaskinos Papandreou in the same issue, p. 71-76.

[2]This point, however, was clearly underscored by the Faith and Order

Orthodox theologians conceive the function of creeds in a way that has little in common with the above quotation from *Concilium*. Within Orthodoxy, a symbol of faith has a purpose other than to proclaim the believer's concern, however deep and sincere it may be, to redress social and political ills. Nor is it an Orthodox conviction that salvation is wrought by God through various kinds of social and political change. Of course the divine will that seeks transfiguration of the created order seeks as well social and political justice. This is evident and beyond any question. The purpose of the Church's symbols of faith, nevertheless, is to proclaim in concise, lapidary form the *Gospel of salvation*: the liberation of man from sin and death through the self-sacrificing love of the Holy Trinity. The symbol is not an exhortation directed at the moral conscience of the individual. It is an inspired revelation of God, an actualization of the divine Word, in which the confessing community believes and in which it participates.

The aim of this chapter is to examine one such confessional statement, the troparion known as the *Monogenēs*, in an effort to clarify first the abiding value of traditional Orthodox creeds, and second the quasi-sacramental character of the creed that enables the confessing Church to participate existentially in the Truth she proclaims.

I.

The Church's creeds originated as confessions of faith pronounced by the catechumen prior to baptismal illumination.[3] How did they come to be known as "symbols," and what is their "symbolic" meaning in the experience of the Church?

The symbol is a concept known throughout the history of religions. Originally the term designated a sign or a token

Commission of the WCC ("Towards a Confession of the Common Faith," FO paper 100, 1980): "Communion in faith is at the heart of the communion the Churches are seeking to recover."

[3]This has been amply demonstrated by J.N.D. Kelly, *Early Christian Creeds*, London, 1960.

used to establish recognition. An object (in ancient Greek practice, a coin or bone) was broken in half by two contracting partners who then went their separate ways. At some later date the two rejoined halves would serve as a sign of mutual recognition.

As Mircea Eliade has shown,[4] in religious usage the symbol manifests the presence of the sacred in pagan rituals, where the transcendent realm becomes accessible through some material "symbolic" representation. From a simple sign of recognition, the symbol gradually became known as a *means of mutual participation* between two parties, human and divine, who had entered into alliance with one another. Here συμβάλλειν signifies a "meeting" or an encounter between man and God, mediated by the σύμβολον, a material object that enters into contact with the realm of the sacred and thereby communicates divine power to the realm of the profane. Through the object, become itself sacred by virtue of its contact with the transcendent sphere, human life has access to divine reality and participates in it. In a cultic context, it was an easy and natural process to transfer symbolic value from material objects to verbal expressions such as incantations and consecratory formulas. An established form of *verbal symbols* thus came to communicate the presence and power of the divinity in the context of ritual worship.[5]

In Christian practice, this symbolic, mediatorial function occurs through word and gesture as well as through material objects. The sacraments—particularly baptism, chrismation and eucharist—attribute symbolic quality to the material substances water, oil, bread and wine. Their ritual gestures of immersion, unction, consecration (by the sign of the Cross) and communion, together with the prescribed ritual formulas, are perceived as elements essential to the mediation of sacramental grace. The crucial difference between Christian sacraments and pagan rites lies in the fact that the sacraments are

[4]In numerous works, e.g., *Rites and Symbols of Initiation, the mysteries of birth and rebirth,* New York, 1958.

[5]Recall the Hebrew belief in the power and irreversible character of blessings and curses (e.g., Gen 27:35).

effected wholly by divine initiative and by divine invitation. They are God's gifts to the Church, in which God is the unique source and acting agent. In pagan rites such as the Hellenistic mystery religions, on the other hand, the initiative lies with man in his quest for participation in the (impersonal) realm of the sacred. Rather than offer the traditional ritual formulas as an expression of invocation and adoration, the adept use them as magical incantations in an attempt to manipulate the divine.[6]

Common to both pagan rites and Christian sacraments, however, is the conviction that the ritual act enables the worshiper to *participate* directly and personally in divine reality. In the language of the Church, this participation as effected through baptism can be expressed as "regeneration" (Tit 3:5) or "new birth from above" (Jn 3:5), the creation of a "new man" in the Spirit (Rom 5; 1 Cor 15).

It is significant that from the time of St Cyprian of Carthage (d. 258), the term *symbolon* has been used to designate not only the sacramental rite but also the *confessional formulas* pronounced by the candidate for baptism.[7] As used of the rite itself, the term can be synonymous with "type" or "image," a prophetic figure of a future antitype or transcendent archetype.[8] In his Mystagogical Catechisms, Cyril of Jerusalem interprets the candidate's turning from West (the realm of Satan) to East (towards the light) as "symbolic" of the eschatological reopening of Paradise (*cat.* 19:9 = MC 1:9). In the following lecture he speaks of the ritual gestures accompanying baptism as "symbols" of an actual participation in the events of Christ's life, a participation that transforms the "Old Adam" in the "New Man."[9] Eusebius speaks of the sacraments as "mystical symbols," images of

[6]Such "playing with the powers" was condemned throughout the biblical period (Lev 19:26; Dt 18:10-14; Ezek 13:18; Ac 16:16-19; Eph 6:12; etc.) and explains why the Orthodox Church to our day strictly forbids such activities as divination, sorcery, astrology, druidism, and, in general, delving into the realm of psychic phenomena.

[7]Cyprian, Ep. 69:7; Kelly, *op cit*, p. 52ff.

[8]Cf. Justin, *dial* 42:1, 4 (PG 6, 565ac) on the "symbolic value" of OT types.

[9]Cf. Col 3:9; Rom 6:3ff; Gal 3:27 and 2:19-20, where "crucified with Christ" is an allusion to baptism.

heavenly reality.[10] Theodore of Mopsuestia affirms that baptism is a "symbol" of death and resurrection.[11] His contemporary in the Antiochian school, John Chrysostom, speaks in similar terms,[12] declaring that the "symbols" of our covenant with God are fulfilled in baptism (θεῖα τελεῖται ἐν αὐτῷ σύμβολα), in which burial and death, resurrection and life occur simultaneously. In his catechetical lectures,[13] Chrysostom calls the rising up from the baptismal waters a "symbol" of the resurrection, and he exhorts the newly illumined Christian to implore Christ's divine assistance. Finally, in a related passage,[14] he speaks of the water and the blood that issued from Christ's side as a "symbol" of baptism and the eucharist.

If we recall Chrysostom's aversion to allegory, it is clear that to his mind such a symbol is not a mere "sign" that simply indicates or points to a given transcendent reality. Nor is it to be understood metaphorically. For its symbolic quality relates, indeed *unites* the liturgical object, gesture or formula to its historical prototype. In the experience of the Church, for example, the power of the Holy Spirit transfigures the baptismal water into the waters of the Jordan and into the tomb of the risen Lord. It is the Spirit who transforms the sign into a true symbol and thereby enables the baptismal candidate to share directly in Christ's own baptism, death and resurrection.

Such examples drawn from the writings of the Fathers can easily be multiplied. Those we have mentioned, however, suffice to illustrate the *participative character* of the symbol in the context of sacramental ritual. By the power of the Holy Spirit, the symbol "represents," that is, renders present and accessible, its historical prototype. This is the case not only with regard to material elements (e.g., bread and wine that become the Body and Blood of Christ). It holds true as

[10]*Eccl hist* 10:3, 4 (PG 20, 860).

[11]Frag. 21 in Jo 3:4ff; R. Devreesse, *Studi e Testi* (Vatican) 141 (1948) p. 321.

[12]Hom 25:2 in Jo; in B. de Montfaucon, *Joannis Chrysostomi opera omnia* (Garme) Paris 1834-39, 8:146c.

[13]II Bapt Cat 29:7; *Sources Chrétiennes* 50 bis.

[14]III Bapt Cat 16:7; *ibid.*

well of liturgical formulas. The liturgical Word participates symbolically in the historical reality as antitype to prototype, "re-presenting" or rendering present in every particular "now" or existential moment the historical event that lies behind it. The "Word of the Cross" (1 Cor 1:18), for example, actualizes and renders accessible to faith the crucifixion of Christ, just as the Words of Institution (with the whole of the Anaphora) unite every eucharistic celebration to the Last Supper.[15]

Such observations suggest that we should considerably broaden our traditional understanding of the symbolic character of confessional formulas. A symbol or rule of faith is not simply a concise statement of belief. As a sacramental Word whose formulation is inspired by the Spirit and transmitted by conciliar decree, a symbol of faith is nothing less than a *salvation event.* On the one hand, it permits the believer to affirm identity of faith with the One, Holy, Catholic and Apostolic Church. At the same time, it renders present in the life of the *ekklēsia* the reality which it confesses (e.g., the eternal Trinity, the historical events of Christ's redemptive death and resurrection, the person and mission of the Holy Spirit). Thereby it enables the community to participate directly and personally in the object of its faith.

Holy Scripture has the power to communicate salvation by virtue of the living Word who speaks through it. The Church's confessional statements affirm and actualize that same Word by proclaiming in different and more concise language the same divine truth. Consequently, they, like the Word of Scripture, can serve the Spirit as instruments of saving grace.

It is axiomatic that no symbol of faith can be considered a legitimate expression of the Church's belief if it does not conform to the teachings of Scripture. Even the use of non-biblical language is enough to throw the validity of a confessional statement into question. If the Nicene Creed was for years the focal point of intense theological controversy, this is because the crucial term ὁμοούσιον, used to define the relationship of the Son to the Father within the Godhead,

---

[15]See chapters 1 and 2 above.

was not to be found in the canonical writings. Only after the Church as a whole came to accept *homoousios* as a complete and accurate expression of scriptural revelation did the confession of Nicea-Constantinople (C) achieve universal acceptance. The conclusion to be drawn from the Nicene controversy is evident: a symbol of faith can be accepted for use by the Church only if it conforms with the content and, insofar as possible, with the language of divine revelation as found in Holy Scripture. Other terms or formulas are permissible only to the degree that they faithfully reproduce the *meaning* of the biblical witness. Thus in the definitive version of C the term *homoousios* was approved and its explanatory phrase "of the essence of the Father" (inserted in the original formulation [N] of 325) was omitted, because *homoousios* was finally acknowledged to be, in and of itself, 1) a concise and valid expression of the scriptural witness concerning the relationship of the Son to the Father; and, 2) an adequate rebuttal of Arian teaching which denied that the Son was of the same eternal and uncreated nature as the Father. *Homoousios*, then, became accepted as an inspired, global symbol that fully and accurately expresses the consubstantiality of the First and Second Persons of the Holy Trinity.

In its traditional form[16] the Nicene Creed (C) found its way into the eucharistic liturgies of the East during the fifth century, beginning apparently in Antioch under the influence of the Monophysite patriarch Peter the Fuller.[17] Its central place in the Orthodox eucharistic and baptismal liturgies has tended to eclipse other confessional formulas. One of the most important of these from a theological point of view is the *Monogenēs*, a troparion dedicated to "the Only-Begotten Son of God." A remarkably complete and precise statement of Orthodox belief, the *Monogenēs* is a confessional symbol in the fullest sense of the term. Summarizing the faith of the Church in the catechetical portion of the Divine Liturgy, it proclaims the Word of Truth (cf. Jn 17:17) and communi-

---

16That is, without the addition of the clause *filioque*, affirming that the Spirit proceeds from the Father *and the Son,* interpolated into the Creed at the Third Council of Toledo in 589.

17Theodore Lector, *hist eccl* 1:20f (PG 86/1, 175ff.). "C" was not introduced into the Latin rite until the early 11th century.

cates that Truth to the gathered community. Thus it illustrates in an especially clear way the fact that confessional formulas exercise a quasi-sacramental function by transmitting divine grace: through the symbol of faith, a living and personal encounter occurs between God and man.

II.

According to Theophanes the Confessor (d. 818?),[18] the *Monogenēs* is a "prose-hymn" composed by the Emperor Justinian in 535 or 536. Its original aim was to reconcile Chalcedonians and Monophysites in order to ensure doctrinal unity and consequent political harmony within the empire. Justinian inserted the troparion into the Byzantine liturgy, and from there it passed into the Monophysite rite of the Syrian Jacobites. In 1912, Dom J. Puyade attempted to refute this traditional view by comparing the language and thought of the *Monogenēs* with quotations drawn from extant writings of the Monophysite patriarch Severus of Antioch (d. 538).[19] Close parallels between the two sources, together with the fact that the Syriac liturgy explicitly attributes the *Monogenēs* to Severus, convinced Dom Puyade that the hymn had actually been composed by Severus around the beginning of the sixth century and was only subsequently adopted by the Byzantine rite.[20] On this theory, the *Monogenēs* is a Monophysite composition that by inference (one not explicitly made by Puyade) stands in the Byzantine liturgy as a foreign element, inserted as much for political as for theological reasons.

In defense of Justinian authorship, V. Grumel published

[18]C. de Boor, *Theophanis Chronographia* I, Leipzig, 1883, 6028f (PG 108, 477b).

[19]"Le Tropaire *Ho Monogenēs,*" *Revue de l'Orient chrétien,* t. 17, 1912, p. 253-258.

[20]Phrases of the *Mon.* that struck Puyade as specifically Monophysite include a) "immortal" as the antithesis of "mortal," b) the incarnational expressions *sarkothēnai* and *enanthropēsas,* c) the accent upon *atreptōs* "without change," and d) the anti-Nestorian formula "One of the Holy Trinity." While each of these expressions is to be found in Severus' writings, the question remains whether they are specifically and exclusively Monophysite.

an article in 1923, in which he showed that the *Monogenēs* is in fact a concise summary of the christology of the "emperor-theologian."[21] In terms of language and thought, the hymn reproduces formulas that appear throughout Justinian's writings, particularly in his *Confessio rectae fidei*. In addition, Grumel demonstrated that the date of composition could hardly have been prior to 519, and that in 536 it had already found its way into both the Byzantine and Syrian liturgies. The key phrase, in Grumel's view, is the affirmation that the Son is "One of the Holy Trinity." Justinian inscribed this formula into the law of the empire (the *Chronicum paschale* of 15 March 533) as well as into the Church's eucharistic liturgy. His chief motive, once again, was to unify the empire by ensuring confessional unity between the two major parties, Chalcedonian and Monophysite. In theory, the emperor's initiative should have succeeded. By affirming the Son to be "One of the Holy Trinity" who fully shares the glory of the Father and the Spirit, the *Monogenēs* denies a Nestorian dualism between the historical Jesus and the eternal Word.

It also stands in agreement with the Cyrillian theopaschite formula, with which both Severus and the Fifth Ecumenical Council would agree: "One of the Trinity was crucified according to the flesh" (originally put forward by Patriach Proclus [434-446/7] in his *Fourth Epistle*). Anathema 10 of the council declared: "If anyone does not confess that our Lord Jesus Christ, who was crucified in the flesh, is true God and the Lord of glory and one of the Holy Trinity: let him be anathema." Insofar as St Cyril's controversial formula μία φύσις Θεοῦ λόγου σεσαρκωμένη is interpreted according to anathema 8 (by φύσις Cyril was understood to mean ὑπόστασις), there is no conflict between Chalcedonian orthodoxy and the "moderate monophysitism" of Severus.[22]

---

[21]"L'auteur et la date de composition du Tropaire Ho Monogenēs," in *Echos d'Orient*, t. 22, Oct-Dec 1923, p. 398-418.

[22]In fact, a clear distinction should be drawn between the modalistic monarchianism ("patripassianism") of Sabellius in the third century and the "theopaschism" promoted in 519 at Constantinople by John Maxentius and a group of Scythian monks. Both Justinian and even the antimonophysite Leonitus of Byzantium upheld the "theopaschites" in their use of the formula

The theopaschite formula should in fact have served as the basis for reconciliation, since it defends the crucial truth that only a person—and not a "nature" or "flesh"—can be born, suffer, die and be resurrected. And the *Monogenēs* unambiguously affirms this truth.

History records, of course, that reconciliation did not come about and that Severus was excommunicated by the Constantinopolitan Synod of 536. Only recently have theological discussions confirmed that the centuries-old division between Orthodox and "Monophysite" Christians (so-called Eastern and Oriental Orthodox) is due more to the ambiguities of theological language than to substantial difference of faith.

While it seems certain that Justinian inserted the *Monogenēs* into the Byzantine liturgy in or before 536, no existing record stipulates at what point it was to be sung. Juan Mateos notes that by the ninth century it was attached to the antiphons of the Liturgy of the Catechumens.[23] If we can judge from existing rites, the *Monogenēs* was originally intended to be an entrance hymn for dominical celebrations. It normally followed the third antiphon (Ps 94) and, in Monophysite rites, preceded the so-called "christological Trisagion." In this latter context, the *Monogenēs* and the Trisagion together formed a choral celebration of the crucified and exalted Son, the divine Word of God.[24]

"one of the Trinity was crucified." For the relevant literature on the theopaschite controversy, see O. Bardenhewer, *Geschichte der Altkirchlichen Literatur* (Freiburg im Breisgau 1924) 4:202, 299f. Fr John Meyendorff discusses the entire problem in his *Christ in Eastern Christian Thought* (Crestwood, N.Y.: SVS Press, 1975) 69-89. An interesting and important confirmation of the fact that the Chalcedonians and monophysites of Severus' school shared common ground in essential matters is to be found in *Does Chalcedon Divide or Unite?* (Geneva: WCC, 1981). See also Meyendorff, *Byzantine Theology* (New York: Fordham University Press, 1974) 35: "in joining the Orthodox Church, the Monophysites were not required to reject anything of Cyrillian theology, but only to admit that Chalcedon was not a Nestorian council."

[23]*La Célébration de la Parole dans la Liturgie Byzantine,* O.C.A. 191, Rome 1971, p. 50-52.

[24]In the 10th cent. Typicon of the Great Church (J. Mateos, *Le Typicon de la Grande Eglise,* Rome 1962-63), the *Mon.* is prescribed as the hymn of the Lesser Entrance, following the third antiphon. For its similar position in other major liturgies, see F. E. Brightman, *Liturgies Eastern and Western,*

Since the eleventh century, the *Monogenēs* has been sung
as a *perisse* or "appendix" to the second antiphon (Ps 92) of
the Byzantine liturgy.[25] Its only other occurrence is at the office
of the Typica, where it is sung after the second psalm (Ps
145) just before the Beatitudes. This order clearly reflects
that of the Liturgy. The Typica developed as an *obednitsa*
or brief office that replaced the eucharist celebration and is
therefore secondary in relation to the Liturgy itself.[26]

The function of the *Monogenēs* in the Liturgy of the
Catechumens is the same as that of the Nicene Creed in the
Liturgy of the Faithful. The one precedes the Lesser Entrance;
the other follows the Great Entrance and prepares for the
Anaphora or eucharistic Canon. Each is a concise statement
of the Church's belief in the redemptive work of the incarnate,
crucified and glorified Son of God. Each summarizes in confessional form the central message of Holy Scripture. And as
a true symbol of faith, each confession enables the community
to reactualize and to participate in the saving events that it
proclaims.

III.

Is the *Monogenēs* a "legitimate" expression of Christian

vol I, "Eastern Liturgies," Oxford 1896: the Greek Liturgy of St James (p.
33), where it is followed by the Great Litany; the Liturgy of St Mark (p.
116f), where it is followed by the Trisagion; and the Armenian rite (p. 421),
where it is followed by a similar confessional formula. In the Liturgy of
the Syrian Jacobites, the *Mon.* is followed immediately by the "christological
Trisagion" of Peter the Fuller: "Holy art thou, o God/Holy, o mighty/Holy,
o immortal who was crucified for us/Have mercy upon us."

[25]The reasons for its transfer, and the replacement of the *Mon.* by the
troparion "Save us, O Son of God," are discussed by Mateos, *Célébration*,
p. 52-54. Curiously, N. Cabasilas makes no reference to the *Mon.* in his 14th
cent. *Interpretation of the Divine Liturgy*. In his explanation of the first
antiphon, he speaks of a "hymn" that glorifies the Father and the Son
through "the self-emptying of the Son, His poverty, His works and His
suffering in the flesh." (*Sources Chrétiennes* 4 bis, p. 133 and note). This is
usually understood to refer to the antiphon itself (Ps. 91); but the explanation, based upon Phil 2:6-11, is far more appropriate to the *Mon.* than to
the Psalm. There seems, however, to be no firm basis for assuming that the
Mon. was ever attached to the first antiphon.

[26]See *La Prière des Heures* (Horologion), ed. Chevetogne, 1975, p. 325-
329.

belief? Such a question might strike some Orthodox faithful as impertinent or even blasphemous. Yet we are obliged to respect the axiom stated above, that every authentic symbol of faith must conform to the teachings of Scripture. Doctrinal interpretation of the biblical witness can lead to a new and deeper understanding of revealed truth. It can express that truth in new and more precise language. Holy Scripture alone, however, remains canonical or normative for determining the content of Church Tradition. When Jesus announced to His disciples that the Spirit of Truth would "lead them into all the truth" (Jn 16:13), He was not speaking of "new revelation," the communication of new doctrines. The Spirit "will not speak on His own authority," but He will speak only what He hears from the Son, the glorified Word. This only will He communicate to the Church: in new language and in developed form, but with complete faithfulness to the original revelation of divine truth communicated by Jesus Himself.

We have already noted the political motives behind Justinian's promulgation of the *Monogenēs*, and it is well known that similar impulses guided Constantine and the Fathers of the First Ecumenical Council in elaborating the original Nicene Creed. Do such motives invalidate these confessional statements? The answer is obviously that they do not, for the inspirational power of the Spirit transcends and transforms even the sinful acts and intentions of His human agents. Yet the question remains: to what degree is the *Monogenēs* an authentic witness to biblical revelation? If certain scholars can attribute its authorship to the Monophysite Severus, does it truly reflect the theological convictions of the Chalcedonian Fathers? Is it, in other words, a genuinely "Orthodox" creed? And if so, does it betray the Orthodox as being "crypto-Monophysite," as they have often been called?[27] To answer this question, we shall have to look more closely at the hymn

[27]G. Dix, *The Shape of the Liturgy*, London, 1945, p. 450, asserts that Justinian composed the *Mon.* at the close of his "pro-Monophysite" period. He continues to affirm, in contradiction to the facts, that "the Monophysite rites of Syria and Egypt do not contain this hymn" because "the Syrians and Egyptians soon came to execrate him (Justinian) as the incarnation of Byzantinism." To the contrary, for the *Mon.* in the Syrian rite, see Brightman, *op cit*, p. 33, 77; and in the Egyptian Liturgy of St Mark, p. 116f.

itself, paying particular attention to the relationship between its poetic structure and its doctrinal content.

Brightman divides the troparion into ten lines, alternately long and short.[28] While this arrangement provides symmetry, it tends to obscure its various doctrinal components. Two slight changes in Brightman's text give us the following versification.

```
1        Ὁ μονογενὴς Υἱὸς καὶ Λόγος τοῦ Θεοῦ
2                  ἀθάνατος ὑπάρχων
3 καταδεξάμενος διὰ τὴν ἡμετέραν σωτηρίαν σαρκωθῆναι
4    ἐκ τῆς ἁγίας θεοτόκου καὶ ἀειπαρθένου Μαρίας,
5      ἀτρέπτως ἐνανθρωπήσας σταυρωθείς τε
6      Χριστὲ ὁ Θεὸς θανάτῳ θάνατον πατήσας
7             εἰς ὢν τῆς ἁγίας Τριάδος
8  συνδοξαζόμενος τῷ Πατρὶ καὶ τῷ ἁγίῳ Πνεύματι
9                  σῶσον ἡμᾶς
```

```
1        Only-Begotten Son and Word of God
2              Thou who art immortal,
3 Who condescended for our salvation to become incarnate
4    Of the holy God-Bearer and Ever-Virgin Mary,
5   Who without change became man and was crucified,
6        O Christ God, destroying death by death,
7        Thou who art one of the Holy Trinity,
8 Glorified together with the Father and the Holy Spirit,
9                  Save us!
```

A striking resemblance exists between the *Monogenēs* and the well-known Christ-hymn of Philippians 2:6-11. The oldest extant Christian liturgical pericope, this hymn was probably composed within a decade of the crucifixion. While it may stem from the hand of St Paul himself, it is clearly an independent element that the Apostle has inserted into his letter to the church at Philippi. In so doing, he has altered the original meaning and purpose of the hymn by transforming it from a primitive christological statement into a parenetic illustration of humble obedience.[29]

---

[28]*Op cit,* p. 116f, 365f; cf. p. 33, where he reproduces it in prose form with commas.

[29]In addition to the critical commentaries on Phil., see also R. Martin,

Of all New Testament christological formulas, the Philippians hymn has exercised the greatest influence upon the structure of the Church's confessions of faith. Both the Old Roman Creed (R) and the Nicene Creeds (N and C) adopt its basic form, while developing one or another of its central affirmations concerning the redemptive work of Christ.[30] In the case of the *Monogenēs,* the internal movement is identical to that of the Pauline hymn. The most important differences occur where the *Monogenēs* uses stereotyped formulas of the post-apostolic Church that attempt to define with greater precision than Philippians 2 the person of Christ and the means by which He accomplished His divine mission.

The structural relationship between the two hymns can be summarized as follows: Each begins with a statement of Christ's eternal, divine status, and continues with 1) His voluntary abasement: descent, incarnation and crucifixion for our salvation; 2) His victory over death and consequent exaltation; and 3) His glorification as God.

With regard to the person of Christ, both hymns clearly affirm His divine nature or condition.[31] The Philippians hymn begins by recalling that Jesus Christ was in "the form of God" (ἐν μορφῇ Θεοῦ ὑπάρχων), an expression that marks an explicit parallel with His incarnational condition in "the form of a servant" (μορφὴν δούλου λαβών).[32] However

---

Carmen Christi (Phil. 2:5-11 in recent interpreation and in the setting of early Christian worship), Cambridge, 1967; and A. Feuillet, *Christologie paulinienne et tradition biblique,* 2e partie, "L'Hymne christologique de l'Epitre aux Phil. (2, 6-11)"; Paris 1973, p. 83-161, with abundant bibliographical references. For a recent Orthodox contribution, see G. Galitis, "The Christological Hymn of the Philippians and the Psalm 109," in *Bulletin of Biblical Studies,* Athens, vol 1, no 2, 1980, p. 86-98 (in Greek).

[30]See the comprehensive study by J. N. D. Kelly, *Creeds, op cit,* chs. 4, 6, 7.

[31]To demonstrate convincingly that the Phil. hymn, and the NT as a whole, affirm the full divinity of Christ would require an exegetical study which is beyond the scope of this chapter. It is important to recall, however, that the question has only been raised in recent times by certain biblical scholars whose hermeneutic presuppositions place them outside of Orthodox-Catholic tradition. See, e.g., R. Bultmann, "The Christological Confession of the World Council of Churches," in *Essays Philosophical and Theological,* London, 1955, p. 273-290.

[32]The only other NT usage of *morphē* is found in Mk 16:12, where Jesus "was manifested in another form" to two of His disciples, an evident summary of the Emmaus encounter of Lk 24. For a discussion of recent

we may interpret the term μορφή, the Pauline hymn clearly proclaims the same message as the prologue of the Gospel of St John: the Word, of eternal divine origin, assumes "flesh," that is, the fulness of human existence, by an act of voluntary self-abasement (ἑαυτὸν ἐκένωσεν, Phil 2:7/ ὁ λόγος σὰρξ ἐγένετο, Jn 1:14; cf. Col 1:22). Obediently identifying Himself with fallen man, He enters into the realm of human existence in order to liberate humanity from the destructive forces of sin and death by the power of His divine life (Phil 2:8f; Jn 1:14; cf. Heb 5:8f). Because of Christ's obedient acquiescence to the divine will for man's salvation, God (the Father) raises Him out of the domain of death and highly exalts him (ὑπερύψωσεν, Ph 2:9) above the created order, so that every creature might praise and worship Him as Kyrios, the Lord. This exaltation to universal Lordship reveals Him to be what He is, was and eternally shall be by virtue of His immutable divine nature: "one with God" (ἴσα Θεῷ, Ph 2:6).

Using different but corresponding language, the *Monogenēs* makes a similar proclamation. Beginning with a firm affirmation of the divinity of Christ, it passes to His self-humiliation and identification with mankind, His victory over death by death, and His subsequent exaltation and glorification as "One of the Holy Trinity." What concerns us particularly are the differences between the troparion and the hymn of Philippians 2. To what degree are these differences justified by other christological statements of the New Testament?

We should note first of all that festal troparia in Orthodox tradition are normally composed in the second rather than the third person. Kerygmatic formulas such as Philippians 2 (cf. Ac 2f; 1 Cor 15:3-5), and confessional symbols such as R and C, are essentially catechetical. Their purpose is to affirm and to transmit the truth, divine revelation, in a form that can be easily committed to memory. The dogmatic liturgical hymns called torparia also have this function. But they include another dimension that gives them a unique value and

attempts to interpret the meaning of "form" in Ph 2, see A. Feuillet, *op cit*, p. 101ff.

importance within the life of the worshiping Church: addressed in the second person, they are essentially *prayers*.[33] As such, they not only affirm the personal and collective faith of the members of the earthly community. More importantly, they unite the praise and supplication of the gathered faithful with that of the Communion of Saints in a universal expression of adoration. In this sense, the *Monogenēs* is a true troparion, a christological statement of Orthodox faith composed in the form of prayer: "Only-Begotten Son and Word of God . . ., save us!"

To what extent, then, does this "confessional prayer" reflect not only the language but also the meaning of the biblical witness?

IV.

The troparion opens with two christological titles, "Only-Begotten Son" and "Word of God." Both titles were taken from the prologue of the Fourth Gospel, where the Logos is described and glorified as being of divine origin. The expression πρὸς τὸν Θεὸν (Jn 1:1f), usually translated "with God," suggests more than mere personal presence or moral orientation. It affirms that the Word participates in the very life of God: He shares both the divine being and the divine will concerning creation and redemption. "The Word was God" is synonymous with "being one with God" as that essential unity is expressed in Philippians 2.[34]

[33]Troparia can be addressed to Christ, to the angelic powers or to the saints, including the Mother of God. In the last example, the saint in question may be directly addressed in a request to pray for the Church, e.g., "O blessed Father Sabbas, pray Christ our God to save our souls" (5 Dec.); "Hail, full of grace, thou Virgin-Mother of God, . . . Rejoice thou also, o righteous Elder (Simeon)" (2 Feb). More often, however, the troparion celebrating a saint is addressed directly to Christ, e.g., "Thy martyr (N.), O Lord, by his struggle, has received from Thee the incorruptible crown . . . Through his entreaties, o Christ our God, save our souls!"

[34]The expression "Word of God," *ho logos tou theou*, is used in the NT to refer to the divine commandments (Mk 7:13), the saving proclamation of the Gospel (Lk 5:1; 8:11, 21), and the Scriptures of the former alliance (Jn 10:35). In the mind of the primitive Church, and in particular the Johannine communities, Christ is the "Word of God" insofar as He reveals and embodies the divine economy of salvation.

The term *monogenēs*, on the other hand, appears as a christological title only in the Gospel and First Epistle to John (Jn 1:14, 18; 3:16, 18; 1 Jn 4:9). Scholars have long argued over the precise meaning of the term as it is applied to Christ. If it stresses "uniqueness," then it should be translated "only Son."[35] It would then simply affirm that Jesus was without siblings. To support this interpretation, exegetes refer to other usages of the term *monogenēs*, found only in Luke (7:12, in reference to the deceased son of the widow of Nain; 8:42, to Jairus' dying daughter; 9:38, to an unidentified man's spirit-possessed son) and in Hebrews (11:17, in reference to Isaac). Closer consideration of these passages, however, reveals another, deeper dimension. The one designated as *monogenēs* has a particular relationship to the parent not only as the uniquely engendered offspring, but also as the *beloved child*. The Septuagint employs *monogenēs* to translate *yahid*, "unique" or "solitary," in Jud 11:34. In Gen 22:2, 12, 16, however, *yahid* is translated by ἀγαπητός, "beloved," in reference to Isaac, the son of Abraham.[36] As Abraham is a type or prophetic image of God the Father, so Isaac, the freely offered, innocent victim, is an image of God the Son. Thus he, like Jesus Himself, can be designated "only son" (ὁ μονογενὴς) or "beloved son" (ὁ ἀγαπητός), the two terms being synonymous (cf. Mk 1:11 and par.).

The qualities "unique" and "beloved," however, do not exhaust the rich meaning of *monogenēs* either in Johannine literature or in the Church's symbols of faith. In Jn 1:14, the incarnate Word, in His condition as *monogenēs*, reflects and reveals the divine glory He has received from the Father. A

[35]In defense of this view, see D. Moody, "God's Only Son," *Journal of Biblical Literature* 72, Dec. 1953, p. 213-219; his art. "Only Begotten," *Interpreter's Dictionary of the Bible* III, 604; and R. Brown, *The Gospel According to John*, I-XII, New York, 1966, p. 13, 17.

[36]Cf. the prophetic oracle of Zach. 12:10, where the people of Israel shall mourn "him whom they have pierced, they shall mourn for him, as one mourns for an only child (*agapēton*)." The early Church took up this messianic prophecy (originally referring to the Suffering Servant?) and applied it to Christ: cf. Jn 19:37; Ac 1:7. See Th. C. De Kruijf, "The Glory of the Only Son (John 1:14)," in *Studies in John*, Leiden 1970, p. 111-123, and esp. p. 121ff, where the author discusses the soteriological significance of *monogenēs* in John.

similar thought is expressed in 1 Jn 4:9—the Father sends "His Son, His *monogenēs*" to "manifest His love." The Son is thus the bearer, the very incarnation of divine love and glory, as He is of divine grace and truth (Jn 1:14). In offering to sacrifice Isaac upon the altar in the wilderness, Abraham demonstrated that his love for God was utterly disinterested. His gesture prophetically announced the love of the Father in offering His own beloved Son upon the altar of Golgotha. Abraham's offering was supreme; for what father would not prefer to die himself rather than witness or, indeed, cause the death of his own son? In the fullest sense, Abraham offered not only Isaac, but also his own life and hope. His sacrifice was a self-offering of love, the most complete and perfect sacrifice that can be made. God demanded such an offering as proof of Abraham's total and perfect devotion. And He did so to prepare His "beloved children" of Israel for a still greater sacrifice of which He Himself would be the author. Because of His ineffable love for the world, God "gave His Son, His Only-Begotten" as a sacrifice of forgiveness and reconciliation, offered to those who, through faith, seek adoption as "sons" or "children" of God.[37]

Are we justified, however, in rendering *monogenēs* as "only-begotten"? Although many interpreters reject this translation,[38] it nonetheless seems warranted by the Johannine emphasis upon the *pre-existence* of Christ. In Jn 8:58, Jesus makes the paradoxical affirmation, "before Abraham was, I AM." The principal accent here is upon the expression "I AM" (ἐγὼ εἰμί), which in Ex 3:14 is revealed to be the divine name, the name of God. The pre-existent Son, who bears that divine name (Jn: "I AM"/Phil.: KYRIOS), is designated *monogenēs*. Yet His uniqueness is not merely num-

[37]Jn 3:16; 1:12 *tekna theou*. In Johannine writings the term *huios* is restricted to Jesus Christ as a further affirmation of His uniquely divine status as "only-begotten Son." On the other hand, Jn uses the verb *gennaō* in reference to all of God's (human) children (1:13; 3:3; 3:5-8; I Jn 2:29; etc.), while St Paul refers to Christians as *huioi theou* (Rom 8:14, 19; Gal 4:6) adopted through baptism (Gal 3:26f). To both Paul and John, adoption as children of God occurs by means of an act of divine engendering (*gennethēnai anōthen*, Jn 3:7) accomplished by the sacrament of baptism.

[38]Cf. e.g., D. Moody, who argues against the rendering of the King James Version, "only-begotten"; IDB III, 604.

erical; it is qualitative. To use non-biblical language that nevertheless captures the Johannine nuances of the term, the title *monogenēs* expresses a *relationship of ontological identity* between the Father and the Son.[39]

By selecting this title to begin his christological symbol, Justinian remained faithful not only to the New Testament witness, but also to the Church's confession of essential identity (*homoousios*) between the Father and the Son.[40] His hymn proclaims at its outset the divine condition of the Son,

[39]In classical Greek usage, *genei huios* designates a son by birth as opposed to an adopted son. The *genos eklekton* of I Pet 2:9 (cf. Isa 43:20f), usually translated "chosen race," also suggests "birth," those "born of God." As in Jn 3, the underlying thought is that of baptismal rebirth: "regeneration from above." Despite Moody's arguments, *arts cit,* the term *"mono-genēs"* clearly expresses the "generation" of the Son from the Father. In the Nicene Creed (N), the term *monogenē* is synonymous with the preceding formula *gennēthenta ek tou patros.* See also Kittel, TWNT IV, p. 748-750; and the commentary on the Fourth Gospel by H. Strathmann, NTD (Göttingen) 1963, p. 39, who correctly maintains that *monogenēs* in Joh 1:18 designates Jesus' divine being: "Bei Johannes meint der Ausdruck eine metaphysische Wesensbezeichnung jenseits oder oberhalb aller irdischen Geschichte. Es bezeichnet also das gottheitliche Wesen Jesu."

[40]A similar doctrinal concern governed the usage of the title *monogenēs* throughout the early Church's history. Apart from the Johannine writings (or quotations: e.g., Ep ad Diognet 10), the term is rarely found before the end of the 2nd cent. (Justin, dial 105; Martyr Poly 20:2). Around 180, St Irenaeus takes it up again and wields it as a polemical weapon against gnostic subordinationism (adv haer III.16.1). In the gnostic system of Valentinus, "incarnation" evaporates in a haze of metaphysical speculation. There the divine emmanation *Monogenēs* (also called "the Father") is clearly subordinate to the supreme deity *Bythos.* Mon. alone has knowledge of *Bythos* and he alone can reveal him to the other aeons (cf. Jn 1:18). See R. McL. Wilson, *The Gnostic Problem,* London 1958, p. 128f, 150. Against such speculation Irenaeus insists that the *Mon.* is ontologically identical with the historical person of Jesus. The *Mon.* is not only pre-existent; He assumes human nature through His Incarnation, without in any way abandoning the divine essence. In the language of Nicea, He remains eternally *homoousios* with the Father, language that faithfully reflects NT christology. As in the Fourth Gospel, so in the theology of the Greek Fathers the term *monogenēs* could serve as a confessional symbol to express the relationship not only of love but also of *identical essence* between the First and Second Persons of the Holy Trinity: the Father is eternally "unbegotten," while the Son is eternally and uniquely "begotten," *monogenēs.* Cf. Gregory Naz., Theological Discourse III.2 (*Sources Chrétiennes* 250, Paris 1978, p. 180f): "The Father is the Begetter and the Emitter (*gennetor kai probleus*); without passion of course, and without reference to time; and not in a corporal manner. The Son is the Begotten (*gennēma*) and the Holy Spirit the Emission (*problēma*)." (tr. NPNF vol. VII, p. 301).

affirming with John 1:18, that He who reveals God to the world is Himself no less than God (μονογενὴς Θεός).[41]

V.

Following the initial christological titles, the troparion makes a series of statements concerning the nature, the means and the purpose of the incarnation. In the first of these, the Son and Word of God is declared to be "immortal." The expression does not appear in the New Testament. There we find only the noun "immortality" (ἀθανασία), attributed to the transfigured resurrection body in 1 Cor 15:53f, and to God (the Father) in the doxology of 1 Tim 6:16. In this latter case, God is described as "Lord of lords, who alone possesses immortality, who dwells in inaccessible light." In the context of the chapter, a clear distinction seems to be drawn between God and "our Lord Jesus Christ" whom God will "make manifest at an appointed time" (6:14f). It is true that the New Testament does not explicitly affirm ontological identity between the Father and the Son. Yet as St Athanasius maintained, such an identity is clearly presupposed by the biblical writers, despite the absence of metaphysical language in their writings.[42]

Apart from statements ascribed to Jesus Himself,[43] christological hymns such as Phil 2, Col 1:15-20 and 1 Tim 3:16 declare that the Son is able to reveal the Father because He, the Son, partakes fully of the divine glory. In 1 Tim 6:14, Jesus Christ bears the title "Lord" (cf. Phil 2:9-11), which, as we have seen, is the Name of God in the Septuagint. If 1 Tim declares that God dwells in "inaccessible light," elsewhere Jesus is expressly identified with the light, the divine

[41]Against Büchsel (TWNT, art cit, p. 748, n. 14), the RSV and many modern translations, the most recent critical editions of the NT prefer the reading *mon. theos* to *mon. huios* (Nestle, ed. 25, 26; Aland-Black). This reading is preferable on the basis of manuscript evidence and as the more difficult variant. Its parallel with the preceding phrase accords well with Johannine thought: no one can come to the Father except through the Son, for only God can reveal God to men.

[42]Athanasius, de decret Nic syn 21 (PG 25.453).

[43]Jn 10:30; 14:9; 17:11, 22; cf. 5:18f.

glory from the Father that enlightens the world (Jn 1:4-9; 8:12; etc.). Certainly it would be anachronistic to read into the biblical passage metaphysical concepts developed during the christological controversies of the fourth century. It would be equally false, however, to maintain that the identity between the Father and the Son, as it is affirmed in the New Testament, refers only to a moral unity, a mere identity of purpose or will. If the divine Name is bestowed upon the exalted Christ, it is because He shares fully in the divine life. His essence is divine essence. Attributes proper to the Father, such as Light, Glory, and Immortality, are thus equally proper to the Son.

Of immortal divine nature (Ph 2:6), Christ assumes or "recapitulates" the human nature of Adam, the "former man" (Eph 1:10; cf. Rom 5:15-19). By submitting to a voluntary death upon the Cross, He enters freely into the domain of death to liberate those held in captivity.[44] By the power of His Resurrection, He overwhelms death ("by death He tramples down death," θανάτῳ θάνατον πατήσας) and raises baptized humanity with Himself (cf. 1 Pet 3:21), conferring upon mortal man the gift of His own immortality (Jn 5:24; Rom 6:3-11; Col 1:13).

The closest parallel between the troparion *Monogenēs* and the hymn of Phil 2 is to be found in this affirmation of the voluntary abasement of the divine Son to liberate man from death. This holds true despite the fact that the Philippians hymn does not explicitly state the motive behind Jesus' "kenosis" (ἑαυτὸν ἐκένωσεν, 2:7—lit. "He emptied Himself" of all divine prerogatives and power, in full acceptance of the conditions of human existence).[45] For the hymn focuses

---

[44]Christ is raised *ek nekrōn*: not "from death" only, but "from the realm of the dead," Ac 3:15; Rom 4:24 et passim; cf. the confessional phrase *descendit ad infera (inferos)* of R, based upon I Pet 3:19f.

[45]J. Jeremias' argument (TWNT V, art. *pais theou;* "Zu Phil. 2:7," in *Novum Testamentum* IV, 1963, p. 182-188), that *ekenōsen* refers not to the incarnation but to the crucifixion, cannot be accepted. *Ekenōsen* is a global term that expresses Christ's relinquishment of divine power and prerogative to assume the conditions of human existence including mortality (the consequences of the Fall). To express the utter humility of Christ in assuming the most shameful of deaths, Phil 2 uses the term *etapeinōsen eauton*. The parallel between the two expressions (*eauton ekenōsen/etapeinōsen eauton*)

upon the divine humility that leads to exaltation. Its purpose is to depict the obedience and glorification of the Suffering Servant, rather than to proclaim the particular benefits of Christ's death on behalf of mankind. Implicitly, however, it accords fully with the rest of the New Testament and with the *Monogenēs* in affirming that the Son of God deigned for our salvation to become incarnate, to suffer upon the Cross, and to vanquish both the power and the consequences of death by His own innocent death. In the words of the Orthodox Easter troparion: "Christ is risen from the dead/By His death He has trampled down death/And to those in the tombs He has given life."[46]

This act of condescension and personal abasement (ἑαυ-τὸν ἐκένωσεν/καταδεξάμενος) is a divine act that can be assumed only by Him who, by His very nature, is God. This "ontological imperative"—the necessity that He who assumes and glorifies our humanity be Himself divine—explains and justifies the non-biblical references in the *Monogenēs* to the *Theotokos*, the Mother of God and Ever-Virgin Mary.

VI.

At the beginning of the troparion, Jesus is designated by two christological titles, the "Only-Begotten Son" and "Word of God." Similarly, His Mother is qualified by two adjectives, "God-bearing" and "ever-virgin," that in the course of fifth-century christological controversies crystalized into

is intentional. It affirms that by His Incarnation "unto death upon the Cross," Christ identifies fully with the fallen human condition: "If I descend to Sheol, Thou art there!" (Ps 138:8, LXX).

[46]Based upon affirmations of Christ's resurrection *ek nekrōn* and passages such as I Cor 15:54-57; Heb 2:14f; and II Tim 1:10, the Church Fathers incorporated into their teaching the antinomy "destroying death (or trampling down death) by death." In the middle of the 4th cent., Cyril of Jerusalem proclaimed, "Christ has overthrown (the power of Satan), having partaken with me of flesh and blood, that through these He might destroy death by death (*katargēsei thanatō ton thanaton*, Myst Cat I:4). When Justinian incorporated the phrase into the *Mon.*, it had become a common theological and liturgical formula. For the patristic references, see G. W. H. Lampe, *A Patristic Greek Lexicon*, Oxford 1961, p. 611f.

fixed mariological titles: "Mother of God" and "Ever-Virgin" (θεοτόκος/ἀειπάρθενος).

The Virgin Birth of our Lord is explicitly attested in Mt 1 and Lk 1.[47] St Paul presupposes the tradition in Gal 4:4: "In the fullness of time, God sent His Son, born of a woman. . . ." Here the correspondence between "Son of God" and "born of a woman" expressly affirms the unique, divine origin of Mary's child. The pre-existent Son[48] enters into human history to destroy the "powers of this world" (Gal 4:2; cf. Col 2:8). Renouncing force, He accomplishes His mission through humility. As the eternal, divine Son, He "assumes flesh": He becomes a man among men, accepting fully the condition and consequences of fallen human existence. His Incarnation is real and complete. The Son of God, He is equally the Son of Mary. For only by being "born of a woman" (not ἐν, but ἐκ γυναικὸς) can He enter unconditionally into human life. Only thus can He "recapitulate" humanity (St Irenaeus) and bestow upon those created in the image of God the gift of divine sonship (Gal 4:5).

The title *Theotokos,* used since at least the time of Origen,[49] is essentially a *christological* affirmation. God in the hypostasis of the Son has indeed "assumed flesh" (Jn 1:14), which signifies the whole of human nature.[50] The incarnational term ἐκένωσεν of Phil 2:7 thus finds its equivalents in σάρξ ἐγένετο and ἐσκήνωσεν ἐν ἡμῖν of Jn 1:14, ἐν ἡμῖν meaning not only "among" but "with" us, in the sense of a full *participation* in human life and destiny.

The title *Theotokos* was officially adopted by the Council of Ephesus in 431 and was reconfirmed at Chalcedon twenty years later. Its chief advocate, Cyril of Alexandria, defended its use as an unambiguous affirmation that "the Word is united hypostatically [καθ᾽ ὑπόστασιν] to the flesh."[51] In the lan-

---

[47]Only Mt has been shaped by the problematic LXX rendering of *'almah* (young girl, young woman) by *parthenos* (virgin) in Isa 7:14. The correct translation of *'almah* is *neanis,* "maiden," whether single or newly married.

[48]Cf. Rom 1:3f; 8:3, 29, 32; I Cor 8:6; II Cor 8:9; Ph 2:6; Col 1:13-16.

[49]Socrates, *hist eccl* VII:32.

[50]See J. Meyendorff, *Christ in Eastern Christian Thought,* SVP, New York 1975, p. 21-22.

[51]Ep. 17, second of twelve anathemas against Nestorius, who preferred

guage of Chalcedon, Christ was and remains eternally "of
two natures" (ἐν δύο φύσεσιν), fully God and fully man,
and thus He was able to unite human nature to His divinity.
Only such an ontological, hypostatic identification between God
and man, between divine and human existence, could bring
about the redemption of the children of God. For, in the
words of St Gregory of Nazianzus, "what is not assumed is
not healed; but what is united to God is saved."[52]

To the Eastern Church Fathers, the biblical witness to
Christ as the pre-existent Son of God, who became incarnate
in the person of Mary, justifies and, indeed, necessitates the
use of the title *Theotokos*. To refuse Mary honor and venera-
tion as "Mother of God" is tantamount to denying the reality
of both the Incarnation and our salvation.

Is it equally necessary to affirm Mary's perpetual virginity?
While the New Testament clearly states that Mary conceived
Jesus "without human seed," the infancy narratives focus
attention upon the supernatural character of her conception
rather than upon her virginity as such.[53] And they nowhere
suggest that her virgin state remained intact during the birth
and throughout her later life.[54]

If Orthodox theology is adamant in its defense of the
perpetual virginity of Mary, it is due rather to the necessity
of the doctrine imposed by the logic of the Incarnation. St

the title *Christotokos*. (See J. N. D. Kelly, *Early Christian Doctrines*, London
1960, p. 324; J. Meyendorff, *op cit* p. 18-22, 30f.)

[52]Ep. 101 ad Cleodonium (PG 37.181c-184a); J. Meyendorff, *op cit*, p. 15.

[53]The oldest extra-canonical reference to the Virgin Birth is found in
Ignatius' letters to the Ephesians (19:1) and Smyrniotes (1:1), written
around A.D. 110. In the former he speaks of the virginity of Mary, together
with the birth and death of the Lord, as three mysteries accomplished "in
the silence of God." On the question of biblical and extra-canonical evidence
for the Virgin Birth, see R. Brown, *The Virginal Conception and Bodily
Resurrection of Jesus*, New York 1973, p. 47ff.

[54]Many exegetes see contrary evidence in references to Jesus' "brothers"
(e.g., Mk 3:32 par.). The Protogospel of James, a mid-second century
panygeric of Mary, is the oldest extant work that teaches her perpetual
virginity. There Joseph is portrayed as an elderly man and Jesus' "brothers"
as Joseph's children by a former marriage. St Jerome rejected this view on the
theory that the *adelphoi* were in fact Jesus' cousins. Textual and linguistic
evidence of the New Testament is inconclusive.

Athanasius, who was apparently the first to link the two titles *theotokos* and *aeiparthenos*,[55] explains it in these terms: "[Jesus Christ] takes [assumes] our body, and not only so, but He takes it from a sinless and spotless Virgin, who knew no man; a body pure and free from human intercourse."[56] This is not, as it has often been taken to be, a condemnation of human sexuality inspired by monastic asceticism. Virginity is honored as the ideal state by St Paul as well as by the later Church, not because sexual relations are inherently sinful, but because the virgin state reflects human perfection before the Fall and after the final Resurrection.

By her divine conception, Mary becomes the mediatrix between God and man. In her person and from her flesh the Son of God unites our humanity to His divinity. "The holy Virgin," declares St John of Damascus, "gave birth not to a mere man, but to Him who is truly God; not naked, but clothed with flesh; not as a body descended from heaven and passing through her as through a conduit, but taking from her [ἐξ αὐτῆς] flesh of the same nature as our own."[57] This hypostatic union of divine and human "flesh"—which signifies the whole of personal existence[58]—is the essential condition of our redemption. Reconciliation between God and man is not merely a juridicial affair, as certain currents of Protestant theology have often affirmed. The "righteousness of God" (δικαιοσύνη) does not mean that God simply pronounces man innocent despite his enduring condition of sinfulness. "Justification" in the Pauline sense includes an ontological dimension: "For our sake He [the Father] made Him [the Son] to be sin [ἀμαρτία ἐποίησεν] who knew no sin, so that in Him we might become the righteousness of God" (2 Cor 5:21, RSV). If Christ "takes away the sin of the world" (Jn 1:29), it is because He has entered into the realm

---

[55]Exp Ps 84:11 (PG 27.373a).

[56]De incarnatione 8:3. Greek text: F. L. Cross, London 1939/1963.

[57]De fide orth XII; cf. G. Florovsky, "The Ever-Virgin Mother," in *The Mother of God*, London 1949/1959, p. 54.

[58]Cf. St Augustine: "The meaning of the Word being made flesh, is not that the divine nature was changed into flesh, but that the divine nature assumed our flesh. And by 'flesh,' we are here to understand 'man' . . ." (Enchiridion XXXIV, in W. J. Oates, *Basic Writings of St Augustine*, vol I, p. 678; New York, 1948.

of sin; He has "become sin," in order to transform sinful humanity into His divinity that knows no sin. In patristic language, "God became man [ἐνηνθρώπησεν] so that we might be made divine [θεοποιηθῶμεν]."[59] This participation of God in human life is, once again, a real "fleshly" participation. He has assumed human nature as a whole. And He has done so in the only way ontologically possible: by taking human flesh in the womb of a woman. It was no ordinary man that Mary conceived and bore; it was and is God Himself, the fullness of divine life, in whom dwelt "the fullness of the Godhead bodily" (Col 2:9). She, a simple adolescent, uninstructed in the formal sense and subject to temptation and the consequences of sin, is nevertheless "full of grace," beloved and chosen by the Father to bear "this little child, the eternal God" (Kontakion, Feast of the Nativity).

While the New Testament remains silent in this regard, the later Church knows and venerates Mary as Ever-Virgin because of the miracle of the Incarnation that was accomplished in and through her person. To her, the Savior is also a Son. She has imparted to Him her humanity; and the Church confesses that He has communicated to her His divinity, a communication realized as a consequence of her Dormition. Yet already within her womb there occurred a veritable *perichōrēsis,* a "circumincession" or inter-penetration of natures, human and divine. While Mary remained a human person in the full sense of the term, her *fiat* signified a choice, freely made, to devote herself entirely and uniquely to her Lord and her God. This divinely inspired self-offering is symbolized by the Gospel reading selected for most feasts dedicated to the Mother of God: Luke 10:38-42; 11:27-28. Like Mary of Bethany, the mother of Jesus seeks "the good portion," which means total devotion to the Word of God. Such devotion is expressed by the body as well as by the mind. It is above all an attitude of the heart that seeks nothing other than to "please the Lord" (1 Co 7:32). "Virginity," affirms Fr Georges Florovsky, "is not simply a bodily status or a physical feature as such. Above all it is a spiritual

[59]St Athanasius, De incarnatione 54:3.

and inner attitude," acquired by *apatheia,* freedom from lustful desires.[60] By grace, every passion can be transformed into "a-patheia," which means not a lack of feeling and emotion, but rather a pure love and an ardent longing for God and for God alone. It is the recognition of this pure and ardent devotion of the Mother of God toward her Son and Lord that leads the Church to affirm with St John of Damascus, "In mind and soul and body, Mary remains ever-virgin [ἀειπαρθενεύουσαν]."[61]

Although the titles Theotokos and Ever-Virgin are absent from the New Testament, they are by no means foreign to its witness. Strict application of the principle *sola scriptura* would eliminate them as unjustifiable extrapolations of the biblical evidence. Orthodox Marian doctrine, however, belongs to the very essence of the Church's faith because it is founded upon experience. In its celebration of feasts dedicated to Mary, and in its awareness of her perpetual protection and intercession, the community of believers knows and proclaims her to be the ἀειπαρθενομήτηρ, the Ever-Virgin Mother of God.

VII.

On the basis of this ecclesial experience, the *Monogenēs* proclaims that the immortal Son and Word of God deigned to assume human life in order to save man from death. Taking flesh from His Virgin Mother, He "loved His own to the very end" (Jn 13:1), fulfilling His voluntary abasement by a scandalous and agonizing death upon the Cross. The consequence of His death is the defeat of Death itself. Redemption is accomplished, fallen Adam is raised to new and eternal life by the power of His Resurrection, and He Himself is glorified by all creation as "One of the Holy Trinity."

The *Monogenēs* concludes with a cry from the heart: "Save us!" The risen and exalted Lord is both God and Savior. Yet He remains forever ὁ ἐσταυρωμένος, "the

---

[60]G. Florovsky, *op cit,* p. 60-61.
[61]Hom 6:5 (PG 96.668c).

crucified One" (Mk 16:6). As God, He enters again and again into the darkness of human existence, penetrating to the very depths of hell, in order to release every Adam from the consequences of sin and death. But only because He is, was, and forever shall be: God. The Church never ceases to affirm the "ontological necessity" of His divinity. "If Christ is not risen from the dead," St Paul reminds us, "we are the most pitiful of all men" (1 Cor 15:12-19). And if Christ is not God, we must add, then we have no share in divine life. The *Monogenēs* recognizes this imperative and expresses it with a term foreign to the hymn of Philippians 2 and to the New Testament as a whole: ἀτρέπτως, "without change."

"*Without change* you became man and were crucified, O Christ God, destroying death by death . . ." Does this unequivocal declaration of Christ's perfect and eternal divinity render the *Monogenēs*—and the whole of Orthodox christology—"crypto-Monophysite"? Or does it rather bear witness to an essential truth that in recent years has often been distorted and denied?

The gravest doctrinal danger of our day—and the most serious obstacle in the way of confessional unity—is precisely the denial, explicit or implicit, of the divinity of our Lord. By depicting Jesus as a prophet, as an example of moral rectitude or as a political liberator, contemporary theological trends distort not only His image but the very image of God. The Divinity has revealed itself to be a Trinity of Persons who act in concert for the salvation of man and creation. For this reason, Orthodox confessions of faith must unceasingly and unequivocally glorify the Son as "One of the Holy Trinity." During the period of His earthly life His words were prophetic and His comportment exemplary. Without question, His mission was to liberate mankind: from injustice, poverty and oppression; but also and especially, from the spiritual death that man brings upon himself. And this He could accomplish only because He is and forever shall be both Lord and God.

If Orthodox symbols of faith remain inflexible in their insistence upon the divinity of Jesus Christ, it is because nothing less than the salvation of the world depends upon that confession. In the liturgical life of the Church, confession of the "truth"—ἀλήθεια, the divine "reality" such as God reveals it to the world—renders possible an immediate and personal participation in that truth. The quest for an "ecumenical" confession of faith is justified only insofar as any new formulation affirms and defends that divinely revealed truth in all its fullness. If such creeds degenerate into ethical maxims, political slogans or reductionist heresies —proclamations of "a different Gospel" than the one announced "from the beginning" (Gal 1:8; 1 Jn 1:1)—then they can no longer be accepted by the Orthodox Church as true "symbols." For then the *sacramental, participative character* of the symbol would be lost, and the "confession" would be nothing more than "winds of doctrine" (Eph 4:14), words devoid of meaning because they no longer correspond to the reality they seek to confess.

The Orthodox Church firmly believes that it is called by God to defend and proclaim the truth of the Gospel as that truth is interpreted and transmitted by Holy Tradition. This conviction explains why Orthodoxy considers the Creed of Nicea-Constantinople to be the most important of all symbols of faith. If changes are to be made in its content, they can be accepted by the Church only insofar as they express with greater depth and clarity that same divinely revealed truth: by declaring the full divinity of the Holy Spirit, for example, or emphasizing God's inexhaustible love as the motive of the divine economy.

Any further statement concerning *man's response* to divine love, however, is not really appropriate to a symbol of faith, even though that response is essential for the salvation of the individual and the mission of the Church in the world. The function of the symbol, in other words, should not be confused with the equally necessary but separate function of *statements of commitment.* It is these latter formulations that should express the fundamental concern of Christian people for social and political justice together with unqualified respect for the rights of man. To confuse the two is to risk obscuring or distorting divine revelation by seeking to create a symbol of faith that is "relevant," one that addresses itself to a limited situation within a particular moment of history, however crucial and urgent that situation might be. As a relative concept, the problem of relevance should be addressed rather by statements of commitment that change with time and circumstance. An authentic symbol of faith, however, articulates absolute, immutable truth. It thus provides the indispensable foundation upon which every affirmation of ethical concern, as well as every concrete proposal for Christian action, should be built.

The troparion *Monogenēs,* perhaps more than the Nicene Creed itself, serves as an ideal model for any attempt to reformulate and reinterpret symbols of faith in the language of today. Composed five hundred years after St Paul addressed his letter to the Christians at Philippi, it complements the christological hymn of Philippians 2 while remaining faithful to holy tradition. Any new confessional statement must do the same, for its sole purpose and justification can only be to proclaim the gospel of Jesus Christ as that gospel is interpreted in the Church by the Holy Spirit. Insofar as it remains faithful to that goal, a symbol of faith becomes for the confessing community a source of life-giving grace. Like the gospel itself, it becomes "the power of God for salvation to all who believe" (Rom 1:16).

CHAPTER VII

The Word as Image: Paschal Iconography

No one could describe the Word of the Father; but when He took flesh from you, O Theotokos, He accepted to be described, and restored the fallen image to its former state by uniting it to divine beauty. (Therefore) we confess and proclaim our salvation in Word and Images.

—Kontakion, tone 8
Sunday of Orthodoxy

I.

As the sacred image of Orthodox tradition, the icon exercises a twofold function in the life of the Christian community: it serves both as a medium of revelation and as a channel of saving grace. Through it, the Word of God comes to expression in form, color and light.

On the one hand, the icon gives dogmatic expression to divine truth; on the other, it communicates that truth to the worshiper by uniting him in faith to the subject it depicts: the incarnate (and therefore visible and representable) Word of God, His Virgin Mother, angelic beings, or the saints. Blessed and sanctified by the power of the Holy Spirit, the icon renders present in the liturgical worship of the Church the archetype that stands behind it. It creates a mystical communion between the image and the believer, between heaven and earth, and thereby it enables the worshiper to participate in transcendent, divine life. It is this latter, grace-transmitting aspect, known in the experience of the Church above all through miracle-working icons, that constitutes the "sacramental" nature of the sacred image.

This dual revelatory, grace-communicating function can be illustrated by comparing the icon to a window. Many interpreters have viewed these painted panels, frescoes or mosaics as hallowed casements that open out upon eternity, revealing to mortal eyes a glimpse of the invisible world and granting to the limited mind an intelligible conception of transcendent reality. Yet a window not only looks out upon a distant horizon. It also permits light to enter and to fill the room, illuminating everything within it. In similar fashion, the icon offers a vision of the divine glory that lies beyond every horizon; and it allows that glory to pass through its inherent transparentness to fill and enlighten the lives of those who pray before it.

This iconographic penetration of divine grace and glory into the created and fallen world is perhaps nowhere more evident than in the several icons that depict the mystery of Easter or Holy Pascha. Pascha is both the event and the celebration of our salvation, accomplished by the self-abasing love of the second Person of the Holy Trinity. Its theme is given eloquent expression in the familiar "Christ-hymn" of Philippians 2:6-11. Retaining His full divinity yet abandoning every claim to divine majesty, the Son assumes in kenotic obedience "the likeness of men, the form of a servant." As the Servant of servants, the Lord of those enslaved by sin and death descends to earth, to take upon Himself the suffering of the lowly and the shameful, agonizing death of the outcast. Descending into the uttermost depths of fallen creation, He bursts asunder by the power of His immortal life the portals of hell that enclose the first and every Adam in the darkness of death. There He banishes the darkness by the splendor of His divine light, and in the brightness of the paschal dawn He reaches out to grasp the outstretched hand of fallen man, raising him with Himself and enabling him to partake of the glory of His divinity.

Thou hast descended into the depths of the earth, O Christ, and hast broken down the eternal portals which imprison those who are held captive; and after three days, like Jonah from the whale, Thou hast risen from the tomb.

O my Savior, who as God hast offered Thyself of Thine own will to the Father as a living and unslain sacrifice, by rising from the tomb Thou didst raise up Adam and all his race.

—Paschal Canon, Ode 6

This image of the descending-ascending Son of God is beautifully and poginantly depicted in the traditional paschal icon entitled "The Descent Into Hell" (fig. 1). Unlike Western art that proclaims the resurrection by showing Christ rising victoriously from the tomb,[1] Orthodox Iconography preserves a paradoxical yet vital balance between suffering and joy, humiliation and victory, death and life. "Through the Cross joy has come into all the world," declares the Troparion of the Resurrection.[2] Because of the fall of man, by which the first Adam willfully rejected grace and with it life, the Author of life must enter by His own free will into the realm of death in order to release Adam from capitivity and unite him to Himself, thereby imparting to him the gift of eternal, divine life. "What is not assumed," the Fathers affirm, "cannot be saved." Therefore "our Lord Jesus Christ, the Word of God, of His boundless love, became what we are that He

[1]Since there were no witnesses to the actual resurrection of Christ, but only to the empty tomb and to the appearances of the Risen One, Orthodoxy has never considered this motif to be an appropriate iconographic theme. The resurrection is a transcendent mystery that ultimately defies graphic representation.

[2]Resurrection hymn sung at Matins; also a post-communion prayer of the clergy and is included in the Easter Canon of St John of Damascus. Its paradoxical theme stands at the center of the mystery of death and redemption.

might make us what He is";[3] "The Word became man in
order that we might be made divine."[4]

In becoming man, the Son not only assumes the earthly
limitations of human existence, exposing Himself to the conditions of space and time, temptation and bodily need. He
must also descend with man into the depths of his nothingness, the abyss of annihilation where the flame of the divine
image within flickers with threatened extinction. The full
extent of Christ's voluntary self-emptying only becomes visible, therefore, upon the Cross. For this reason, the "icon of
the Resurrection" never depicts the event of the resurrection
as such. Rather, it takes up the theme of the descent into hell,
mentioned only in passing in the Scriptures,[5] but known in
the experience of the Church to be the very cornerstone of
redemption. The paschal icon thus proclaims to eyes of faith
that Life itself has penetrated into the realm of death to
perform a new act of creation: a transformation of the old
Adam into a perfect likeness of the new Man, the glorified
Son of God.[6]

O Christ our Defender, Thou hast put to shame the
adversary of man, using as shield Thine ineffable
Incarnation. Taking man's form, Thou hast now bestowed upon him the joy of becoming Godlike: for it

[3] St Irenaeus, *Adv. haer.* V praef.

[4] St Athanasius, *De Incarn.* 54:3, *theopoiēthōmen.* Cf. St Basil, *De Sp.
Sanc.* IX.23 (*Sources Chrétiennes* 17 bis, p. 328) who defines the aim of
Christian life as "to become God" (*theon genesthai*). The same idea, deriving
from Plotinus (*Enneads*), appears in his *Contra Eunomius.*

[5] I Pet 3:19, cf. Acts 2:22-36. An addition to the apocryphal Gospel of
Nicodemus includes a marvelous dialogue between Hades and Satan, in
which Hades expresses to the Prince of Darkness his dread at the coming
of Jesus, who frees men from the tomb "with only a word." "I have pain in
the stomach. Lazarus who was snatched from me before seems to me no
good sign . . . I adjure you by your gifts and mine, do not bring him
(Jesus) here. For I believe he comes here to raise all the dead." (Text in E.
Hennecke, *New Testament Apocrypha,* Vol. I, p. 473; London 1963). There
follows a vivid description of the despoiling of hell, with Christ raising
Adam, the prophets, martyrs and all the saints to paradise. This fanciful
narrative is late (3rd cent.?), but it represents the oldest extant detailed
commentary on the theme of the *descensus Christi ad inferos.*

[6] Rom. 5:1-6:11; I Cor 15.

was in the hope of this that of old we fell from on high into the dark depths of the earth.[7] (cf Gen 3:5)

II.

Paschal iconography, however, embraces themes other than the descent of Christ into hell. The paschal motif itself is implicitly expressed by festal icons of the Nativity and of the Presentation of Our Lord in the Temple, as well as by the more obvious images of the Raising of Lazarus and of the Myrrhophores or Spice-bearing Women.

The icon of the Nativity of our Lord (fig. 2) focuses above all upon the mystery of the Incarnation. Yet a number of its more significant details foreshadow the coming passion of the "Word made flesh."

Contemplating the mystery of the pre-eternal God who has come as a little child, the worshiper finds his eyes drawn at once to the figure of the newborn infant. He lies not in a manger, but in a cave, a black hole carved into the heart of the created and fallen world. In Orthodox iconography there is a highly developed "theology of the abyss" that finds expression in the major events of Christ's life. Here the cave is transformed into the abyss, as is the Jordan River in many icons of the Theophany. Leonid Ouspensky sees in this detail a figure of "this world stricken with sin through man's fault, in which 'the Sun of truth' shone forth."[8] The abyss, however, is a universal symbol for death and for the power of hell. This is evident in those Theophany icons in which Christ descends into the black waters of the Jordan—the realm of primeval chaos and thus an image of hell—and by His sanctifying power banishes Satan from his own domain. Clearly there is an intentional parallel between the cave of the nativity, the water of baptism, the tomb of Joseph of Arimathea,

---

[7]Nativity Canon, Ode 7 (second canon) in *The Festal Menaion*, tr. by Mother Mary and Archimandrite K. Ware, London, 1969; p. 279. All quoted passages from fixed feasts are taken from this source.

[8]Ouspensky and Lossky, *The Meaning of Icons*, Boston, 1969; p. 159. But cf. P. Evdokimov, *L'Art de l'icône*, Desclée de Brouwer, 1970; p. 232.

and the infernal abyss into which the crucified Lord descends to set free those held in the bondage of death.

This interpretation is confirmed by the image of the Christ child Himself. In the Nativity icon, He is not merely clothed in the apparel of an infant; He is wrapped head to foot in swaddling bands that envelop His body like a shroud. As Lazarus shall be, He is bound with the garment of the dead, prefiguring His own burial in the tomb of the noble Joseph. Nor is the child simply laid upon a bed of straw. Instead, His cradle is given the form of a sacrificial altar, upon which the Son of God is born to die as a life-giving offering for the sins of the world.

In the icon reproduced by Ouspensky and Lossky,[9] the Theotokos or Mother of the newborn Christ looks away from the infant and gazes with compassion at Joseph, who is tortured by doubt concerning the origin of her child.[10] In other representations she is shown looking directly at the infant Jesus or directing her regard towards eternity. In each case, her solemn expression and her passive, reclining figure (usually draped in the deep red that symbolizes both sacrifice and resurrection) suggest that she is contemplating not the joyous event of the Savior's birth, but rather the ultimate consequences of her *fiat* that will one day place her at the foot of the Cross.

Certain late composite icons of the Nativity include further prophetic images of the passion.[11] Here the joy of the Christ-child's birth is poignantly diminished by the tragic massacre of the innocents (Mt 2:16ff), in which the shed blood of blameless children prefigures the murder of the innocent Righteous One (Acts 3:14ff),[12]

[9]*Op. cit.*, p. 161; 15th cent. Novgorod School.

[10]For a discussion of the identity of the figure standing before Joseph, see Ouspensky and Lossky, *op. cit.*, p. 163 (the devil); G. Drobot, *Icône de la Nativité*, Bellefontaine, 1975; p. 287 (a shepherd); and N. Osoline, "L'Icône de la Nativité" in *Contacts* XXVIII, No. 96 (1976); p. 327ff (a shepherd). Fr. Osoline traces the metamorphosis of this figure in Russian iconography from a simple shepherd announcing the good news to an image of Satan, who sows the seeds of doubt in Joseph's mind.

[11]As, e.g., in the 17th c. icon reproduced by Ouspensky and Lossky, *op. cit.*, p. 162.

[12]The Proto-gospel of James (mid-second cent.?) develops the theme of

The purpose of the incarnation is succinctly summarized in its relation to Christ's redemptive work by a passage from the Epistle to the Hebrews, read at the Ninth Royal Hour of the Vigil of the Nativity:

> Since the children [of God] share in flesh and blood, He Himself likewise partook of the same nature [lit.: "of the same things"], that through death He might destroy him who has the power of death, that is, the devil, and deliver all those who through fear of death were subject to lifelong bondage . . . Therefore He had to be made like His brethren in every respect, so that He might become a merciful and faithful High Priest in the service of God, to make expiation (*hilas-kesthai*) for the sins of the people. For because He Himself has suffered and been tempted, He is able to help those who are tempted.
>
> —Hebrews 2:14-18 (RSV)

III.

The feast of the Meeting of Our Lord in the Temple (*Hypapantē/Srētenie,* 2/15 Feb.) follows chronologically upon the Nativity, although the Orthodox Church separates the two with the celebration of Theophany or the Baptism of Christ in the Jordan (6/19 Jan.).[13] The icon of the Meeting (fig. 3) places the Theotokos and the Righteous Simeon with

---

the suffering innocents still further. The righteous Elisabeth hides the infant John in a divinely opened cleft in the rock (ch. 22). And her husband, the priest Zachariah, is murdered before the altar in the temple for refusing to betray the whereabouts of his son. Interestingly, the narrative reports that his blood turned to stone, but that his body was not to be found—an apparent type or prophetic image of Christ's resurrection (ch. 23f). According to this tradition, Zachariah's successor was the righteous Elder Simeon, who, as we shall point out, further prophesies the Lord's passion and saving death.

[13]The Roman Catholic Church, together with some churches of the Reform, celebrate on this day a composite feast that commemorates primarily the Visit of the Magi and secondarily the Baptism of Christ together with the Wedding at Cana. Rather than stress the "meeting" of our Lord on 2 Feb., the Catholic celebration focuses upon the "Purification of the Holy Virgin."

the Christ child in the foreground, leaving Joseph and the prophetess Anna standing apart as secondary figures.

As in the icon of the Nativity, a number of important details foreshadow the Savior's passion. The theme of the icon, as of the feast itself, is the meeting of the two Testaments before the altar of the Lord. No other sacred image so directly and so touchingly expresses the relation of "promise" and "fulfillment" that links the old and new Covenants. Filled with the Spirit during his earthly life, the Elder Simeon[14] is led by that same Spirit into the Temple, there to encounter and to receive in his arms the promised Messiah.

In the Nativity scene, the presence of the Magi witnesses to the universal character of Christ's saving work. Salvation indeed is from the Jews (Jn 4:22), but the Jewish Messiah is destined to die as an expiation for the sins of the entire world (1 Jn 2:2; Jn 3:16f). Accordingly, the Canticle of Simeon, the *Nunc Dimittis* sung at every Vespers service of the Orthodox liturgical year, proclaims that this child shall be a "light to enlighten the Gentiles" as well as "the glory of [the] people of Israel."

The victory of that Light over the world-pervading darkness, however, can only be accomplished through a sacrificial death. The theme of redemptive suffering, therefore, is interwoven throughout both the hymnography and the iconography of the feast. In obedience to Mosaic Law (Lev 12), Mary comes to the Temple on the day of her purification to present her child as an offering of first-fruits to the Lord (Num 18). Before the altar, the table of sacrifice,[15] Simeon stretches forth his hands to receive the fulfillment of the hope that for so long had burned within him and within the collective consciousness of the righteous Israelites whom he represents. Concluding his prophetic canticle, Simeon blesses the parents of the child. Turning to Mary, he pronounces curious, ominous words, not of joy and gladness, but of coming conflict and

[14]Lk 2:25, a sign of his stature as a prophetic witness to the coming Messiah. Cf. Jesus' use of the prophecy of Isa 61 to proclaim, in words almost identical to those applied to Simeon, that "The Spirit of the Lord is upon me" (Lk 4:18). For the (historically dubious) tradition that Simeon was high priest, see above, note 12.

[15]See the above comments on the altar-image in the icon of the Nativity.

suffering. In conclusion he adds almost parenthetically, still addressing the Virgin Mother, "and a sword will pierce through your own soul also" (Lk 2:35). The note of joy mingled with grief, observed in the expression and attitude of Mary at the nativity of her Son, reappears in this first scriptural prediction of our Lord's passion.

> "And a sword shall pierce thy heart, O all-pure Virgin," Simeon foretold to the Theotokos, "when thou shalt see thy Son upon the Cross, to whom we cry aloud: O God of our fathers, blessed art Thou!"
>
> —Meeting Matins, Ode 7

The Holy Theotokos presents her Son in fulfillment of the obligation to make an offering of her first-born male child. The deeper sense of her offering, however, intimated by Simeon's prophetic words, points to the Cross and to the victory to be achieved through sacrificial death. Thus the megalynaria (Ode 9) of the feast declare:

> The pure Dove, the Ewe without blemish, brings the Lamb and Shepherd into the temple.

The Lytia verses of Great Vespers proclaim the meaning of the sacrifice accomplished by the holy Mother and awaited by her Son:

> Now the God of purity as a holy child has opened a pure womb, and as God He is brought as an offering to Himself, setting us free from the curse of the Law and granting light to our souls.

The light granted to the nations and to the soul of every believer is ultimately the divine, uncreated Light of the triune Godhead. As Isaiah received purification through a fiery coal taken from the altar by a Seraph (Isa 6), so the Righteous Elder receives purification and the knowledge of salvation from the hands of the Virgin, as she entrusts to him the

"Lord of light that knows no evening."[16] Touching the
Light, he himself is filled with light. Like future generations
of those who dwell in that Light, Simeon is nourished by the
very body of the Lord, receiving Him as a prototype of the
bloodless sacrifice of the holy Eucharist.

As he takes his leave, the Elder is made to utter a final
prophecy that links this feast directly to the descent of Christ
into hell.

"I depart," cried Simeon, "to declare the good tidings
to Adam abiding in hell and to Eve . . ."[17]

To deliver our kind from dust, God will go down
even unto hell: He will give freedom to all the captives
and sight to the blind, and will grant the dumb to
cry aloud: O God of our fathers, blessed art Thou!"

—Matins, Ode 7

IV.

At the threshold of Holy Week, the Church remembers
liturgically the stupendous miracle that raised Lazarus from
the dead. Here, on the day before Christ's triumphant entry
into Jerusalem, we find a further prophetic announcement of
resurrection: not only of our Lord, but of all those who seek
in Him the source of eternal life.

By raising Lazarus from the dead before Thy passion,
Thou didst confirm the universal resurrection, O Christ
God! Like the children with the palms of victory, we
cry out to Thee, O Vanquisher of death: Hosanna
in the highest! Blessed is He that comes in the name
of the Lord![18]

---

[16]Meeting Matins, Ode 5.
[17]The Hebrew word *adam* means "man," "mankind."
[18]Troparion of Lazarus Saturday (6th Sat. of Great Lent) and of Palm
Sunday (The Entrance of Our Lord into Jerusalem). The use of this troparion
for the two juxtaposed feasts clearly illustrates their theological unity. In his

FIGURE 1
"The Descent Into Hell"

FIGURE 1 BIS.
"The Descent Into Hell"

FIGURE 2
"The Nativity of our Lord"

FIGURE 3
"The Presentation (Meeting) of our Lord in the Temple"

FIGURE 4
"The Raising of Lazarus"

FIGURE 5
"The Myrrhbearing Women"

FIGURE 6
"*Philoxenia* or Hospitality of Abraham"

FIGURE 7
"Rublev's Icon of the Holy Trinity"

The icon of the feast gives graphic expression to even the smallest details of the Gospel narrative (John 11). Although Christ Himself is the central figure, our attention is immediately drawn to the side of the image (fig. 4). There Lazarus, bound in white bands reminiscent of the shroud-like swaddling clothes of the nativity scene, stands in vivid contrast to the surrounding blackness of the tomb. The garb of the dead is a burst of light, shining forth from the darkness. Lazarus stands at the mouth of the abyss, his body slightly stooped in a humble bow before the Giver of Life. His face is serene; his open eyes gaze in worshipful wonder toward the One whose all-powerful Word has just summoned him to "come forth." Significantly, no other figure but Jesus looks at the man who, moments before, lay in death. The attention of the crowd is fixed upon the Worker of the miracle, not upon the miracle itself.

Mary and Martha, the bereaved sisters, fall at the Lord's feet, each now drawn with single-minded devotion to "the one thing needful" (Lk 10:42).

A few of the bystanders cover their faces with upraised arms in anticipation of the stench of death ("Lord, by this time there will be an odor . . .").[19] Jesus delayed four days in coming, and as a result of His apparent indifference, their friend and brother died. The crowd thus gathers more out of curiosity than conviction, as though summoned by the Church's liturgy for the burial of the dead:

> Draw near, you descendants of Adam, and gaze upon him who is laid low in the earth, made after our own image, all beauty stripped away, dissolved in the grave by decay, consumed in darkness by worms, and hidden by the earth . . .

book, *Worship* (Dept. Rel. Ed., Orthodox Church in America, 1976; p. 84), Fr Thomas Hopko stresses that "Lazarus Saturday is a paschal celebration. It is the only time in the entire Church year that the resurrectional service of Sunday is celebrated on another day. At the Liturgy of Lazarus Saturday, the Church glorifies Christ as 'the Resurrection and the Life,' who, by raising Lazarus, has confirmed the universal resurrection of mankind even before his own suffering and death."

[19]Ouspensky interprets this gesture to mean that there was in fact an odor of decomposition (*op. cit.*, p. 177). The Gospel narrative—and the icon

Expecting the odor of decay, they encounter instead the miracle of life. Every aspect of human existence that was formerly subjected to the corrupting power of death is now transformed by a greater power. There is no stench, for the victory is total: death is vanquished, and its every consequence is overcome.

A festal verse on the Vespers Psalm "Lord, I Call" expresses the means by which this victory is accomplished: the raising of the dead man Lazarus, like the calling to life of the first man Adam, is effected by the *creative power of the divine Word*.

> O Lord, Thy voice destroyed the kingdom of hell!
> The Word of Thy might raised the dead one from the tomb. Lazarus thus becomes the saving foretaste of eternal life.

The *stichera* of the Praises recall that Lazarus was Jesus' friend. Exegetes have often seen in Lazarus an image of the faithful Christian,[20] and consequently they are inclined to interpret the Lord's grief ("Jesus wept," Jn 11:35) as an expression of devotion for "His own."[21] To one steeped in Orthodox liturgical tradition, however, Jesus' friendship for Lazarus represents a specific example of the divine love that embraces all men: "May Christ our true God . . . have mercy on us and save us, for He is good and loves mankind." By resuscitating Lazarus to renewed earthly existence, Jesus foretells the resurrection, not of a chosen few, but of the world as a whole. The divinely conceived purpose of His own victory over the power of death is to enable all men to "come forth" from the tomb, some indeed to a resurrection of judgment, but others to a resurrection of life (Jn 5:29). Yet paradoxically, those who believe in Him and His Word have already passed beyond judgment. Even now, in this earthly

itself—however, suggest that the miracle worked a complete restoration to Lazarus' former state: "Did I not tell you that if you believed you would see the glory of God?" (Jn 11:40).

[20]See e.g., Raymond Brown's commentary, *The Gospel According to John* I, New York, 1966; p. 436.

[21]Cf. Jn 17:9.

life, they delight in a foretaste of the Kingdom of heaven. Through the miracle of God's redeeming and forgiving grace, they prophetically, yet actually, participate in the glory of eternal life (Jn 5:24).[22]

> Christ—the joy, the truth, and the light of all, the life of the world and its resurrection—has appeared in His goodness to those on earth. He has become the image of our resurrection, granting divine forgiveness to all.
>
> —Kontakion

V.

On the third Sunday after Holy Pascha, the Church celebrates the mystery of the Empty Tomb as depicted by the icon of the Myrrhbearing Women (fig. 5). The Gospel reading for the Divine Liturgy is Mark 15:43-16:8, the most sober and the most perplexing of all accounts of the resurrection.

The reading begins with a brief mention of Jesus' burial by Joseph of Arimathea, "a respected member of the Council [Sanhedrin], who was also himself looking for the Kingdom of God." The emotional tension experienced by this faithful follower of the Lord is set in relief by the simple statement, "he took courage" in approaching Pilate to ask for Jesus' body. Lowering the corpus from the Cross, Joseph, together with some of the women, carried it to a tomb newly hewn in the rock: a cavern similar to the one in which, according to iconographic tradition, the incarnate Son of God was born. There they washed blood, dirt and spittle from the wasted flesh, anointed it with a preliminary coating of precious ointment, and hurriedly wrapped it in a linen shroud. Their haste—and, significantly, their inability to complete the burial

[22]This theme of so-called "realized eschatology" is often wrongly attributed to St John's Gospel alone. It appears throughout St Paul's writings (e.g., Rom 6:1-11; Col 2:6-15; Gal 2:19f; cf. Tit 3:5ff; I Jn 2:20, 27; 3:9) and elsewhere in the NT, usually in a baptismal context. Thus on Lazarus Saturday, as on other special feast days of the liturgical year, the baptismal hymn (Gal 3:27) replaces the Trisagion at the Divine Liturgy.

ritual that included further anointing and clothing of the deceased in fine garments—was due to the fact that "the sabbath was beginning," when no faithful Jew could undertake such work. "On the sabbath they rested according to the commandment" (Lk 23:56).[23]

If it is true, as many claim, that the famous Shroud of Turin is actually the "fine linen cloth" in which Jesus was buried, then it represents indeed the "icon of icons," the ultimate sacred image "not made by human hands."[24] Imprinted upon this shroud is the (photographically negative) image of a crucified Jew, almost certainly of the first century A.D. Numerous books and articles give the details that support the thesis of its authenticity. For our purposes, we need mention only two points that bear upon the question and possibly link the Turin Shroud with the icon of the spice-bearing women.

First it should be noted that the body which was wrapped in the shroud was hastily buried shortly after crucifixion on a Friday afternoon. This is the only time of the week that would have allowed no opportunity for proper anointing and dressing of the dead man. (The expensive quality of the cloth alone is enough to show that those who performed the burial rites would hardly have left them incomplete for any lesser motive than to observe the sabbath.) And it is equally clear that the shroud was removed from the body before the following Sunday morning, at which time friends of the deceased would certainly have completed the burial according to Jewish custom (as the myrrh-bearing women planned to do).

[23]For a detailed—and highly illuminating—account of Jewish burial practice and the probable way in which Jesus was laid to rest, see P. Barbet, *A Doctor at Calvary*, New York, 1963; esp. pp. 154-175. Dr. Barbet presents a well-reasoned case defending the view that the Shroud of Turin is the burial shroud of our Lord.

[24]The "image not made by human hands," representing the "Holy Face" of Christ, was, according to early Church tradition, imprinted by Jesus Himself upon a cloth that was subsequently used to heal King Abgar of Edessa. A similar tradition exists in the West. The fifth Station of the Cross venerated in the Roman Catholic Church recalls the imprinting of Jesus' image upon the veil of Veronica (the name "Veronica" means "veritable icon" or "true image," suggesting that the tradition has an etiological origin).

The second and most significant point to note is that the evidence of the shroud suggests that it could not possibly have been removed from the body by normal means. Whereas the image itself is photographically negative, the bloodspots on the shroud are positive. Blood from the wounds (that correspond precisely to the wounds of Jesus mentioned in the Gospel narratives) penetrated the cloth and dried there, causing the material to adhere to the body. The striking fact is that these bloodspots are completely intact, showing no signs of cracking or other damage that would necessarily occur if the shroud had been stripped away from the wounds.[25]

The evidence is circumstantial, and the theory of the shroud's authenticity defies scientific proof. That evidence does clearly indicate, however, that the cirumstances under which the body in question was buried were identical to those surrounding Jesus' own burial, and above all, that the shroud was not removed from the body, but that the body "disappeared" or "de-materialized," leaving the shroud lying in the manner of Jesus' own shroud as described by the Gospel of John (20:6f): "Simon Peter . . . entered the tomb, he saw the linen clothes lying there, and the napkin, which had been on His head . . . rolled up in a place by itself."

The icon entitled "The Myrrh-bearing Women" is in fact an icon of the Holy Shroud. The shroud itself forms the conceptual center of the image. To the left, the women stand in mute awe, gazing at the quiet yet eloquent message proclaimed by the empty cloth, still rolled as if to wrap a corpse, still showing the outline of the figure it enveloped some hours before. The time is "very early in the morning." The women return to the sepulchre at daybreak to find that the stone has been rolled back from the tomb, not to permit removal of the body, but to reveal its resurrection. The empty shroud proclaims a new daybreak, the "dawn of the eighth day," in which the work of redemption is complete.

An angel[26] confirms to the women the miracle that their

---

[25]A fact easily verified by removing a bandage from a bloody wound: the dried blood inevitably cracks and the bandage itself bears evidence of the damage done to the scab.

[26]Two men or angels, according to Luke and John. For the theological significance of the two angels posted at opposite ends of the stone ledge (an

eyes perceive but their minds refuse to comprehend. "Why
do you look for the living among the dead? He is not here;
He is risen. Go . . . announce!" Proclaim to His disciples and
to the world that the tomb is empty. Declare that the abyss
has rendered up its dead, not to recall them again as it will
Lazarus, but to release them to a greater power, a greater
authority that death can in no wise oppose.

Angelic voices proclaimed the nativity of Emmanuel, and
an angel declares that Christ is risen. This is no tradition of
men, no guileful invention of disillusioned disciples or fig-
ment of wishful thinking. Nor is it a ruse, designed to mask
the secret theft of Jesus' body in a desperate effort to feign
fulfillment of His own predictions that "after three days the
Son of Man will rise again." This is rather a divine witness
to truth. The angel's message is the basic *kerygma* of Christian faith: "Do not be amazed. You seek Jesus of Nazareth,
who was crucified. He has risen, He is not here . . . go, tell
His disciples."

The Greek word *estauromenon*, here translated "who was
crucified," means literally "the Crucified One" (Mk 16:6).
As the festal icon depicts the sublime mystery of the empty
tomb, whose core is the empty shroud, it is evident that the
Risen One must forever remain *estauromenos*, He who is
crucified. Although the victory over death is complete, Christ
could only "trample down death" by voluntarily submitting
to His own death. The way to resurrection for the glorified
Lord, and thus for all those who seek eternal life in Him, is
inevitably the way of the Cross and of the blood-stained
shroud.

> The noble Joseph, when he had taken down Thy most
> pure body from the tree, wrapped it in fine linen,
> anointed it with spices, and laid it in a new tomb. . . .
> The angel came to the myrrh-bearing women at the
> tomb and said: Myrrh is fitting for the dead; but
> Christ has shown Himself a stranger to corruption!
> So proclaim . . . Christ is risen from the dead! *By His*

antitype of the *kapporet* or "mercy seat" of the Ark of the Covenant), see
P. Evdokimov, *op. cit.*, p. 274.

death He has trampled down death; and to those in
the tombs, He has given life!

—Paschal troparia

VI.

To complete this sketch of the paschal mystery as expressed by iconographic tradition, it is necessary to speak of
one other icon that may seem to have little to do with our
subject. It is the well-known icon of the *Philoxenia* or Hospitality of Abraham, painted in the early 15th century by the
Russian monk Andrew Rublev (fig. 7). Detailed interpretations of this spiritual masterpiece have appeared elsewhere,[27]
and we need concern ourselves only with a few of its pertinent details.

Behind the icon stands the event of the meeting between
Abraham and three angels or divine messengers as recounted
in Genesis 18. The Greek title *philoxenia,* meaning "love of
strangers," expresses Abraham's welcome to his guests, who
announce to him the covenant promise made by God, that his
aged wife Sarah would bear him a son to insure his posterity.
Abraham addresses his guests now in the plural, now in the
singular. To the early Church Fathers, this peculiar variation
revealed the presence of divinity and, especially, of the tri-
unity of the Three Persons of the Godhead.[28] Consequently,

[27]Apart from the discussion by Ouspensky and Lossky (*op. cit.,* p. 201-
207) and P. Evdokimov (*op. cit.* p. 205-216), see M. Alpatoff, "La Trinité
dans l'art byzantin et l'icône de Roublev," *Echos d'Orient* 26 (1927), p. 150-
186; L. Thunberg, "Early Christian Interpretation of the Three Angels in
Gen. 18," *Studia Patristica* VII (1966), p. 560-570; M. Zernov, "The Icon
of the Holy Trinity," *Sobornost* VI, No. 6 (1972), p. 387-394; G. Drobot,
"L'Icône de la Trinité de Roublev," *Contacts* XXVI, No. 88 (1974), p.
332-337; and A. Riou, "L'Icône de la Trinité," *Contacts* XXVI, No. 88
(1974), p. 338-348.

[28]L. Thunberg, *art. cit.,* shows that patristic interpretation of Gen. 18
took three major forms. The first saw in the messengers simply three angels
(Jewish and Antiochian exegetes); the second gave a christological interpretation, whereby the three were Christ and two angels (Novatian, Tertullian,
Hilary, Justin, Origen, Athanasius); and the third offered the trinitarian
interpretation represented by the Rublev icon (generally favored by Alexandrians). As Thunberg points out (p. 565), "a Trinitarian interpretation of
the Mamre scene is far from self-evident in the Early Church."

the image that represents this scene has come to be known as the "Icon of the Holy Trinity."

Interpreters have taken very different approaches in their attempts to analyze the Mamre scene and to explain its spiritual significance. Yet even where they adopt a trinitarian view, iconographers have always depicted the three figures as angels, the visible form in which they appeared to Abraham. Those images that deliberately place Christ the Pantocrator in the center, with a scroll in His hand and a cross in the nimbus, must simply be regarded as uncanonical.[29]

According to Athonite canons, the icon of the *Philoxenia* should be painted with the following details: "a house and three angels sitting at table; the main dish with bread and the head of an ox, other dishes of food, bottles of wine and goblets. To the right of the angels, Abraham carrying a covered dish, to the left Sarah bringing in a roast bird."[30] This prescription was carefully followed in the oldest icons of this type, and it continued to guide painters well after the time of Rublev. The 16th century icon of the Cretan School reproduced here (fig. 6) retains the original theme of Genesis 18 (substituting the head of a calf for that of an ox); yet it also reflects the tri-unity of the three central figures in an obvious attempt to symbolize the three divine Persons.

With inspired genius, Rublev transformed the setting from the historical site by the oak of Mamre to the eternal, heavenly plane. The table has become an altar, whose reliquary niche represents the earth. The figures of Abraham and Sarah have been eliminated; the patriarch's tent has become the

---

[29]Ouspensky and Lossky, *op. cit.*, p. 207, n. 8. A vastly more serious and dangerous distortion appears in those "icons" that depict the Father as an old man, accompanied by the Son and the Spirit (or a dove). This popular motif represents heresy of the worst kind, in that it blatantly contradicts the testimony of Scripture ("No one has ever seen God," Jn 1:18; 1 Jn 4:12) and the apophatic element of Orthodox theology. This is equally true of those images of the Cross in which the Holy Face (of Christ) above the corpus has been replaced by the "face" of the Father. Such representations are plainly iconoclastic: they undermine the defense of sacred images made by the 7th Ecumenical Council, based upon the truth that the "image" of the Father is revealed only in the Son and hence only the incarnate Second Person of the Holy Trinity is "representable."

[30]G. Schafer, ed. *The Painters' Handbook of Mt Athos*, 1855, p. 114; quoted by D. Wild, *Holy Icons*, Berne, 1961; plate 18.

heavenly sanctuary, and the oak has been replaced by the tree of life that grows from the central figure like a shoot from the stump of Jesse (Isa 11:1).

The figures themselves, while retaining the aspect of angelic beings, show by their attitude and harmonious interrelationship that a deeper meaning lies concealed beneath their outward form. They represent the members of the Divine Council, by whose decree man was created in the image and likeness of God (Gen 1:26). Here they engage in silent contemplation of the new creative act by which fallen man is redeemed and restored to his original glory. Is it possible to determine their identities, other than to affirm that they symbolize the Three Persons of the Holy Trinity?

Paul Evdokimov has argued eloquently for the view that the central angel represents God the Father, the source of divine life.[31] Following St Irenaeus, he identifies the figures to the left and right as the Son and the Holy Spirit, the "two hands" of the Father.

More recently, G. Drobot and A. Riou[32] have warned against any attempt to label the individual figures, maintaining correctly that no absolute identity between them and the divine Persons was ever intended either by the Genesis passage or by the iconographer. They tend, however, to overstate their case; and in so doing, they obscure the essential *dogmatic* element inherent in every genuine iconographic motif. As we stressed at the outset, the icon is a medium of revelation. By its very nature it represents ("renders present" and intelligible) some aspect of ineffable divine Truth.

But what precisely is the content of that Truth in the Rublev icon? Holy Tradition has accepted this depiction as a graphic statement of trinitarian dogma. Hence it has become an icon of the feast of Pentecost, on which that dogma is celebrated in the Church's liturgy. In support of the trinitarian theme, Evdokimov finds the basic geometric form of the icon to be a circle, the symbol of eternity and unity, that circumscribes the three figures. While this is an accurate perception, still another form—that of the *eucharistic chalice*—more

[31]*Art. cit.,* he is followed in this interpretation by M. Zernov (see note 27).
[32]*Arts. cit.,* see n. 27.

clearly illustrates the basic teaching of the image. For the
Rublev icon is above all a proclamation of the paschal mystery
as it is reactualized and experienced in the eucharistic celebration of the worshiping Church.

In agreement with accepted iconographic tradition, Ouspensky states that "the Angels are grouped on the icon in
order of the Symbol of Faith, from left to right: I believe
in God the Father, the Son and the Holy Spirit." Following
this interpretation, we can only see in the central figure the
Person of God the Son.[33] Many details confirm this view.
Vested in the sacerdotal colors of a purple-red hue, He wears
the stole of High Priest. The solidity and vivid color of His
garments, compared with the transparency of those worn by
the other two figures, reflect the material, human nature assumed by the Incarnate Son. From behind (or within) Him
who is the source of life, there springs forth the tree of life;
while His right hand forms the priestly blessing with two
fingers, signifying His two natures, human and divine.

On the table stands a single object: no longer a bowl
holding the head of an ox or a calf, but a chalice in which
lies a sacrificed lamb. To the left and right of the icon, the
two figures of the Father and the Holy Spirit rise in complementary sweeps that likewise form a eucharistic cup. The
Son, the Crucified One and eternal High Priest, blesses the
lamb-bearing chalice, while the Father and the Spirit form
a second chalice that contains the "Lamb slain from the foundation of the world" (Rev 13:8).

The deep red vestments of the Son recall His sacrificial
blood shed upon the Cross. The stole borne upon His
shoulder represents the unique high priestly office of Him
who is both Celebrant and Sacrifice, the Offerer and the
Offering, of the eucharistic mystery. His head is bowed in
humble submissiveness to the will of the Father, in whom
the paschal mystery finds its ultimate source and meaning.

The vestments of the Father are all but transparent,
symbolizing the infinite transcendence of Him who embodies

---

[33]Ouspensky and Lossky, *op. cit.,* p. 204; cf. L. Thunberg, *art. cit.,* p. 570,
who refers to R. Mainca's opinion "that the middle figure on the icons is
always Christ rather than God the Father."

the source of all divine life, from whom the Son is eternally begotten and the Spirit eternally proceeds. Yet the transparency of His vestments also expresses the mysterious and tragic role He plays within the paschal drama: because of His infinite love for mankind, the Father remains silent, hidden in an apparent act of abandonment, during the passion and crucifixion of His beloved Son.

A paschal benediction originates in the right hand of the Father and passes as a divine line of force to the right hand of the Son. From the Son the blessing descends to consecrate the lamb-bearing chalice. Yet the angle of the fingers suggests a second movement, toward the dove-shaped hand of the Spirit. From there the movement continues downward toward the rectangular figure in the center of the altar table that symbolizes the created world. The Father, as the eternal source of all life, divine and human, offers His blessing of love through the Person of the true paschal Lamb. That blessing, transmitted to the world by the Holy Spirit, reposes upon the Church as the sacramental power of the new creation.

The paschal mystery thus finds its fulfillment in the descent of the Spirit at Pentecost. Indeed, the blessing whose movement forms the center of the Rublev icon, is nothing less than the gift of the Spirit Himself. "I will pray the Father, and He will give you another Counselor (Paraclete) to be with you forever, even the Spirit of Truth . . ." (Jn 14:16f). It is this Spirit who creates and sustains the Church as the Body of Christ, nourished by the transfigured elements received from the eucharistic cup.

> We offer unto thee this reasonable and bloodless worship, and ask Thee and pray Thee and supplicate Thee: Send down Thy Holy Spirit *upon us* and upon these gifts here offered.
>
> —Epiklesis, Liturgy of St John Chrysostom

The sanctifying, consecrating power of the Spirit transforms not only bread and wine. It also effects a metamorpho-

sis, a transfiguration of fallen humanity.[34] In fulfillment of
the paschal mystery, the Third Person of the Holy Trinity
descends ever again upon the eucharistic assembly to unite
the faithful in a mystical communion with the divine life of
the risen and glorified Lord.

> As the bread from the earth, having received the
> invocation of God, is no longer plain bread, but Eu-
> charist, constituted of two realities, earthly and heaven-
> ly, so our own bodies that participate in the Eucharist
> are no longer corruptible, but possess the hope of
> resurrection.
>
> —St Irenaeus, Adv. Haer. IV.18.5

It is this unquenchable hope of resurrection that creates
of the various icons of the paschal mystery a beautiful and
harmonious mosaic. Their composite theme is that of salvation and eternal joy offered to mankind through the suffering
of the Cross. Into the dark abyss of our fallen existence has
come the incomprehensible yet unconquerable Light of the
incarnate Son of God. Standing at the mouth of our tomb,
hewn by our own hand, He summons us by the power of
His Word to "come forth" into the splendor of a new day
that knows no decline. Rendered ever present upon the altar
of our earthly sanctuary, He preserves and nourishes His
new creation with the heavenly manna of His own Body
and Blood. He is our victory, our life, our hope, and our joy.
But as such, He forever remains the Crucified One. In His
eternal passion, He shares both the suffering and the longing
of those who know that eucharistic communion is only a
foretaste of a greater joy and a greater glory to come.

O Christ! Great and most holy Pascha!
O Wisdom, Word, and Power of God!

---

[34]For the liturgical history of epikleses that invoke the Spirit upon priest
and congregation, see E. G. Cuthbert F. Atchley, *On the Epiklesis of the
Eucharistic Liturgy and in the Consecration of the Font,* London, 1935; esp.
p. 106-107.

Grant that we may more perfectly partake of Thee
In the never-ending Day of Thy Kingdom!

—Hymn of the Resurrection